Land Rover Series II and IIA

Specification Guide

LAND-ROVER

1966
THE QUEEN'S AWARD
TO INDUSTRY 1966

THE WORLD'S MOST VERSATILE VEHICLE

Land Rover Series II and IIA

Specification Guide

James Taylor

THE CROWOOD PRESS

First published in 2010 by
The Crowood Press Ltd
Ramsbury, Marlborough
Wiltshire SN8 2HR

enquiries@crowood.com

www.crowood.com

This impression 2024

British Library Cataloguing-in-Publication Data
A catalogue record for this book is available from the British Library.

ISBN 978 1 84797 160 9

Typeset and designed by D & N Publishing
Baydon, Wiltshire.

Printed and bound in India by Parksons Graphics Pvt. Ltd.

contents

introduction and acknowledgements

Enthusiasts have preserved and restored Series I Land Rovers for many years now, but it has taken time for the Series II and IIA models to attract the same sort of interest. Gradually, I am pleased to say, it is now happening. People are recognizing that these were the vehicles that shaped the Land Rover utilities as we know them today, and their association with the 1960s – a decade that has become fashionable and interesting again – has done the rest.

However, these Land Rovers spent so long as little more than sources of spares or the basis for off-road specials that few bothered to record or even notice what they were really like. So the point of this book is to show as accurately as possible what the Series II and IIA models were like when they were new. It is intended to be useful to restorers, and to anyone else with an interest in these models.

The 1960s were an extraordinarily prolific decade for new ideas as far as the Land Rover was concerned. There were all kinds of fascinating, might-have-been projects, which are beyond the scope of this book, but which I have chronicled in *Land Rover, 60 Years of the 4×4 Workhorse* (The Crowood Press, 2007). There were also forward control models and military half-tons (more familiarly known as lightweights), and these are also given their place in the current book alongside the mainstream models.

In fact, there is still little known about some of those mainstream models, especially those built overseas. Chapter 10 attempts to pull together the overseas story, but I am conscious of the huge gaps in it. Perhaps somebody reading this book will be able to fill them in. If so, please do get in touch with me through the publishers.

Let me add a few words of warning. Throughout this book you will find dates and chassis numbers that indicate when certain changes are recorded as having occurred. The record – often a service bulletin issued to dealers – may have been made a month or more after the change had actually been made on the assembly lines. Do bear in mind, too, that changes were rarely as exact as this makes them appear. Even the change from Series II to Series IIA specification was a little more gradual than the change of name suggests.

There were several reasons for this. First, vehicles did not come down the assembly lines in strict chassis number order. So, for example, although chassis number 12345 was the first one down the lines to incorporate a particular change, numbers 12346 and 12347 might already have been built and would therefore not have had it. Secondly, human error could creep into the process of recording changeover points, as Rover service literature sometimes shows. And thirdly (as an example), after a sidelight had been 'officially' changed from one type to another, it is quite possible that another box of the old ones would have been found in the stores at Solihull and fed into the assembly lines to be used up.

I must also point out that this book cannot be described as definitive. It simply reflects the best information available at the time of publication, and research continues; if we were to wait until that research was complete the book would never get published.

I have been working intermittently on this book since 1999, and in those ten years a huge number of people have contributed to the store of knowledge that it contains. I cannot blame any of them for any errors in it – and I am sure that there will be some – but I can thank them for the contributions they have made. I would not be able to list all their names even if I tried, but the contributions by a few have been very important and I must acknowledge that. So here are special thanks to:

Jochen von Arnim of the Deutscher Land Rover Club
Philip Bashall of the Dunsfold Collection
Richard Brotherton, formerly of BMIHT
John Cranfield, American enthusiast
Roger Crathorne at Land Rover
Bill Davis at Great Basin Rovers
Richard Green of the (Australian) Register of Ex-Military Land Rovers
John Mastrangelo of the Ex-Military Land Rover Association
George Mitchell at Land Rover
Tim and Christopher Race, formerly African contributors to *LAND ROVER enthusiast* magazine
Mark and Ian Rumsey of the Series II Club
Glenn Smith at Land Rover Australia
Stephen Stansfield of the (Australian) Register of Ex-Military Land Rovers
Patrick Sutcliffe, *LRe*'s Australian Correspondent
Jan Valentino at BMIHT
Dan Warden of the One Ton Register, and
Pat Ware of *Classic Military Vehicle* magazine

James Taylor
Oxfordshire, April 2009

1

the life and times of the Series II and IIA

The press shot of the 109 showed a very early vehicle, probably one of the pilot-production batch. The elegant truck cab was all-new. The 109s always had the so-called 'de luxe' bonnet with its rolled leading edge, and this one also has flashing turn indicators, which were an optional extra. The side-mounted spare wheel marked a departure from Series I practice.

It is hard now to establish a start point for the development of the Land Rover that became the Series II when it was announced in April 1958. The main reason for this is that the Rover Company – which then made Land Rovers – seems to have thought of the model as no more than a logical evolution of the existing Land Rover until quite late in the day. In fact, the first written record of the Series II name dates from June 1957, when it appeared in the minutes of the Rover Board meeting during a discussion about future products.

Until that point, Land Rovers had simply been Land Rovers, and the different varieties were distinguished by their mechanical and dimensional characteristics. So the original 80in of 1948 had been succeeded by a 2-litre 80in in 1950, that in turn had given way to 86in and 107in models in 1953, and then there had been 88in and 109in models from 1956, with 88 and 109 diesels from 1957. The Land Rover was a commercial vehicle, and Rover probably thought that it had no need of exciting-sounding titles in the way that cars did.

The catalyst for change was almost certainly the arrival at Rover's Solihull headquarters of news that the Austin division of BMC was planning to introduce its own light 4×4 as a competitor for the Land Rover early in 1958. This was serious news: BMC was a much bigger company than Rover and was likely to be able to promote its new product in ways that Rover simply could not afford. This was bound to damage sales of the Land Rover, which until then had been the only British-built light 4×4 on the market.

So what probably happened was that the Land Rover engineers were encouraged to pull together all their plans for improvements to the vehicle and to prepare them as a package that could be promoted as a new Land Rover. The minutes of the Rover Board meeting for 28 February 1956 show that a plan to introduce 'New Style' Land Rovers was then in place. Calling these Series II models would draw attention to the package of improvements that they embodied, and would help to counter BMC's promotional efforts for their new Austin Gipsy.

DESIGNING THE SERIES II

There were several improvements under development in the middle of the 1950s, but the two that were likely to grab the most attention were a new petrol engine and bodywork that had for the first time been 'styled' – designed to look good rather than to be purely functional.

The new engine had been in the planning stages since 1956 or possibly earlier, and was to be a 2.25-litre 4-cylinder with a modern overhead-valve layout. It had been drawn up in tandem with the diesel engine that had been announced in April 1957 and used the same basic architecture. Rover's Chief Engine Designer Jack Swaine had prepared the diesel engine for introduction with a 2-litre capacity (actually 2052cc), using 'wet' cylinder liners. For the petrol engine, the capacity was raised to 2.25-litres (actually 2286cc) simply by omitting these liners. With a different cylinder head, designed with assistance from the tuning specialist Harry Weslake, and other changes such as a distributor where the diesel had a rotary fuel pump, the transformation was complete.

The new petrol engine – always known as the 'two-and-a-quarter' at Solihull – brought measurable improvements. Despite having a relatively large swept volume for a 4-cylinder engine, it was also commendably smooth and quiet in operation, at least when new and properly maintained. The increase in power to a gross 77bhp not only added nearly 50 per cent to the paper figures but also increased the maximum road speed by about 15mph (24km/h) to around 68mph (110km/h). As for torque, the 25 per cent increase to 124lb ft from the 101lb ft of the old IOE 2-litre petrol engine meant that the Land Rover accelerated faster on the road and towed better in all conditions. However, it is important to remember that the Land Rover was a commercial vehicle, not a car, and its acceleration was leisurely compared with that of small family saloons from the period.

The story of the styling changes seems to be rather more complicated. No documentation has so far been discovered to explain what happened, but it appears that the Series II styling grew out of another project that was dear to Technical Director Maurice Wilks's heart. This was the Road-Rover, which had started life in the first half of 1952 as a utility estate car with a shortened Rover car chassis and a no-frills functional body in the Land Rover idiom. The wheelbase seems to have been close to the 86in of the Land Rover that was by then under development, but it looks as if Wilks had decided to try a larger vehicle by 1955. The easiest way of doing this was to use a long-wheelbase Land Rover chassis, and Wilks seems to have asked his recently-appointed stylist David Bache to draw up a more car-like estate car body on the basis of that.

Bache obliged, and the resulting vehicle – which wore a Rover rather than Land Rover grille badge – was a strikingly handsome creation. It never became a Road-Rover, because that project changed direction in mid 1956 and subsequent prototypes were built on a 98in wheelbase, car-derived chassis. However, Rover was proud enough of it to lend the prototype to the Royal Family for a number of years. As for the styling ideas, Wilks earmarked those for an eventual replacement for the Land Rover 107in Station Wagon. That was exactly what happened to them, albeit with a few modifications, and David Bache (who by this time had his own department and a small team of assistants) drew up variants of the same style to suit the short-wheelbase and pick-up Land Rovers. So enduring did that styling prove that it was still in use fifty-one years later on the Land Rover Defender models in 2009.

Most of the lower body of the Station Wagon design was retained for the other variants, but Bache and his team did have to draw up a new truck cab. The existing type was a purely functional construction that bolted to the standard open bodywork and offered very poor visibility for reversing. Perhaps Bache was instructed specifically to improve that aspect in his new design. But one way or another, what he came up with was neat, attractive and functional, featuring curved rear quarters that contained glass panels to give the driver an excellent view to the rear of the vehicle.

The other changes that made up the Series II package were largely evolutionary. Pendant pedals reduced the amount of dust that got into the vehicle through

This press picture introduced the Series II 88 to the world. In fact, it shows the fifth prototype, 88/2S/5, which has some differences from the production models. Note, for example, the narrow-track Series I rear axle with semi-floating hubs!

the holes in the toeboard on older Land Rovers. A hydraulically operated clutch gave smoother operation. Making flashing indicators standard equipment for most territories simply reflected the inevitable progress of owners' expectations. And wider-track axles were added to make the Land Rover more stable on side slopes while reducing the size of its turning circle.

However, there were to be no new derivatives in the Series II range. As with the earlier models, which were now retrospectively christened Series Is, the range consisted of short-wheelbase (88in) and long-wheelbase (109in) chassis, each with the same basic body types as their predecessors. So there were to be: basic open pick-ups (usually seen with the canvas 'full' tilt in temperate climates, but often delivered elsewhere without); hardtop, van-type options; a 'window hardtop' for export; truck cab pick-ups with the separate 'three-quarters' canvas tilt; and, of course, the Station Wagons. Special bodies by outside concerns would be built on either rolling chassis (which were always delivered with the front bulkhead and seat box in place) or on chassis-cabs (which were exactly what the name suggests), but these simply required deletions during the assembly stage.

SERIES II PROTOTYPES

Not much has been discovered about the prototypes of the Series II, although there seem to have been at least seven 88in types and at least five 109in types. Most of these were probably built in 1957, and they carried an 'S2' identifier in their chassis numbers as a clear indication of what they were. However, some earlier vehicles run by the Engineering Department certainly incorporated elements that would become Series II features, among them an 86in Series I registered in March 1956 that had a prototype 2.25-litre engine.

A problem that Solihull faced as the Series II models came closer to production was that its Drawing Office was overloaded. Also scheduled for introduction in 1958 – in fact, in the autumn – was the new Rover 3-litre saloon, and it is clear that the attempt to get both this and the Series II Land Rovers through the system at the same time led to difficulties. There were delays on the car (which were probably the main cause of some quite serious deficiencies in the first examples) and delays on the Land Rover as well. There were also delays in getting production of the new 2.25-litre engine up to the required volumes.

So the introduction of the Series II models was staggered. Rover had chosen the date of April 1958 for the launch of the new models, partly because this was hot on the heels of the announcement of the new Gipsy and partly because it was ten years to the month since the first Land Rover had been announced. Rover's thinking was that the media were likely to latch on to this fact and to give the new models a correspondingly greater amount of coverage. However, April 1958 was too early for the long-wheelbase Station Wagons (the Drawing Office did not complete work on them until April or May) and so these were held over until the autumn as 1959 models. The shortage of engines was dealt with by offering the more powerful new 2.25-litre only in long-wheelbase models (which, being heavier, needed it most) and by fitting short-wheelbase models with the existing 2litre IOE engine. Then, at the same time as the new Series II 109 Station Wagons were announced, the 88s were also upgraded with the new 2.25-litre type.

SERIES II AND SERIES IIA

The Series II Land Rovers were built not only at the Rover Company's factory in Solihull but also in several overseas locations, using kits of parts sent out from Solihull. There were also dozens of minor specification changes to the Series IIs over the three years of their production, and those changes that form part of this book's subject matter. However, the next round of major changes came in 1961, when a series of modifications introduced at the same time prompted a change to the Series IIA designation. As far as it is possible to tell, these modifications had been developed and tested on otherwise standard Series II models that belonged to the Engineering fleet at Solihull, and it was these vehicles that served as the Series IIA 'prototypes'.

There were far more differences between the Series II and the Series IIA models than it appears at first sight. The most obvious was the change from a 2-litre diesel engine to a 2.25-litre type, which shared its larger bore with the petrol engines. Others included the relocation of the battery under the seat box instead of under the bonnet, a higher-mounted water pump and bulkhead ventilators attached by spot-welds instead of the screws used on Series IIs.

This special Station Wagon was designed by David Bache and built in 1956 on a Series I chassis. It seems to have been intended as a concept study for the Road Rover project, but Rover management liked it so much that its design was set aside for the Series II models – and in fact the chassis was numbered 109/2/52, which made it the second Series II 109 prototype. The vehicle itself was lent to the Royal Family. Note the Viking-ship grille badge, always associated with Rover cars rather than Land Rovers.

THE NEW SERIES II
REGULAR
LAND-ROVER
TTR 117

THE
NEW SERIES II
LONG
LAND-ROVER

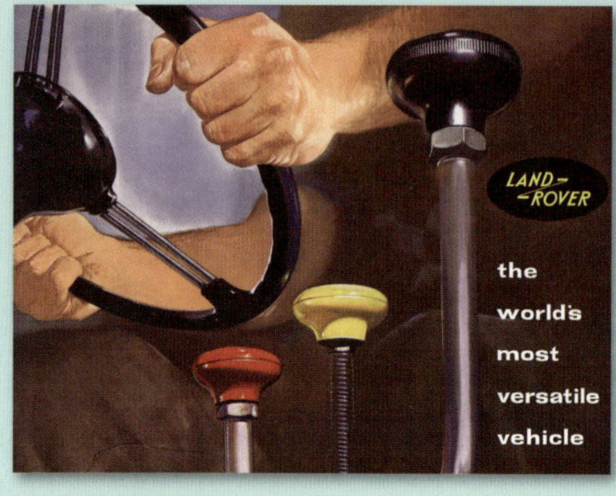
LAND-ROVER
the
world's
most
versatile
vehicle

LAND-ROVER
the world's most
versatile vehicle

LAND-ROVER
LEADS ON THE LAND
YAC 654

LAND-ROVER
LEADS ON THE LAND

the world's most versatile vehicle
LAND-ROVER

ROVER $2\frac{1}{4}$ LITRE DIESEL ENGINE...
221 HKE

Preliminary Information

6 CYLINDER

109" WHEELBASE LONG LAND-ROVER

LAND-ROVER

NOW LAND-ROVER TAKES THE SMOOTH WITH THE ROUGH

New 6-cylinder option for the 109" range makes the Land-Rover comfortably at home cruising down the motorway. A 6-cylinder, 2.6 Litre petrol engine that gives Land-Rover power to cruise faster, accelerate quicker, run quieter. All this and improved fuel economy.

And this new power is matched by a host of other improvements to the 109" range. There's a heavy duty 9½" diaphragm spring clutch to cope with the extra power. It bristles with new safety features. Servo-assisted brakes. Safety-belts. Laminated windscreen and twin horns.

The door sealing has also been improved to make the Land-Rover cosier. A new speedo and temperature gauge have been incorporated in the re-styled facia and de-luxe trim adds the finishing touch.

The Land-Rover has 38 body styles with options of 4- or 6-cylinder petrol engine or 4-cylinder diesel engine. So see your Land-Rover dealer now. He's the man in the know.

Forward-Control models joined the range in 1962, and are covered in Chapter 11. This is an early example on the 109-inch chassis; from 1966, the wheelbase became 110 inches.

A special airportable 'Lightweight' version of the 88 was developed during the 1960s for the British armed forces, and is covered in Chapter 12 of this book. The example pictured is an early prototype, with a number of differences from the production models that started coming off the lines in 1968.

RIGHT: Among the new features on the Series IIs in 1958 were this car-type bonnet catch. Series Is always had military-style external bonnet catches, which the military demanded again when it bought Series IIs and IIAs.

BELOW: Another new feature on the Series IIs was an external fuel filler: on Series Is, the fuel tank had always been under the seat and was filled after removing the seat cushion. There was an extending neck as well, to make filling from a can easier.

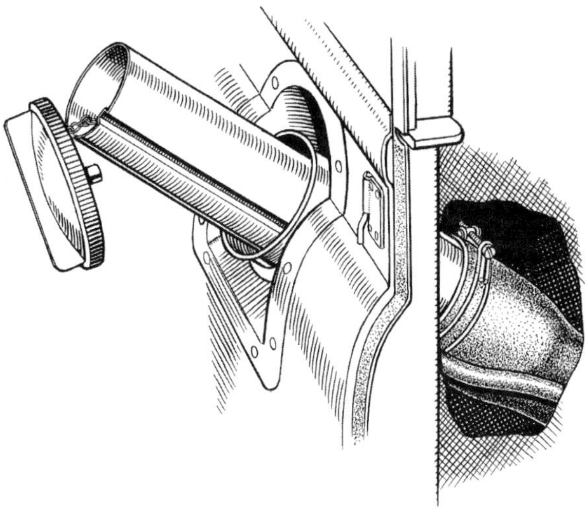

The use of the Series IIA designation also reflected a new vehicle and component numbering system that was introduced at Solihull in autumn 1961 for the 1962 model year. A letter suffix was added to the end of the unit number. Subsequent changes to the specification, which were of importance when servicing the vehicle, would be indicated with a new suffix letter. The idea was to make life easier for dealerships servicing vehicles, and was applied to Rover cars as well as Land Rovers.

Because the first letter applied to Land Rovers was an A (actually, a lower-case letter in the beginning), the new models obviously became Series IIAs. However, Land Rovers remained Series IIAs when the chassis suffix letter was changed to a B (again a lower-case letter was actually stamped into chassis plates) and were still IIAs when the last chassis suffix of H (a capital letter was introduced with suffix C) was introduced during 1970. So the final Series IIA models, some military specials apart, built in 1971 were actually Series IIA Suffix H types.

Although Solihull remained the primary assembly plant, Series IIAs were constructed from kits of parts in even more overseas locations than the Series IIs had been. The Series IIA family also expanded to include a greater variety of types than the Series II family had done. Most notable among these were the Forward Control models that were introduced in 1962, the military-only 'Lightweights' that entered production in 1967, the 6-cylinder 109s that arrived the same year and the 109 One Ton models that were announced in 1968. There were also, inevitably, many more minor specification changes during the ten-year production life of the Series IIAs than there had been during the

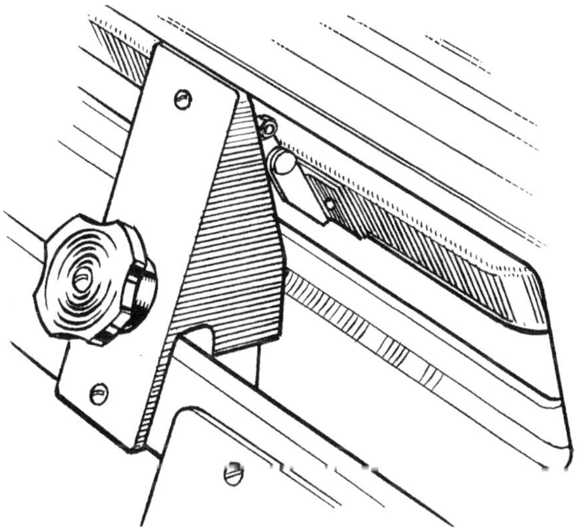

Series Is had bulkhead ventilators that were either open or closed. On Series IIs, a screw adjuster was introduced.

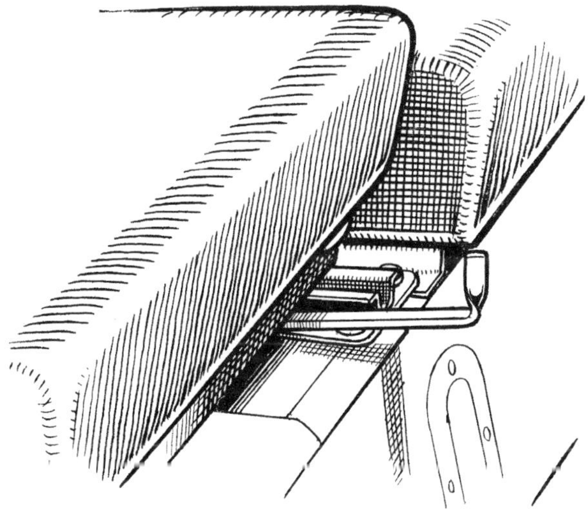

Another great step forward in 1958 was a driver's seat that was adjustable for reach.

three-year production life of the Series IIs.

APPROVED CONVERSIONS

During the Series II and Series IIA era the Land Rover remained as adaptable as it had always been, and the number of aftermarket conversions and adaptations expanded enormously. This was mainly due to the work of the Special Projects Department, which had been established in 1957 under the name of the Technical Sales Department.

Run by George Mackie throughout the period of the Series IIs and IIAs, Special Projects had the responsibility of liaising with aftermarket conversion specialists, testing their work to make sure that it would not compromise the performance of the Land Rover in any way and then awarding a formal 'Land Rover Approval' for each conversion – or, of course, rejecting it. Between the start of Series II production in 1958 and the end of Series IIA production in 1971, scores of conversions and items of special equipment were assessed, and those which gained the coveted Land Rover Approval are the subject of Chapters 7 and 8.

THE LEYLAND MERGER

When the first Series II Land Rovers were built the Rover Company had been a small but highly respected independent manufacturer. However, a series of mergers and take-overs within the British motor industry during the early 1960s saw two major groupings form – one centred on the Leyland truck and bus company and the other on the old BMC (British Motor Corporation) organization. Rover belonged to neither, with the result that BMC's purchase of the independent Pressed Steel Company, which produced all Rover's car bodyshells, left it with a problem. Whether it stayed with Pressed Steel or turned to the Leyland group for its bodyshells it would, in effect, be using a rival company as a major supplier.

Choosing to negotiate from a position of strength while they still could, the Rover Board approached the Leyland Motor Corporation towards the end of 1966. Their joint decision was that a merger would be in the interests of both parties, and so in the early part of 1967 the Rover Company was absorbed into Leyland.

A year later, the Leyland Motor Corporation itself merged with British Motor Holdings (the old BMC group, plus Jaguar) and the new conglomerate called itself the British Leyland Motor Corporation. Within BLMC, Rover (and with it Land Rover) proved to be one of the few successful components of the BLMC empire and was therefore left to get on with its own business in relative peace. At first, the only real difference was that its board was supplemented by two directors from the BLMC main board.

Things began to change in the early 1970s, and by the start of 1971 BLMC was working on plans to eliminate product duplication by merging the Rover and the Triumph saloon car range. However, once again Land Rover engineering was left alone, and the impact of British Leyland on the Series IIAs was undetectable except in the appearance of the Leyland 'flying wheel' logo on sales and advertising material.

One of the Land Rover's strongest selling points was its versatility. This 1965 line-up shows all the options then available from the factory – including the Forward Controls.

Where Were They Made?

The majority of all Series II and Series IIA Land Rovers were assembled in Britain at the Rover company's plant in Lode Lane, Solihull, in the West Midlands. However, in this period Solihull was primarily an assembly plant and depended on components manufactured at a number of 'feeder' plants that Rover owned. These components were all brought to the Solihull plant by road.

The feeder plants were:

Acocks Green diesel engines and 6-cylinder petrol engines
Bordesley Green (north-east Birmingham) sundry parts
Clay Lane (Coventry) cabs and hardtops
Garrison Street (north-east Birmingham) doors and interior trim
Percy Road transmissions
Perry Bar (north-west Birmingham) axles
Tyburn Road (north-west Birmingham) suspension, bell-housings and gearbox casings
Tyseley 4-cylinder petrol engines

Substantial numbers of Land Rovers were assembled from kits of parts shipped to overseas assembly plants from Solihull. These were known as CKD (Completely Knocked-Down) vehicles, and Chapter 10 has more information about them.

2 vehicle identification

The truck cab was characteristic of the Series II re-design. It is seen here on a very early 88, the third home-market model, now restored by the Dunsfold Collection.

The Series II and IIA Land Rovers were available in two wheelbase lengths to suit different load requirements. The short-wheelbase models had an 88in wheelbase and the long wheelbase models had a 109in wheelbase. Rover called them 'regular' and 'long' models, respectively, throughout the Series II and IIA era, but these names have fallen out of use. Most people today call them 88s and 109s.

There were several different varieties of body, all available on both the 88 and the 109 chassis:

Open a pick-up with an open cab, commonly supplied with a full canvas hood; sometimes known as 'full tilt' models, these were popular with military buyers.

Truck cab a pick-up with an enclosed cab; the back body could be fitted with a canvas hood ('three-quarter tilt') supported on hood sticks.

Hardtop a van constructed by adding a metal roof and upper body to the open model; the standard tailgate was usually fitted, together with a top-hinged upper 'door', but from March 1960 the Station Wagon side-hinged door could be ordered as an alternative.

Window hardtop a hardtop with fixed windows in the upper body sides; 88s had one window on each side and 109s had two; they were normally supplied only for export markets because British regulations would have classed them as cars and made them subject to purchase tax, although some were sold to special order; they could have either the standard tailgate with top flap or the side-hinged tail door.

Station Wagon the 88 Station Wagon added upper rear body sides with opening windows, a full-length roof with Alpine lights and (usually) a 'tropical' roof to the open 88 model; the 109 Station Wagon had extra side doors, a special back body, a full-length roof with Alpine lights and (usually) a 'tropical' roof panel.

CHASSIS NUMBERS

All Series II and Series IIA Land Rovers carried a vehicle identification plate (usually known as the chassis plate). This was attached to the cab side of the bulkhead by screws, just above the gearbox cover. The plate has instructions for the use of the transfer gearbox and identifies the vehicle as a Series II or Series IIA type. The chassis number (now known as the VIN in Britain) is stamped into the plate.

As these plates were removable, Land Rover also stamped the chassis number into the outer surface of the right-hand chassis side rail, just behind the front bumper and above the spring

LEFT: The truck cab is seen here on a late 109, with headlamps in the wings and the 'cross'-shaped grille. Note the side stowage for the spare wheel.

BELOW: The hardtop body turned the Land Rover into a van. This 1958 example was new to the Liverpool City Police in 1958.

RIGHT: This 109 hardtop was new to London's Metropolitan Police in 1966 and had the optional Station Wagon-type rear door. The windows in the tail panels alongside were standard.

hanger. (On some models assembled overseas, as in Australia, the number is sometimes located elsewhere on the frame.) This number can be hard to locate because it was first covered by black chassis paint and then by any additional chassis protection material (for instance, underseal) that was applied. Sometimes, the number is covered by extras that have been bolted on, such as a winch mount or winch bumper.

The chassis number identifies the vehicle type and will show whether it was built with RHD or LHD, a diesel or a petrol engine, at Solihull or from CKD. On Series II models the chassis number will also reveal the model-year (*see* below) when the vehicle was built. On Series IIA models it will reveal details of its mechanical specification but will not reveal the date of manufacture.

It is possible to discover the date on which a Solihull-built Land Rover left the assembly line by consulting the archives of the British Motor Industry Heritage Trust, held at the Heritage Motor Centre in Gaydon, Warwickshire (01926 641188). The archives contain the records of the Solihull Despatch Department, which recorded against the chassis number of each vehicle its original body colour, the date when it left the assembly line (and therefore entered the Despatch Department) and the date when it was 'despatched-out' to a dealer, converter or customer.

These records also show the Line Number. Land Rovers were not built in chassis number order but were often grouped in batches of a similar type for convenience and each one was allocated a Line Number as it joined the assembly lines. The Line Number is meaningless by itself, but by comparison with the numbers allocated to other vehicles built at the same time it can indicate whether a given vehicle was built before or after another.

Sometimes, dates recorded as 'into Despatch' seem to contradict the evidence of the Line Number. One reason for this may be that a vehicle had a fault

Hardtops were normally equipped with a top tailgate that hinged upwards. The standard lower tailboard remained in place.

For export only, a window hardtop was available. This Series II has the option of a Station Wagon-type tail door. Like all early 88 hardtops, it has no windows in the tail panels alongside the door.

when it reached the end of the assembly line; it would then be taken on one side for rectification before it was passed from the Production Department to the Despatch Department. In the meantime, vehicles behind it on the assembly lines would, of course, enter the Despatch Department ahead of it.

It is important to recognize that the build-year and the model-year are not necessarily the same. The Land Rover model-year (often called the 'season' during the 1950s and the 1960s) began in September and ended in July, so that a vehicle built in September 1959 would actually be a 1960 model, as would one built in July 1960. A Land Rover built in September 1960 would be a 1961 model and so on. August usually saw the production lines close down and staff took their annual summer holiday in this period, except for some of those in the Production Department who prepared the assembly lines for the new season's models.

UNDERSTANDING A SERIES II CHASSIS NUMBER

Series II Land Rover chassis numbers have a four-digit type identifier prefix followed by a five-digit serial number. The serial numbers in each sequence began at 00001. The four-digit prefix (such as 1418) decodes as follows:

1 Land Rover
4 Series II 88in
  5 Series II 109in
1 petrol engine, home market (RHD)
  2 petrol engine, RHD export
  3 petrol engine, RHD CKD
  4 petrol engine, LHD
  5 petrol engine, LHD CKD
  6 diesel engine, home market (RHD)
  7 diesel engine, RHD export
  8 diesel engine, RHD CKD
  9 diesel engine, LHD
  0 diesel engine, LHD CKD
8 1958 model-year
  9 1959 model-year
  0 1960 model-year
  1 1961 model-year

Note that a Series II chassis number does not identify the original body type fitted to the vehicle.

SERIES II CHASSIS NUMBERS

These figures are for model-year ('season'), which ran from September to August.

88in Utilities

1958

- 1418-00001 to 1418-01703 home market, petrol
- 1428-00001 to 1428-01359 RHD export, petrol
- 1438-00001 to 1438-00960 RHD, CKD, petrol
- 1448-00001 to 1448-02288 LHD, petrol
- 1458-00001 to 1458-00840 LHD, CKD, petrol
- 1468-00001 to 1468-00587 home market, diesel
- 1478-00001 to 1478-00243 RHD export, diesel
- 1488-00001 to 1488-00156 RHD, CKD, diesel
- 1498-00001 to 1498-00239 LHD, diesel
- 1508-00001 to 1508-00036 LHD, CKD, diesel

1959

- 1419-00001 to 1419-04072 home market, petrol
- 1429-00001 to 1429-01964 RHD export, petrol
- 1439-00001 to 1439-01822 RHD, CKD, petrol
- 1449-00001 to 1449-04010 LHD, petrol
- 1459-00001 to 1459-01068 LHD, CKD, petrol
- 1469-00001 to 1469-01761 home market, diesel
- 1479-00001 to 1479-00215 RHD export, diesel
- 1489-00001 to 1489-00060 RHD, CKD, diesel
- 1499-00001 to 1499-00355 LHD, diesel
- 1509-00001 to 1509-00294 LHD, CKD, diesel

1960

- 1410-00001 to 1410-04545 home market
- 1420-00001 to 1420-02899 RHD export, petrol
- 1430-00001 to 1430-01671 RHD, CKD, petrol
- 1440-00001 to 1440-06518 LHD, petrol
- 1450-00001 to 1450-00276 LHD, CKD, petrol
- 1460-00001 to 1460-02192 home market, diesel
- 1470-00001 to 1470-00369 RHD export, diesel
- 1480-00001 to 1480-00041 RHD, CKD, diesel
- 1490-00001 to 1490-00494 LHD, diesel
- 1500-00001 to 1500-00047 LHD, CKD, diesel

The 109 window hardtop had two windows in each side. The front sidelights and indicators show that this example started out as a military vehicle.

The 88 Station Wagon was a seven-seater. This example dates from the mid-1960s.

1961

- 1411-00001 to 1411-04450 home market, petrol
- 1421-00001 to 1421-02256 RHD export, petrol
- 1431-00001 to 1431-02302 RHD, CKD, petrol
- 1441-00001 to 1441-05602 LHD, petrol
- 1451-00001 to 1451-00312 LHD, CKD, petrol
- 1461-00001 to 1461-01282 home market, diesel
- 1471-00001 to 1471-00392 RHD export, diesel
- 1481-00001 to 1481-00018 RHD, CKD, diesel
- 1491-00001 to 1491-00704 LHD, diesel
- 1501-00001 to 1501-00054 LHD, CKD, diesel

Station Wagons were numbered within the sequences used for the Series II 88in Land Rovers.

109in Utilities

1958

- 1518-00001 to 1518-00360 home market, petrol
- 1528-00001 to 1528-01153 RHD export, petrol
- 1538-00001 to 1538-00480 RHD, CKD, petrol
- 1548-00001 to 1548-00903 LHD, petrol
- 1558-00001 to 1558-00048 LHD, CKD, petrol
- 1568-00001 to 1568-00261 home market, diesel
- 1578-00001 to 1578-00309 RHD export, diesel
- 1588-00001 to 1588-00132 RHD, CKD, diesel
- 1598-00001 to 1598-00083 LHD, diesel
- 1608-00001 to 1608-00006 LHD, CKD, diesel

1959

- 1519-00001 to 1519-01137 home market, petrol
- 1529-00001 to 1529-03458 RHD export, petrol
- 1539-00001 to 1539-00481 RHD, CKD, petrol
- 1549-00001 to 1549-01911 LHD, petrol
- 1559-series none built LHD, CKD, petrol
- 1569-00001 to 1569-01089 home market, diesel
- 1579-00001 to 1579-00586 RHD export, diesel
- 1589-00001 to 1589-00060 RHD, CKD, diesel
- 1599-00001 to 1599-00362 LHD, diesel
- 1609-00001 to 1609-00030 LHD, CKD, diesel

1960

- 1510-00001 to 1510-01587 home market
- 1520-00001 to 1520-04533 RHD export, petrol
- 1530-00001 to 1530-01922 RHD, CKD, petrol
- 1540-00001 to 1540-03116 LHD, petrol
- 1550-00001 to 1550-00280 LHD, CKD, petrol
- 1560-00001 to 1560-01310 home market, diesel
- 1570-00001 to 1570-00747 RHD export, diesel
- 1580-00001 to 1580-00113 RHD, CKD, diesel
- 1590-00001 to 1590-00565 LHD, diesel
- 1600-00001 to 1600-00005 LHD, CKD, diesel

1961

- 1511-00001 to 1511-01500 home market, petrol
- 1521-00001 to 1521-04909 RHD export, petrol
- 1531-00001 to 1531-02955 RHD, CKD, petrol
- 1541-00001 to 1541-02832 LHD, petrol
- 1551-00001 to 1551-00168 LHD, CKD, petrol
- 1561-00001 to 1561-00911 home market, diesel
- 1571-00001 to 1571-00818 RHD export, diesel
- 1581-00001 to 1581-00156 RHD, CKD, diesel
- 1591-00001 to 1591-00756 LHD, diesel
- 1601-series none built LHD, CKD, diesel

109in Station Wagon

1959

- 1619-00001 to 1619-00106 home market, petrol
- 1629-00001 to 1629-00567 RHD export, petrol
- 1639-00001 to 1639-00025 RHD, CKD, petrol
- 1649-00001 to 1649-00962 LHD, petrol
- 1659-series none built LHD, CKD, petrol
- 1669-series none built home market, diesel
- 1679-00001 to 1679-00006 RHD export, diesel
- 1689-series none built RHD, CKD, diesel
- 1699-00001 to 1699-00026 LHD, diesel
- 1709-series none built LHD, CKD, diesel

1960

- 1610-00001 to 1610-00101 home market
- 1620-00001 to 1620-01188 RHD export, petrol
- 1630-00001 to 1630-00063 RHD, CKD, petrol
- 1640-00001 to 1640-01267 LHD, petrol
- 1650-00001 to 1650-00024 LHD, CKD, petrol
- 1660-series none built home market, diesel
- 1670-00001 to 1670-00020 RHD export, diesel
- 1680-series none built RHD, CKD, diesel
- 1690-00001 to 1690-00073 LHD, diesel
- 1700-series none built LHD, CKD, diesel

1961

- 1611-00001 to 1611-00134 home market, petrol
- 1621-00001 to 1621-01314 RHD export, petrol
- 1631-00001 to 1631-00180 RHD, CKD, petrol

ABOVE: This 1967 Series IIA 109 Station Wagon shows the standard 'tropical' roof and the folding side-steps fitted for some markets.
LEFT: The One Ton version of the 109 was readily identifiable by its larger 9.00×16 tyres.

- 1641-00001 to 1641-01366 LHD, petrol
- 1651-00001 to 1651-00006 LHD, CKD, petrol
- 1661-00001 to 1661-00004 home market, diesel
- 1671-00001 to 1671-00080 RHD export, diesel
- 1681-series none built RHD, CKD, diesel
- 1691-00001 to 1691-00067 LHD, diesel
- 1701-series none built LHD, CKD, diesel

Understanding a Series IIA Chassis Number

Series IIA Land Rover chassis numbers had a three-digit-type identifier prefix followed by a five-digit serial number and a letter suffix. The serial numbers in each sequence began at 00001.

The letter suffix indicates major design modifications, which are of importance when servicing the vehicle and was introduced to aid dealer workshops in identifying the correct replacement parts. The suffix letter is in lower case on Suffix A and B models and in upper case from Suffix C onwards. The major changes introduced with each letter suffix are listed below; capital letters are used throughout for consistency.

The three-digit prefix (such as 276) does not decode in the same way as on Series II models. To identify a vehicle type, refer to the tables in this chapter.

Series IIA 88in chassis numbers did not identify the original body type fitted to the vehicle until 1965, when Station Wagons were given their own type identifier prefixes. However, chassis numbers for the other models still did not distinguish between (for example) a truck cab model and a hardtop type.

SERIES IIA: SUFFIX LETTER CHANGES

4-cylinder Models

Suffix A

As introduced in 1961, the Suffix A Series IIA models had a number of differences from Series IIs. A 2.25-litre diesel engine replaced the 2-litre type, and there were several revisions to the petrol engine as well. The battery was relocated under the seat box to make way for a wider radiator (although diesels still had one battery under the bonnet) and the bulkhead ventilators were attached by spot-welds instead of the screws used on Series IIs.

Suffix B

Suffix B was introduced for both 88 and 109 models in March 1963. It brought wider-spaced ratios in the main gearbox to improve low-speed performance and a taller Low ratio in the transfer box; lower-geared steering to reduce steering effort, and larger diameter fixings on the steering unit; bigger propshaft UJs; and modified shackle plates to take 9/16in shackle pins. Petrol models had a modified carburettor linkage with clips on the control rod between relay shaft and carburettor, and non-adjustable ball joints on the control rod between bell crank and carburettor. Diesel models had simplified controls with the electrical services switch combined with the starter and glow-plug switch, so that only one key was needed.

There were redesigned headlamps and new side, flasher and rear lamps without a separate bezel. A combined stop-tail and number-plate illumination lamp replaced the two separate lamps on earlier models and a curved apron panel replaced the flat type.

Suffix C

The Suffix C models were introduced in August 1965. The key modifications were a new, all-plastic steering wheel fixed to the steering column on a tapered spline in place of the earlier straight spline, and a modified rubber seal on the transfer lever to eliminate interference between seal and lever. Midway through Suffix C production seat belts became an option and a longer handbrake lever was introduced to ensure that a belted driver could reach it.

LEFT: The chassis number is stamped into a plate attached to the bulkhead, just above the transmission tunnel. Note the red warning plate directly underneath it. This is on a 1958 Series II 88.

ABOVE: Later chassis plates differed: note the reference to Solihull and to the model type. This plate is from a 1965 Series IIA Suffix C 88.

ABOVE: The engine number on a 2.25-litre 4-cylinder petrol is stamped into the left-hand front of the cylinder block. LEFT: Location of the gearbox number.

SUFFIX D

Suffix D changes were introduced in May 1967. Central to them was the change to a negative-earth electrical system. Twin wipers operated by a single motor replaced the earlier system with separate motors, and the new black instrument panel had a revised dial and switchgear layout and damped fuel and water temperature gauges. Petrol-engined models now had a key start system and diesels had a new key starter switch on the instrument panel. There were redesigned door locks with an extended barrel lock.

At the same time, the 4-cylinder petrol engine (now Suffix J) took on a Zenith 36IV carburettor in place of the Solex; the diesel engine had a reshaped front exhaust pipe to give more clearance; a 9.5in diameter diaphragm spring clutch became standard on diesel models (both at Suffix H); and the gearboxes (now Suffix E) had a modified bell housing with repositioned cored holes accommodating a grommet instead of a dust cover.

Chassis changes affected the handbrake relay mounting and the axle check strap mountings (now flat plates instead of angled), while there was a larger hole for the PTO in the front cross-member (although the rear one was unchanged).

SUFFIX E

Suffix E was introduced in March 1968 for diesel models only; 4-cylinder petrol models retained Suffix D. At the same time, the diesel engines switched to Suffix K.

There were improvements to reduce oil consumption: lip-type oil seals for the valve guides replaced O-rings and there were new compression rings with a chrome insert. Other measures simplified timing: a timing pointer on the front cover and a timing mark on the crankshaft pulley replaced marks on the flywheel and an aperture in the flywheel housing, and a new distributor pump also allowed external timing.

The diesel engines also gained a dustproof crankcase breather and a new injection system with leak-off provision at the top rather than the side. The injectors changed to flanged types from clamped types and the fuel filter was an improved reverse-flow type. There was a redesigned starter motor with better sealing.

SUFFIX F (JANUARY 1969)

A key change with Suffix F was a flat-bodied heater (which was still an optional fit). This put out 3.5kW as against the older type's 2.5 kW, and had a two-speed fan. Its increased size meant the transfer lever had to be cranked slightly to clear it and a vertical hand-throttle replaced the earlier horizontal type for the same reason. There was a new permanent magnet wiper motor with an improved rack tube to give quieter running and a mechanical stop-light switch replaced the hydraulic type. The brake pedal, bracket and spring were all modified to suit, as was the wiring harness, and there was an additional anchor plate for the De Luxe trim, again to suit the new switch. Flashers were standardized for most markets.

SUFFIX G (APRIL 1969)

The major change at this point was the relocation of the headlamps in the front wings. A larger, cross-shaped mesh grille was fitted and the front number plate was relocated from the wing to the centre of the bumper on a support plate. There was also a new Lucas 8FL flasher unit.

The 4-cylinder petrol engine had a higher compression ratio of 8:1 (and a new numbering series with a 241- prefix), although the 7:1 engine was still available to order. The high-compression engines were rated at 81bhp at 4,250rpm and 127lb ft at 2,500rpm.

SUFFIX H (FEBRUARY 1971)

The final Series IIA suffix change brought a switch to metric (16mm) wheel studs. British-market 88 and 109 Station Wagons gained an all-synchromesh gearbox (numbered from 910-00001A) and these models also had a large cut-out in number 3 chassis cross-member to accommodate the associated new bell housing and slave cylinder.

The standard ('Rover type') differentials now had revised pinion housings to make them common with Range Rover type housings, while some export 109s and all 109 Station Wagons for Britain had stronger Salisbury rear axles (numbered from 911-00001A).

6-cylinder Petrol 109s

Suffix A

As introduced in May 1967, these had the heavy-duty 9.5in diaphragm-spring clutch and wider front brake shoes from the Forward Controls, plus a Clayton Dewandre brake servo as standard. There was a semi-sealed cooling system with an overflow bottle on the left-hand side of the radiator. The standard engine compression ratio was 7.8:1, but a low 7.0:1 version was available for export, and there was a single SU carburettor. The double-ended SU fuel pump was mounted on top of the right-hand chassis rail under the seat box.

Suffix G

Suffixes B to F were not used on the 6-cylinder models. It appears that the suffixes were brought into line with those used on 4-cylinder models very soon after production began.

109 One Ton Models

Suffix A

The One Ton model was announced at the Commercial Motor Show in September 1968, but volume production did not begin until April 1969. It was rated to carry a maximum payload of 2,240lb (1,015kg) in cross-country work. Both 4-cylinder and 6-cylinder petrol engines were available, although, in practice, all had the 6-cylinder engine apart from twenty-two vehicles delivered to the military, which were bodied by HCB-Angus as TACR-1 airfield crash rescue tenders.

The gearbox had an extended mainshaft but was otherwise standard, and there was a special low-ratio transfer box, together with heavy-duty ENV axles front and rear and 9.00×16 tyres on 6.5×16 wheels. The chassis frame had extended spring shackles ('drop-shackles') to increase the ride height by 2–3in (50–75mm) and heavy-duty springs and dampers were fitted. The 6-cylinder models had a rear-mounted fuel tank, but the military TACR-1s had fuel tanks in the conventional position. The steering box ratio was lower than on standard 109s. Standard equipment included a hydraulic steering damper and a Girling brake servo.

Suffix G

Like the 6-cylinder 109s, the One Tons moved straight from Suffix A to Suffix G. Chassis number 13 had an A suffix, but chassis number 20 had a G suffix.

SERIES IIA CHASSIS NUMBERS

The Land Rover model year once again ran from September to August. These tables are based on the records of the Despatch Department, now held by the Heritage Motor Centre, but do not include CKD models after December 1964. Where figures have been discovered for CKD models, these are indicated in brackets, and where the suffix letter of the final chassis is not known, its absence is indicated with 'x'.

88in Utilities

- 1722-00001 to 1722-00003
  RHD diesel, 1961 prototype batch
- 1772-00001 to 1772-00004
  LHD diesel, 1961 prototype batch
- 241-00001A to 241-42494H
  home market, petrol
- 242-00001A to 242-13449H
  RHD export, petrol
- 243-00001A to 243-08207x
  RHD, CKD, petrol (highest known 243-15651D)
- 244-00001A to 244-45282H
  LHD, petrol
- 245-00001A to 245-02629x
  LHD, CKD, petrol (highest known 245-05701D)
- 271-00001A to 271-15263H
  home market, diesel
- 272-00001A to 272-02707H
  RHD export, diesel
- 273-00001A to 273-00294x
  RHD, CKD, diesel (highest known 273-00930D)
- 274-00001A to 274-07561H
  LHD, diesel
- 275-00001A to 275-00355x
  LHD, CKD, diesel (highest known 275-01388D)

Note: Station Wagons were numbered in the main 88in sequences until 1965, but had their own sequences thereafter.

88in Station Wagons

- 315-00001B to 315-00782H
  home market, petrol
- 316-00001B to 316-01652H
  RHD export, petrol
- 317-series (no records)
  RHD, CKD, petrol (highest known 317-00329D)
- 318-00001B to 318-09216H
  LHD, petrol
- 319-series (no records)
  LHD, CKD, petrol (highest known 319-02616D)
- 320-00001B to 320-00041H
  home market, diesel
- 321-00001B to 321-00228H
  RHD export, diesel
- 322-series (no records)
  RHD, CKD, diesel
- 323-00001B to 323-01653H
  LHD, diesel
- 324-series (no records)
  LHD, CKD, diesel (highest known 324-00786D)

109in Utilities

- 251-00001B to 251-22019H
  home market, 4-cylinder petrol
- 252-00001A to 252-34662H
  RHD export, 4-cylinder petrol
- 253-00001A to 253-11218x
  RHD, CKD, 4-cylinder petrol (highest known 253-29622D)
- 254-00001A to 254-39150H
  LHD, 4-cylinder petrol
- 255-00001A to 255-00541H
  LHD, CKD, 4-cylinder petrol (highest known 255-12565D)
- 276-00001A to 276-13140H
  home market, diesel
- 277-00001A to 277-07673H
  RHD export, diesel
- 278-00001A to 278-01273x
  RHD, CKD, diesel (highest known 278-03799D)
- 279-00001A to 279-08620H
  LHD, diesel
- 280-00001A to 280-00462x
  LHD, CKD, diesel (highest known 280-03300D)
- 345-00001A to 345-02100H
  home market, 6-cylinder petrol
- 346-00001A to 346-01232H
  RHD export, 6-cylinder petrol
- 347-series (no records)
  RHD, CKD, 6-cylinder petrol (highest known 347-07906G)
- 348-00001A to 348-02149H
  LHD, 6-cylinder petrol
- 349-series (no records)
  LHD, CKD, 6-cylinder petrol (highest known 349-00378D)

109in Station Wagons

- 261-00001A to 261-03542H home market, 4-cylinder petrol
- 262-00001A to 262-11569H RHD export, 4-cylinder petrol
- 263-series (no records) RHD, CKD, 4-cylinder petrol (highest known 263-03507D)
- 264-00001A to 264-18516H LHD, 4-cylinder petrol
- 265-series (no records) LHD, CKD, 4-cylinder petrol (highest known 265-00876D)
- 281-00001A to 281-01453H home market, diesel
- 282-00001A to 282-01649H RHD export, diesel
- 283-00001A to 283-00081x RHD, CKD, diesel (highest known 283-00369D)
- 284-00001A to 284-04326H LHD, diesel
- 285-00001A to 285-00042H LHD, CKD, diesel (highest known 285-00150D)
- 350-00001D to 350-01625H home market, 6-cylinder petrol
- 351-00001D to 351-01133H RHD export, 6-cylinder petrol
- 352-series (no records) RHD, CKD, 6-cylinder petrol (highest known 352-00696D)
- 353-00001D to 353-02191H LHD, 6-cylinder petrol
- 354-series (no records) LHD, CKD, 6-cylinder petrol (highest known 354-00096D)

109in NADA Station Wagon

- 343-00001A to 343-00811A

109in One Ton

- 222-00001A to 222-00052H RHD export, 6-cylinder petrol
- 223-00001A to 223-00064H LHD, 6-cylinder petrol
- 229-00001A to 229-00170H home market, 6-cylinder petrol
- 231-00001G to 231-00022G home market, 4-cylinder petrol

HOW MANY WERE THERE?

It is possible to give precise production totals for Series II models. However, it is currently possible to give only approximate totals for Series IIA types because no CKD records for the years from 1964 have been found.

After 1964, CKD 'sets' went straight to a company sub-contracted to ship them to their destination. They no longer passed through the Despatch Department at Solihull and were therefore not recorded in that department's ledgers, which are the source of most of our information about production dates and totals. Despite this absence of records for CKD models, it is possible to make some educated guesses about totals from references in Service Bulletins and from the chassis numbers of surviving vehicles.

Production Breakdown

Series II

TOTAL SERIES IIs 110,067
88s 60,456 (20,592 home; 39,864 export, of which 9,957 CKD)
109s 42,032 (8,155 home; 33,877 export, of which 6,836 CKD)
109 SWs 7,579 (345 home; 7,234 export, of which 598 CKD)
1958 models 12,146 (8,411 88s; 3,735 109 utilities)
1959 models 26,427 (15,621 88s; 9,114 109 utilities; 1,692 109 SWs)
1960 models 35,966 (19,052 88s; 14,178 109 utilities; 2,736 109 SWs)
1961 models 35,528 (17,372 88s; 15,005 109 utilities; 3,151 109 SWs)
diesels 18,114 (9,539 88s; 8,299 109 utilities; 276 109 SWs)
petrols 91,953 (50,917 88s; 33,733 109 utilities; 7,303 109 SWs)

GRAND TOTALS
88in (all types) 60,456
109in (all types) 49,611

Series IIA

TOTAL SERIES IIAs around 430,000

Nobody knows exactly how many Series IIA Land Rovers were built. Solihull's Despatch Department records account for 343,298 vehicles, but it is clear from an October 1969 Service Bulletin issued to Land Rover dealers that 63,825 CKD vehicles built after December 1964 had not been recorded by the Despatch Department. Added to the total recorded vehicles, this gives 407,123.

At a calculated average of 12,765 CKD vehicles a year, there would have been another 25,530 CKD models in the two years before Series IIA production ended over the summer of 1971. The grand total of Series IIA models (excluding Lightweights and Forward Controls) therefore works out at 432,653, but this figure cannot be considered definitive.

The figures below are based on the Despatch Department records only. In cases where CKD examples were built, they should therefore be considered as minimum quantities.

88s, including Station Wagons to March 1965 138,241
88 Station Wagons from March 1965 13,572
109 4-cylinder utilities 138,758
109 4-cylinder Station Wagons 41,178
109 6-cylinder utilities 5,481
109 6-cylinder Station Wagons 5,760
109 One Ton 4-cylinder utilities 22
109 One Ton 6-cylinder utilities 286
diesels 66,828 (26,187 88 utilities and Station Wagons to March 1965; 1,922 88 Station Wagons after March 1965; 31,168 109 utilities; 7,551 109 Station Wagons)
petrols (4-cylinder) 264,950 (112,061 88 utilities and Station Wagons to March 1965; 11,650 Station Wagons from March 1965; 107,590 109 utilities; 33,627 109 Station Wagons; 22 109 One Tons)
petrols (6-cylinder) 11,527 (5,481 109 utilities; 4,949 109 Station Wagons; 811 NADA 109 Station Wagons; 286 109 One Tons)

GRAND TOTALS
88in (all types) 151,813
109in (all types) 191,485

3 chassis and running gear

One of the pilot-production Series II 88 chassis is seen here under construction. In the background is an equally early 109.

This chapter deals with the 'rolling chassis' of the Series II and Series IIA Land Rovers: the chassis frame, transmission, axles, suspension, steering and brakes.

THE CHASSIS FRAME

The side-members of the Land Rover chassis frame were first made by welding four strips of metal together to form box-sections. However, with the arrival of Suffix H models in February 1971, side-members were assembled from two C-shaped sections, welded together along their top and bottom edges.

The 88in chassis frame was broadly unchanged between 1958 and 1971, but there were minor variations. So, for example, the mountings for a second battery tray on 1958 chassis were deleted from 1959 and later versions to make room for the wider radiator that came with the 2.25-litre petrol engine.

There were five major variants of the 109 chassis, and within those there were dozens of minor variations. The major variants were for the 109 4-cylinders, the 109 4-cylinder Station Wagons, the 109 6-cylinders and the 109 6-cylinder Station Wagons; the fifth was for the 109 One Ton models and was characterized by its extended spring shackles. Some 109 chassis built for special applications between about 1963 and 1968 (for example, the Australian military and Shorland armoured car) also had extended spring shackles. Chassis frames were always painted in gloss black.

The earliest Series II chassis had a towing attachment bracket on the rear cross-member, but this was deleted in September 1959 and became an optional extra. All 109 Station Wagon chassis were fitted with a folding rear step, which was initially too wide (at 19.5in/495mm) to allow a towing jaw to be fitted to the rear cross-member. From March 1960 the chassis was modified to take an 11.5in (292mm) step, offset from the vehicle's centre-line, so that a towing jaw could be fitted. The change occurred at chassis numbers 1610-00001, 1620-00089, 1640-00088, 1660-00001, 1670-00001 and 1690-00002.

The front bumper, which bolted to the chassis, was unchanged in its basic design although early examples were arc-welded and later ones were MIG-welded. For Suffix G and later models, the top surface was drilled to accept the number plate that the repositioned headlamps had displaced from the front wing.

The 4-cylinder models had a 10gal fuel tank under the right-hand seat, but all 109 Station Wagons and all 6-cylinder models had the tank mounted at the rear of the chassis. The Station Wagons had a 16gal tank, but a narrower tank was fitted to 6-cylinder utilities to make room for the propshaft drive for a rear PTO. This tank had an 11gal capacity.

THE TRANSMISSION

Clutch

The standard clutch on all models up to the end of Series IIA Suffix C was a 9in Borg and Beck coil-spring type. The pressure springs were uprated several times, especially for diesel models. From July 1962 at engine and gearbox Suffix B a self-adjusting clutch was introduced, and larger-diameter clutch hydraulic pipes were used from July 1966.

The 9.5in diaphragm-spring clutch used on Forward Control models was

In this picture of a Series II 109 chassis, the bulkhead, radiator and radiator grille panel are all in place.

On the six-cylinder 109 chassis, the petrol tank was always mounted at the rear of the chassis. This is actually a visually similar Series III type.

The transmission consisted of a four-speed primary gearbox and a two-speed transfer gearbox. In this picture, looking forward, the main gearbox is at top left, and the transfer gearbox is behind it, nearer the camera. The front extension of the transfer box takes the selectable drive to the front axle, and the black-painted drum of the transmission or hand brake is mounted on the output to the rear axle.

made available as a heavy-duty option in June 1965 (*see* Chapter 6), and was also fitted to all models destined for North America from engine number 251-63284. It was fitted to all diesel models from the start of Suffix D and to all 6-cylinder models.

The clutch slave cylinder remained unchanged throughout, although different models had different mounting brackets. A notable change to the bracket occurred in August 1960 when the engines were offset slightly; the change occurred at engine numbers 1460-02358, 1510-23273 and 1560-02148.

The clutch shared its fluid reservoir with the braking system. Very early in production, the original type with outlets at the bottom was changed for one with a side outlet to the brake master cylinder to prevent air locks; this change took place on 88s at chassis numbers 1418-00001, 1428-00376, 1448-00272, 1468-00001, 1478-00126, 1498-00060 and on 109s at 1518-00001, 1528-00115, 1548-00037, 1568-00001, 1578-00019 and 1598-00008.

Main Gearbox

All Series II and Series IIA Land Rovers had versions of the same four-speed, single helical constant-mesh manual gearbox. This is sometimes called the '76mm' gearbox (from the distance between the mainshaft and layshaft centres) and was latterly known as the LT76 (LT standing for Leyland Transmissions). These gearboxes had no synchromesh on first and second gears; however, the all-synchromesh version designed for the Series III models was introduced right at the end of production on Station Wagons for the home market only.

The gearbox number identifies the type and is stamped into the casing. The number consists of a type identifier followed by a serial number. On Series II models the type identifier has four digits; on Series IIA models it has three and the serial number is followed by a suffix letter. This letter identifies variants in specification.

Transfer Gearbox

All Series II and Series IIA models had the same basic design of two-speed transfer gearbox. On Series II and Series IIA Suffix A models, the High Range gearing was 1.148:1 and the Low Range gearing 2.89:1. On Series IIA Suffix B and later models the High Range gearing was unchanged but the Low Range gearing was 2.35:1.

On the 109 One Ton models the transfer box had High Range gearing of 1.53:1 and Low Range gearing of 3.27:1. These transfer boxes also had helical-cut gears to allow a change from High ratio into Low ratio on the move.

Gearbox Identifying Prefixes

Series II

1958 model-year

1418	for 88 (2-litre) petrol models
1468	for 88 diesel
1518	for 109 (2.25-litre) petrol models
1568	for 109 diesel

1959 model-year

1419	for petrol models
1469	for 88 diesel
1519	for petrol models
1569	for 109 Diesel Station Wagon

1960 model-year

1410	for petrol models
1460	for 88 diesel
1510	for petrol models
1560	for 109 Diesel Station Wagon

1961 model-year

1461	for 88 diesel
1511	for petrol models
1561	for 109 diesel

Series IIA

223	(serials commencing 800001B) for 109 One Ton 2.25-litre petrol
223	(serials commencing 900001B) for 109 One Ton 2.6-litre petrol
229	for 109 One Ton 2.6-litre petrol
236	for 88 Lightweight
238	for 109 One Ton 2.25-litre petrol
251	for all 2.25-litre petrol and diesel models, to September 1964
252	for all 2.25-litre petrol and diesel models, from September 1964 (continuation from 251 series after all numbers used)
254	for 2.25-litre petrol models and NADA
255	for 2.25-litre petrol and diesel models from 1971 with modified front oil seals
256	for all 2.25-litre petrol and diesel models; service exchange gearboxes from 1972 on
257	for 109 One Ton 2.25-litre petrol; service exchange gearboxes from 1972 on
259	for 2.25-litre petrol and diesel models for Swiss Army and Postal Service in 1972 model-year
261	for 2.25-litre petrol and diesel models for Swiss Army and Postal Service in 1971 model-year
262	for 2.25-litre petrol models for UNICEF, 1963 model-year
276	for 2.25-litre diesel models
343	for 109 6-cylinder and NADA 6-cylinder
344	for 109 6-cylinder models from 1971, with modified front oil seals
346	for 109 6-cylinder; service exchange gearboxes from 1972 on
347	for 109 One Ton 6-cylinder
348	for 109 6-cylinder models for Swiss Army and Postal Service in 1971 model-year
349	for 109 6-cylinder models for Swiss Army and Postal Service in 1972 model-year
910	all-synchromesh gearboxes, from December 1970 approx.

Production Changes: Gearbox and Transfer Box

Series II

Changes during 1958. The material specification of the transfer box intermediate gear shaft was changed to improve its wearing qualities at gearbox numbers 1418-00135, 1518-00081, 1468-00121 and 1568-00001.

Changes during 1959. In June an oil-level plug on the transfer gearbox casing replaced the earlier oil-level rod, there was also a new oil filler cap with a breather. These changes occurred at gearbox numbers 1469-01901, 1519-13599 and 1569-01295. In October a bolt and nut replaced the clevis pin holding the transfer box change lever to its bracket, at gearbox numbers 1469-02724, 1519-20906 and 1569-02141.

Changes during 1960. The inspection cover on the bellhousing was changed in March to give a better fit, at gearbox numbers 1460-11147, 1510-11025 and 1560-11024. A stowage bracket was also added for the flywheel housing drain plug at gearbox number 1510-11119. In August came a new type of O-ring on the transfer gearchange shaft to improve sealing. This arrived at gearbox numbers 1460-02521 and 1510-24409. There were no recorded changes during 1961.

Series IIA

Changes during 1962. The gearbox transmission damper on diesel models was deleted in February at gearbox number 276-00880. Then in July there was a wider diameter for the transfer box layshaft and intermediate shaft. At the same time, with gearbox Suffix B the oil filler cap was deleted from the main gearbox and replaced by a fixed breather cap, while combined oil filler and level plugs were introduced in place of separate plugs on the transfer box.

Changes during 1963. In March the gear ratios in the main gearbox were lowered to improve low-speed pulling power, and the Low ratio in the transfer box was raised.

Changes during 1964. In February at gearbox number 251-70529B the tie rod bracket and lugs on the bellhousing were strengthened.

Changes during 1965. From gearbox Suffix D in August, the gearbox layshaft was strengthened, with a shoulder replacing the earlier split ring and groove. Set bolts also replaced the studs, springs and washers fixing the bottom cover plate to the transfer box casing. There were no recorded changes during 1966.

Changes during 1967. In May from gearbox Suffix E the bellhousing was modified with repositioned core holes to take grommets instead of the earlier dust covers. Then in August the fixings for the transfer box bottom cover plate that had been changed in August 1965 reverted to the earlier type.

Changes during 1968. An oil catcher was added to the gearbox in March to prevent oil leakage from the speedometer drive housing reaching the transmission brake. Then in December at gearbox number 253-78396E the peg locating the mainshaft bearing housing was deleted and the housing was secured in position by Loctite glue.

Changes during 1969. In January, a caro-bronze distance sleeve for the mainshaft bush replaced the earlier copper lead type. October brought a modified gearbox oil filler cap with enlarged breather holes.

Changes during 1970. In August a plain splined gearbox output shaft, without the earlier step, was re-introduced to reduce noise.

Changes during 1971. The all-synchromesh 'Series III' type gearbox was introduced in February for British-market 88 and 109 Station Wagons, at chassis Suffix H.

The Axles and Propshafts

There were three different types of rear axle, all with fully floating half-shafts. Standard was always the 'Rover' axle, and an ENV type was optional for heavy-duty applications from about 1965 and standard on the 109 One Ton. Then with Suffix H models in 1971 came the option of a Salisbury heavy-duty axle. (Some pilot-build and very early Series II 88s had Series I-type narrow-track axles with semi-floating half-shafts. These are recognizable by a dished hub centre cap.)

The Rover axle can be recognized by the long, ribbed nose of its differential; the ENV axle has a much larger differential casing with a short nose; and the differential casing of the Salisbury axle is cast integrally with the axle casing with a rear cover, which is bolted on.

The 1958 axles had bump-stop plates running along the axle casing, but from 1959 these plates were mounted at 90 degrees to the casing. The design of the hub ends also changed, probably in 1959 or 1960. Early axles had a 'star' pattern end, with raised sections around the retaining bolts. Later axles had a flat end.

Rear axles always had canvas restraining straps, and there were different types to suit each variety of axle.

From axle number 1510-00001 at the start of the 1960 season, the axle casing was reinforced with stiffener members on both arms. Rover axles had half-shafts strengthened by 25 per cent from March 1964.

There were three different front axle types, each one available in both left-hand-drive and right-hand-drive form. One type suited 88s, a second was for the 109 4-cylinders and the third was a unique ENV type for the 109 One Ton. From February 1961 a location stop was bolted to the axle end to hold the jack platform in place when lifting the front axle under the right-hand side.

The steering swivels at each end of the front axle were largely unchanged during Series II and Series IIA production and so were the universal joints inside the housings. However, a four-dowel fixing replaced the original two-dowel type in the swivel pin housings in October 1961 (at axle numbers 1411-09094, 1441-05654, 1511-10744 and 1541-04184), and shortly afterwards an O-ring was added to the steering levers to prevent oil seepage from the swivel housing (at axle numbers 1411-09561, 1441-05977, 1511-11491 and 1541-04522).

The cone and spring damper arrangement on top of each swivel housing was also changed to one with a Railko bush and thrust washer, and a kit to convert earlier vehicles was made available in February 1962. The switch to Railko bushes on production came at axles 241-09241, 244-05089, 251-07786 and 254-04200. Also in February 1962 the $^3/_8$in (9.5mm) steering lever studs were changed to a $^7/_{16}$in (12mm) size; a swivel pin housing conversion kit was also made available to modify early vehicles.

Early Series II front-hub driving members had no filler plug, but one was introduced in September 1959 to allow the front hub bearings to be primed. This change occurred at axle numbers 1419-07805, 1449-04229, 1519-05517 and 1549-02399.

From March 1964, at the same time as the change occurred on rear axles, the front half-shafts were strengthened by 25 per cent.

On both the front and the rear axle the dowel locating the differential housing in the axle casings was deleted in December 1966. Both front and rear hub driving members were modified in March 1968, the oil filler plug being

This 'star' pattern end was used on early rear axles.

Later rear axles had flat-faced ends.

The reinforcement introduced on rear axle casings in 1960 is obvious here.

The first heavy-duty axle was an ENV type, seen here on a One Ton 109.

The 'long' or 'drop' shackle was used for heavy-duty applications, as on this 109 One Ton.

Axle Numbers

Front axles on Series II models had a four-digit identifier followed by a five-digit serial number. The type identifiers were:

Model-year	88 RHD	88 LHD	109 RHD	109 LHD
1958	1419	1449	1519	1549
1959	1419	1449	1519	1549
1960	1410	1440	1510	1540
1961	1411	1441	1511	1541

On Series IIA models they had a three-digit type identifier followed by a five-digit serial number with a suffix letter. The type identifiers were:

241	88 RHD
242	88 RHD from January 1971 (earlier sequence exhausted)
243	88 RHD from December 1966 (earlier sequence exhausted)
244	88 LHD
251	109 RHD
253	109 RHD from October 1966 (earlier sequence exhausted)
254	109 LHD

Rear axles on Series II models had a four-digit type identifier followed by a five-digit serial number. The type identifiers were:

Model-year	88 RHD	88 LHD	109 RHD	109 LHD
1958	1419	1449	1519	1549
1959	1419	1449	1519	1549
1960	1410	1440	1510	1540
1961	1411	1441	1511	1541

deleted from the hub driving members; hubs were already being packed with grease instead of oil on the assembly lines to reduce leakage.

Front and rear differentials always had the same 4.7:1 gearing. From March 1964 their material specification was changed to make them 35 per cent stronger. The pinion adjustment shims were also changed to a single one-piece type instead of the earlier shim-steel type, which had normally been used in pairs. Then from April 1965 a brass joint washer was added to the nose of the differential between the oil seal housing and the differential casing to create an oil reservoir that improved lubrication.

The front and the rear propshaft both have sliding joints, and the front propshaft has a bellows-type gaiter on its shorter front section. The 4-cylinder and 6-cylinder front propshafts differ, and from Series IIA, Suffix B there were different universal joints.

There were different rear propshafts to suit the different wheelbases and different rear axle types. All 88s had the same propshaft, but there were six different types for the 109s: there were different ones for the Rover, ENV or (from Suffix H) Salisbury axles, in each case one for the 4-cylinder and one for the 6-cylinder engines.

STEERING AND BRAKES

The steering box was normally a Burman recirculating-ball type, but for a short time from February 1963 small numbers of RHD 88s and 109s were fitted with Cam Gears or Adamant boxes of a similar type. The One Ton models had a lower-geared steering box.

There were some changes to the fixings that held the steering box to the support bracket on the chassis: there was no stiffening bracket on 2-litre petrol Series IIs, but one was added to 2.25-litre engined examples. Shakeproof washers were added in June 1960 and larger 3/8in bolts between box and support bracket replaced the original 5/16in size at Series IIA Suffix B.

A longer steering column was introduced in October 1960, coinciding with the change to a centre horn push. The column changed again at Series IIA Suffix C to suit the new plastic steering wheel. The column support bracket on the dash changed at Suffix D.

The relay and linkage also remained largely unchanged during this period. However, the track rod ball joints were initially below the rod but were relocated above them in June 1961; this arrangement could cause steering 'kick', and so a pendant ball joint was reintroduced for the lower steering relay lever from May 1962. The steering arms were modified to suit these changes.

The steering relay shaft initially had a filler plug hole and an oilway, but these were deleted in March 1964. More changes arrived in 1970: from September the Tufnol bushes in the steering relay housing had a saw-cut to improve the consistency of their torque rating, and from November all the steering linkage tubes had a new ball joint clip and an additional slot.

The One Ton models had a hydraulic steering damper on the track rod as standard. However, a steering damper was never part of the standard specification on 88s or 109s, although it was available as an option (*see* Chapter 6). By 1969 the chassis bracket for a steering damper was standard.

The brakes have a single-circuit hydraulic system, with a vacuum servo on 6-cylinder models. The wheel brakes were always drums, with a 10in diameter on 88s and an 11in diameter on 109s. The drums were 2.25in wide on 4-cylinder models and 3in wide on 6-cylinders. The 109s always had twin leading-shoe brakes at the front with leading-and-trailing shoes at the rear. Series IIA, Suffix H models had different drums to allow for their different (metric) wheel studs.

On 88s, a redesigned brake back plate (with a pressed projection in place of the shoe steady post and a riveted anchor pin for the brake shoes) was introduced in December 1959 at front axles numbered 1410-01223 and 1440-00936, and at rear axle 1410-02008.

A brake servo was standard on 6-cylinder models, initially a remotely mounted Clayton Dewandre type and from April 1969 (with Suffix G) a Girling type 38 mounted on the bulkhead and operated direct by the pedal.

The brake master cylinder was originally a CB type. However, a CV type was used on 88s from 241-3337D, 244-31622D, 271-08694D and 274-05073D, and with the Girling servo on 109 6-cylinders. The brakes and clutch shared the same fluid reservoir (*see* above, under Clutch); from May 1959 the original rubber-bodied filter for the brake reservoir was changed for a nylon type.

The handbrake always acted on a drum fitted to the rear output shaft of the transfer box. After a modification to the adjuster and new brake shoes in January 1960 (at gearbox numbers 1460-00566, 1510-05187 and 1560-00341) there were only minor changes to this and to its operating rods over the years, but worth noting is that the damper between transfer box and brake drum on 109 diesel models was deleted at chassis number 276-00879. From July 1970 a thicker handbrake relay bracket and larger-diameter relay lever shaft were introduced; these entailed chassis modifications and could not be retrofitted to earlier vehicles.

THE SUSPENSION, WHEELS AND TYRES

Springs and Dampers

The suspension was always by semi-elliptic leaf springs, of which there were several varieties. The dampers were hydraulic telescopic types, and the 88 type differed from the 109 type. There were several different varieties of front springs, each one available for the driver's or the passenger's side of the vehicle to make eight varieties in all. The 88 petrol models had nine leaves (and those for 2-litre and 2.25-litre 88s differed), while those for 88 diesels and all 109s had eleven leaves.

The rear springs on 88s had eleven leaves, while those for 109s had ten. The 109 Station Wagons had a different ten-leaf design, with eight main leaves and two helper leaves to give a softer ride. Again, each type was handed. The rear springs on early 88s tended to hit the bump stops and so their camber was increased by ¾in in December 1960. The new springs were fitted from chassis numbers 1411-00190, 1421-00096, 1441-00148, 1461-00080, 1471-00007 and 1491-00019. Both front and rear spring ratings varied between models, and Land Rovers designed for high-payload conversions usually had heavy-duty springs (*see* Chapter 6).

This view of the left-hand front wheel on a Series IIA 88 shows the arrangement of the steering linkage, the steering swivel and its housing, and the flexible brake pipe. The main brake pipe here is a copper replacement item; when this vehicle was built, it would have had steel pipework.

Wheels and Tyres

The road wheels normally had a 16in diameter and a five-stud fixing; they had 5in rims for 88s and 5.5in rims for 109s. However, 15in wheels with 6in rims were specified for NADA 88s because of supply difficulties with 16in tyres in North America. The same 15in wheels were also specified for special applications (typically military) where sand tyres were needed because no 16in sand tyres were available until quite late in the Series IIA era.

There was only one type of wheel for 88s, but three different types for 109s and a fourth for the 109 One Tons. The road wheels for ordinary 109s were optional on 88s fitted with larger tyres.

Before mid 1968, 109 wheels had a 1¾in offset; from about November 1968, these were superseded by wheels with a 1 5/16in offset, which were the same as those already used on military vehicles. They were identifiable by the military number FV607510 stamped into their outer faces between two stud holes. The third type of 109 wheel was introduced in April 1970, with a material thickness increased from 9 SWG to 8 SWG (3.6 to 4.0mm). The One Ton wheels had wider 6.5in rims, but had a greater offset than the 6.5in Forward Control rims with which they are often confused.

All wheels have a date of manufacture stamped into their outer faces. For wheel colours *see* Chapter 5.

The wheel nuts changed four times over the years. Series IIs and the Suffix A and B Series IIAs had BSF-thread nuts with rounded faces at both ends. These had a 59/64in AF size, and there appear to have been 'long' (1in) and 'short' (11/16in) types, the longer ones being earlier. Next came BSF-thread nuts, ¾in×1 1/16in AF, with a round face at one end only. These

Brakes and clutch shared a fluid reservoir, and below it here can be seen the steering column and steering box. When new, early reservoirs had a Girling decal above the bracket. Brake pipes would have been steel, not copper, when new.

lasted through chassis Suffix F. The hexagon corners of these nuts could dig into the wheel before the nuts were fully tight, so with Suffix G in April 1969 came a new $^{9}/_{16}$in BSF nut with an 18mm hexagon that increased the surface contact with the wheel. Finally, at Suffix H in February 1971 metric (M16) wheel nuts were introduced, to make Land Rovers compatible with the then-new Range Rovers.

Tyres

Several different types of tyre were available as original fitments. The 88 models normally had 6.00×16 or 6.50×16 sizes, and the 109s normally had 7.00×16 or 7.50×16 sizes; 109 One Tons had 9.00×16s. North American 'Federal' 88s had 15in wheels and 7.10×15 tyres from 1968. The known original fitments offered by the Solihull factory are listed below; vehicles built from CKD would often have locally-produced tyres of different types. For the optional fitments 'approved' by Rover, *see* Chapter 6.

88 models

- 6.00×16 Avon TM or Dunlop RK3 (Goodyear Sure Grips seem to have been used on some late models)
- 7.10×15 Goodyear Ultragrip on US Federal models only

109 models

- 7.50×16 Avon Ranger, Goodyear All Service or Michelin XZY

Six-cylinder models had a brake servo, and a cut-out in the wing to accommodate it. When new, the servo would have had a matt silver finish.

The six-cylinder 109 utilities had a special 11-gallon tank, narrower than the Station Wagon type to make room for the rear PTO's propshaft when one was fitted.

4

engine and exhaust

The 2-litre petrol engine was used only on 1958-season 88s. Note the flat-topped radiator with ridges running front to back.

This chapter looks at the engine, the cooling system and the exhaust system of the Series II and IIA Land Rovers.

THE ENGINES

The Series II models were available with the 2-litre petrol engine (1958 88s only), the 2.25-litre petrol and 2-litre diesel engines. The Series IIAs came with 2.25-litre petrol, 2.25-litre diesel and 2.6-litre 6-cylinder petrol types. There was a special high-performance version of the 2.6-litre engine for North America.

2-litre Petrol Engine

This engine had been used in Land Rovers since 1954 and there had been an earlier version with 'siamezed' bores between 1951 and 1953. It had four cylinders, overhead inlet and side exhaust valves, a swept volume of 1997cc (77.8mm bore×105mm stroke) and a 6.8:1 compression ratio. The single carburettor was a Solex PBI-2. Power was 52bhp at 4,000rpm and torque was 101lb ft at 1,500rpm.

This engine was used for only a few months in 1958 on 88in models and there were few production changes. Cylinder blocks were painted Light Admiralty Grey.

Changes during 1958

From engine number 1418-03478 in August, there were new pistons with a double taper top land, two compression rings and one Maxilite scraper ring; these no longer had the stepped scraper ring fitted to earlier engines.

In September at engine number 1418-05400 the access slot in the oil pressure switch was sealed with solder to prevent oil loss if the diaphragm failed.

Service Replacement Engines

From April 1960 engines that had been rebuilt either at Solihull or at the London Service Depot in Seagrave Road, Fulham, carried a small brass identification plate next to the dipstick. This read, 'Engine assembly part number 29216, suitable for the Land-Rover Series I models 1955-58 in the engine number range 5710 and 1706, and the 1958 Series II 2 litre models.'

2-litre Diesel Engine

This engine was first introduced in Series I models during 1957. It was a 4-cylinder with cast-iron block and head, with overhead valves and 'wet' cylinder liners. The fuel delivery was by indirect injection using a CAV pump. The swept volume was 2052cc, the bore 85.7mm and the stroke 88.9mm. The compression ratio was 22.5:1, power was 51bhp at 3,500rpm and torque 87lb ft at 2,000rpm. Cylinder blocks were painted Light Admiralty Grey.

Changes to 1468 and 1568 Series (1958 Season) Engines

The locating screw for the oil pump drive shaft bush tended to work loose, and so from engine numbers 1468-00160 and 1568-00001 in May 1958, this was replaced by a new screw with a nylon locking insert in its thread.

From engines 1468-00372 and 1568-00135 in August 1958 the main bearing caps gained new high-tensile 'waisted' steel fixing bolts, with a plain washer instead of the earlier spring washer. Right at the end of the 1958 season (the change is actually recorded for January 1959) at engines numbered 1468-01056 and 1568-00671, the cylinder block was modified to accept an immersion heater. Both 100–125V and 200–250V types of heater were made available; the modified blocks could be recognized by a large aluminium plug just above the starter motor.

Changes to 1469 and 1569 Series (1959 Season) Engines

Glow plugs were an issue this year. A modified type was introduced on 1 November 1958 at engines 1469-00523 and 1569-00286 to reduce noise levels; the new plugs were identifiable by a 'pimpled' effect inside, and the recommended timing with these was 16 degrees BTDC. Then, from engine numbers 1469-01365 and 1569-00819 in March 1959, glass-sealed heater plugs replaced mica-sealed plugs. These new plugs could also be retrofitted.

In June with engine numbers 1469-01373 and 1569-00826 cast-iron roller cam followers replaced steel roller followers in the tappet assemblies; they could be identified by a chamfer on the inside bore. The final change in this year came in September and was recorded against chassis numbers rather than engine numbers. A KLG type BRQ1 heater plug resister replaced the KLG R2736/Z type, to reduce the warming-up period of plugs from 30 to 10sec.

With the new resister, the warning light did not glow until 2 or 3sec after the key had been turned; with the earlier type it had glowed immediately. The change arrived with chassis numbers 1469-01582, 1479-00196, 1499-00312, 1569-00965, 1579-00511, 1599-00994, 1669-00001, 1679-00004 and 1699-00026, and the new plug resister could be retrofitted to earlier diesel engines.

Changes to 1460 and 1560 Series (1960 Season) Engines

Only a small number of changes occurred during the 1960-season production run. In June, at engine numbers 1460-01592 and 1560-01472, there were newly dimensioned push rod tubes to improve sealing; these could be retrofitted to older engines. Then, within a few days of this change, came a second one at engine numbers 1460-01610 and 1560-01475, when a stud replaced the set bolt in the rear main bearing cap.

Changes to 1461 and 1561 Series (1961 Season) Engines

A reshaped exhaust manifold was introduced in October 1960 to improve the exhaust pipe run. However, its other aim of eliminating the need for heat shields was never met.

The 1961-specification diesel engines had the fuel filter relocated from the engine to the bulkhead where it was fed by black nylon piping. Some models had twin fuel filters, which were relocated in the same way, and in December 1960 a twin fuel filter kit was made available as a retrofit. It was also in December that Parkerized exhaust manifold studs replaced the zinc-plated type.

In May 1961 at engine numbers 1461-01073 and 1561-01010 a modification to the timing chain adjuster piston gave an extra $^1/_{16}$in clearance between the timing chain ratchet and the piston housing. This modification could be retrofitted to older engines.

June brought a new oil dipstick with three marks: High, Low and Minimum. Then in September with engine numbers 1461-02061 and 1561-02154 came an improved crankshaft oil seal, consisting of two oil seal retainer halves with a separate split oil seal and garter spring.

2.25-litre Petrol Engine

The 2.25-litre petrol engine shared its overhead valve design with the 2-litre diesel and later with the 2.25-litre diesel. It was introduced for the Series II models in April 1958. Cylinder blocks were always painted Light Admiralty Grey.

The overhead-valve 2.25-litre petrol engine was new for the Series IIs and remained in production right through to the end of the Series IIAs and beyond.

The 2.6-litre six-cylinder petrol engine was initially announced with an SU carburettor, as seen here, but soon changed to a Zenith.

This is the later six-cylinder with Zenith-Stromberg carburettor, in a 1969 109 One Ton.

The swept volume was 2286cc (90.47mm bore × 88.9mm stroke), the larger bore being achieved by omitting the 'wet' cylinder liners. The compression ratio was 7:1, and the carburettor initially a Solex 40PA; later engines had a Zenith 36IV. Power (quoted to SAE standards) was 77bhp at 4,250rpm and torque was 124lb ft at 2,500rpm. However, the high-compression (8:1) engines introduced in April 1969 were claimed to deliver 81bhp at 4,250rpm and 127lb ft at 2,500rpm.

The fuel pump was always a mechanical type, but an SU electric type was made optional in November 1960. When fitted – which was rarely – it was located next to the bulkhead ventilator inside the vehicle.

Series II

Engine numbers for Series II models had a four-figure type identifier prefix followed by a five-figure serial number. The serial number prefixes are listed below:

1518 1958 109in models only
1519 1959, all models
1510 1960, all models
1511 1961, all models

There were several production changes. The dates given here come from Rover service literature and are generally slightly later than the changes they record.

Changes to 1518 Series (1958 Season) Engines

Only the 109s had the 2.25-litre petrol engine during the 1958 season. A change dated to September 1958 probably affected the last of these engines. This was the replacement of the aluminium water pipe between thermostat and radiator by a cast-iron type to prevent corrosion. Early and late types were completely interchangeable.

Changes to 1519 Series (1959 Season) Engines

In January 1959 at engine number 1519-02521 a Solex 40 PA 10-5 carburettor replaced the original 40 PA 10-4 type, with a shorter throttle control rod to suit. This carburettor could be retrofitted to earlier engines. Also in January the spark plug leads were waterproofed with rubber boots and there were new combined suppressors and covers for the plugs. These changes took place at engine number 1519-05713. Still in January, the cylinder block was modified to allow an immersion heater to be fitted and, when none was fitted, there was a large aluminium plug just above the starter motor. From engine number 1519-06707, in the same month, a rubber O-ring was added between the thermostat and the water outlet pipe.

In March there were several modifications to the carburettor, which nevertheless retained its 40PA 10-5 designation. The choke tube, non-return valve, main jet, correction jet, emulsion tube, pilot jet and economy jet were all changed at engine number 1519-09190. The new carburettor could be fitted to older engines, or the new components could be used to modify an older carburettor.

In June at engine number 1519-09595 cast-iron roller cam followers in the tappet assemblies replaced the original steel followers. The new type could be identified by a chamfer on the inside bore.

There were also two changes in September: at engine number 1519-17549 a nylon fuel pipe was fitted between the pump and the carburettor, with a new clip; then at engine number 1519–19650 the spark plugs were fitted with Lodge M90X suppressors. Both the new pipe and the suppressors could be retrofitted to earlier engines.

Changes to 1510 Series (1960 Season) Engines

A baffle plate was added between the oil filler and the side cover plate and cylinder block at engine number 1510-06048 in January 1960. Then in June at engine number 1510-01646 a stud replaced the set bolt in the rear main bearing cap.

August brought two more changes, both intended to make assembly easier.

The 2-litre petrol engine had a Solex carburettor.

From engine number 1510-23740, new engine mounting feet offset the engine to the right-hand side of the vehicle by 3/8in (this facilitated assembly of the exhaust manifold heat shield). These feet assemblies were not interchangeable with earlier types. The second change came at engine number 1510-23331 and brought longer dowels to prevent the incorrect assembly of the bottom half of the rear main bearing oil seal. These dowels could be retrofitted to earlier engines as well.

Changes to 1511 Series (1961 Season) Engines

From October 1960 the exhaust manifold was reshaped and the downpipe ran inside the engine bay, instead of passing through the wing. This redesign supposedly eliminated the need for heat shields, but heat shields remained in the specification.

From November 1960 a dust-proofed engine breather was available, and when fitted it replaced the standard oil filler cap. In December con-rod bolts with a rolled thread replaced those with a machine-cut thread, and con-rods with these bolts were identified by a drill point at the nut end. Heat shields were also added to the exhaust manifold and exhaust pipe, and it was possible to retrofit these to earlier vehicles.

During January 1961 a wax-filled thermostat was standardized for hot-climate export territories and the new thermostat was available for retrofit as well. With it came a one-piece thermostat housing in place of the earlier three-piece type. Set bolts replaced studs on the inlet and exhaust manifolds in February, and a stainless steel deflector was added to the water pump spindle; this item could be retrofitted as well.

March brought a heater element conversion kit for the carburettor starter box to eliminate icing-up. This could also be retrofitted to older models. Then in June, from engine number 1511-17643, home market and North American models gained a new Solex B40 PA10-6 carburettor, which incorporated such a heater element. With it came a new cold start control to give a fast idle without mixture enrichment.

Other changes in June were a new oil dipstick with three marks (High, Low and Minimum), and an increased

Seen without its air intake attached is the Zenith 36IV carburettor on a 2.25-litre petrol engine.

The labels seen here on a 2.25-litre petrol engine usually degraded quite quickly in service. Some engines may never have had them.

diameter (½in instead of ⅜in) for the four holes in the end branches of the exhaust manifold to cure a cracking problem.

The last production change on the Series II engines came in September 1961 with an improved design of crankshaft oil seal. The new one, introduced at engine number 1511-23197, consisted of two oil seal retainer halves with a separate split oil seal and garter spring.

Series IIA

Engine numbers for Series IIA types had a three-figure type identifier prefix, a five-figure serial number and a letter suffix to indicate important variants. The serial number prefixes on Series IIA 2.25-litre petrol engines for 88s and 109s were as follows.

Early 2.25-litre petrol engines had a 'swan-neck' exhaust, as seen here.

- 220 engines delivered to Santana in Spain (*see* Chapter 10)
- 241 8:1 CR, from January 1969
- 251 7:1 CR, 1961–5
- 252 followed on from 251-series, March 1964–71, from Suffix F
- 253 7:1 CR, from December 1970
- 261 from 1967
- 262 for UNICEF, 1963 models only (no further details available)
- 306 7:1 CR, detoxed for USA 88in models, from Suffix K from December 1970
- 307 8:1 CR, detoxed for USA 88in models from December 1970; for Sweden from January 1971; from Suffix A
- 310 military APGP, 24V, 1963 only
- 315 (no details)
- 351 for France

Other variants of the engine had 236, 237 and 336 prefixes (all for military Lightweights), and 286 and 325 prefixes (both for Forward Controls).

Suffix A 251 Prefix Engines (October 1961– July 1962)

These engines were introduced at the start of Series IIA production. As compared to the Series II variants, they had a whole series of changes and were not interchangeable with these earlier engines. Their cylinder blocks were painted Light Admiralty Grey. The visible differences were a water pump mounted higher up to allow for a larger fan and a new front cover shared with the diesel type. There were a new radiator cowl and a longer fan belt to suit this. The top rocker cover was also modified.

The cylinder block had additional water holes at the rear to cool number 4 exhaust valve and the main bearing locating tabs were relocated and carried narrower bearings. The crankshaft now had the same larger big-end bearings as the diesel engines, but the new con-rods and con-rod bearings were not interchangeable with their diesel equivalents. A four-piece main bearing oil seal replaced the two-piece type used on Series II engines.

The cylinder head had also been redesigned with relocated rocker brackets and two additional water holes at the rear. A single-piece rocker shaft replaced the two-piece type, but this was not shared with the diesel engine. The push-rod length was also changed.

Changes during 1962. New roller followers were introduced in February. These were countersunk on both sides instead of being drilled right through and were interchangeable with the earlier type. An automatic altitude corrector for Solex carburettors (part number 531984) became available in May and was suitable for both Series II and IIA engines used at high altitude. The same month brought the availability of an engine speed governor to suit Series IIA engines with the raised water pump and C40 dynamo.

Suffix B 251 Prefix Engines (July 1962–November 1962)

The Suffix B engines were introduced in July 1962 at engine number 251-19953B. The key difference was a modified vertical drive shaft (for the distributor), which now had a reamed bush instead of a split type. With these engines, the cylinder block colour was changed to Duck Egg Blue.

Suffix C 251 Prefix Engines (November 1962–March 1963)

The Suffix C engines had as standard the wax-type thermostat that had been used on some earlier engines for export. With it came a simplified design of thermostat by-pass elbow.

Suffix D 251 Prefix Engines (March 1963–March 1964)

Suffix D engines had a short-bodied AC 72 oil filter in place of the early long AC FF 50 type.

Changes during 1963. A carburettor conversion kit (part number 542637) was introduced in June to improve low-end torque, although it also reduced the brake horsepower. From August this was made standard with a new Solex 40PA 10-5A carburettor (identifiable by a brass tag under the float chamber cover fixing bolt); carburettors fitted with a heater element had type number B40PA 10-6. December brought changes to the distributor and flywheel. Service literature records the change from a Lucas DM2 distributor to a 25 D4 type at engine number 251-59746, although this number is clearly inaccurate; it was possible to retrofit the new distributor to earlier engines. The flywheel change was designed to render common the components between normal spring and diaphagm spring clutches, and the new flywheel had five drilled holes for the clutch dowels. It may have been used only as a service replacement type.

Changes during 1964. A reinforced, left-hand engine foot was introduced in March with engine number 251-52751D.

SUFFIX F 252 PREFIX ENGINES (MARCH 1964–JUNE 1965)

There were no Suffix E engines. The Suffix F engines were distinguished by a one-piece dipstick tube in place of the two-piece type. There were minor modifications to the cylinder block to accommodate the different fixings.

SUFFIX G 252 PREFIX ENGINES (JUNE 1965–APRIL 1966)

The primary change for these engines was a new distributor drive coupling with a straight drive blade between the distributor drive shaft and the vertical drive shaft, instead of the earlier splined coupling. The distributor adapter plate changed to suit.

Changes during 1966. In February spring washers replaced the lock washers between the engine mounting feet and the cylinder block.

SUFFIX H 252 PREFIX ENGINES (APRIL 1966–MAY 1967)

The Suffix H engines had a modified front cover without locating studs for the water pump.

Changes during 1967. In January the inlet manifold joint washers were changed to corrugated tin items. Earlier engines had the same type of one-piece washer that was used for the exhaust manifold as well.

SUFFIX J 252 PREFIX ENGINES (MAY 1967-MARCH 1968)

The Suffix J engines had a Zenith 36 IV carburettor in place of the earlier Solex. They also had modified rocker shaft brackets for use with shorter set bolts; these could be retrofitted in complete sets.

Changes during 1967. From September a new varnish-coated cylinder head gasket was introduced. This arrived with engine number 252-92992J and had modified water-transfer holes to give more uniform cooling of the cylinder head and could be retrofitted to earlier engines.

Changes during 1968. A semi-sealed water-cooling system with radiator overflow bottle was introduced in January and could be retrofitted to earlier vehicles.

SUFFIX K 252 PREFIX ENGINES (MARCH 1968–END OF PRODUCTION, 1971)

Suffix K engines had lip-type oil seals for the valve guides instead of O-rings. They had new timing arrangements: the new die-cast flywheel had no timing marks and there was no longer a timing aperture in the flywheel housing; instead, there were now a timing pointer on the front cover and a timing mark on the crankshaft pulley. A new coil featured a snap-in connection for the HT lead. The new oil seals and coil could be retrofitted to earlier engines.

Changes during 1968. From April the exhaust studs were made of a new material in order to minimize corrosion. In May came Hypalon HT leads with angled connectors and changes to the distributor and ignition coil to suit. At the same time, the ignition wire carrier and associated clips were deleted. All these changes could be fitted retrospectively to older engines. December brought yet another modified cylinder head gasket, designed to prevent overheating in high ambient temperatures.

Subsequent Changes. The 252 series Suffix K engines remained available until the end of production for territories requiring a low (7:1) compression ratio. However, from April 1969 Britain and most other territories took the more powerful new 241series high-compression (8:1) engines. Production changes to the 252 series engines broadly followed those made to the 241 series types.

SUFFIX A 241 PREFIX ENGINES (APRIL 1969–END OF PRODUCTION, 1971)

The new 241 prefix engines had a higher

This is the angled-top radiator in a 1969 109 One Ton with six-cylinder engine.

FAR LEFT: The early thermostat housing on the 2.25-litre engine had a peculiarly convoluted shape.
LEFT: The original type of thermostat was a tall unit, which demanded that special housing.

compression ratio of 8:1 to deliver more power and torque.

Changes during 1969. From engine number 241-02350A in August, engines for France and Iceland had a modified crankcase emission control system, which now shared parts with the detoxed US Federal engines.

Changes during 1970. In January the Zenith carburettor gained an improved top cover gasket. April brought a new ignition coil with one double male and one double female connector to prevent incorrect LT connections. From June, the con-rod bearing nip limits were increased to 0.004in-0.008in (0.10–0.2mm). Also in June a new exhaust manifold was introduced at engine number 241-24251A. This had plain instead of bowed fixing washers and improved manifold clamps; both could be retrofitted to earlier engines. (The same change was made to 251 series low-compression engines at number 251-08508K.)

Changes during 1971. At engine number 241-40826A in March new Hypalon ignition leads with push-in distributor cap connections were introduced. These leads could be retrofitted to earlier engines in tandem with a new distributor cap.

2.25-litre Diesel Engine

This engine replaced the 2-litre diesel in the Series IIA models in October 1961. It had the same bore and stroke as the 2.25-litre petrol type, again achieved by omitting the 'wet' cylinder liners of the earlier engine: the swept volume was again 2286cc, with a 90.47mm bore and an 88.9mm stroke. The indirect injection system used a CAV pump, and with a 23:1 compression ratio the engine put out 62bhp at 4,000rpm and 103lb ft at 1,800rpm according to SAE ratings. This engine's cylinder block was always painted in the same Light Admiralty Grey as that of the petrol engine. Engine numbering followed the Series IIA component identification system, with a three-figure type prefix, a five-figure serial number and a suffix letter to identify important design changes. The serial number prefixes were as follows:

271 standard
276 special version with alternator
281 special version with alternator
320 special version with alternator

This engine remained in production for many years after the Series IIA models had been superseded. There are versions for later Land Rovers, for Forward Controls (335 prefix) and also versions for marine and other vehicle applications.

Suffix A 271 Prefix Engines (October 1961–Early 1962)

A different top rocker cover and higher-mounted water pump distinguished these engines visually from the older 2-litre diesels. There was a redesigned inlet manifold with its air intake at the front. The radiator cowl was relocated and the engine front cover modified; there was also a longer fan belt to suit.

Other changes, of course, included the larger bore with no wet liners and additional water holes at the rear of the cylinder block to cool no.4 exhaust valve.

The main bearing locating tabs were repositioned with narrower bearings and there were increased fillet radii on the main and big-end journals. A new crankshaft had larger big-end journals and shared its design with the petrol type. However, the diesel cranks were forged rather than cast; it appears that all service replacements were the diesel type, with the result that some petrol engines acquired forged crankshafts. There were also new con-rods and con-rod bearings.

The cylinder head was redesigned with ridges and dimples in the combustion chamber, plus new valve seat inserts, and a single-piece rocker shaft replaced the two-piece type. The distributor pump had a larger plunger; there were smaller injector springs and new injector pipes, plus a simplified shroud for the injector bores. New glow plugs had an improved design. Finally, the flywheel was thicker and heavier and incorporated new timing marks.

Changes during 1962. February brought new roller followers, countersunk on both sides instead of being drilled right through and interchangeable with the earlier type. In July, at engine number 271-02760 the clamping bars for the injectors were modified to eliminate spot-facing; it was possible to retrofit these to earlier engines if longer studs were used.

Suffix B 271 Prefix Engines (Early 1962–November 1962)

It has not been possible to identify the special characteristics of the Suffix B engines.

Suffix C 271 Prefix Engines (November 1962-March 1963)

The key characteristic of the Suffix C engines was the use of a wax-type thermostat instead of the earlier bellows type. Some earlier export models had been fitted with a wax thermostat as well, but of a different type.

Suffix D 271 Prefix Engines (March 1963–March 1964)

The Suffix D 2.25-litre diesel engines were initially characterized by a shorter full-flow engine filter, an AC72 in place of the earlier AC FF 50.

Changes during 1963. Very early in Suffix D production, probably in March, cup-type core plugs replaced the earlier hexagon plugs and joint washers. The front branch pipe of the exhaust manifold was also modified in shape to ease manufacture; this new manifold could not be retrofitted to Series II engines. Thinner joint washers (0.015in/0.38mm in place of 0.062in/1.55mm) improved the fixing of the water pump and front cover mounting, which could work loose.

Changes during 1964. The only change to Suffix D engines during 1964 came in February, when a strengthened left-hand engine foot was fitted from engine number 271-10202D.

Suffix F 271 Prefix Engines (March 1964–January 1967)

Suffix E was not used for these engines, and the Suffix F version arrived in March 1964, initially characterized by a one-piece dipstick tube in place of the two-piece type.

Changes during 1964. In June, the oil feed boss on the cylinder head was repositioned and a longer feed pipe was fitted to suit.

Changes during 1966. There were no changes to the Suffix F engines during 1965; there were then just two in 1966. The first came in February, when spring washers replaced lock washers between the engine mounting feet and the cylinder block. The second came in August when the fan driving pulley and vibration damper from the 2.25-litre petrol engine was standardized on diesel engines as well.

Suffix G 271 Prefix Engines (January–May 1967)

Suffix G appears to have arrived with engine number 271-34792G, which brought a new Borg and Beck clutch plate with strengthened torque reaction springs. The new springs were identified by their dark grey and light green colouring, and the new clutch plate could be retrofitted to earlier vehicles.

Changes during 1967. Shortly after the Suffix G engines were introduced a modification was made to the inlet manifold fixings. Two corrugated tin joint washers replaced the one-piece washer formerly used for both the inlet and the exhaust manifold. Then, near the end of Suffix G production in May, at engine number 271-35560G, a new cylinder head gasket was introduced to improve the gas seal between the combustion chamber and water transfer holes.

Suffix H 271 Prefix Engines (May 1967–Early 1968)

The Suffix H engines came with a front exhaust pipe that had been reshaped to provide adequate clearance between the pipe and the seat base locker. This new exhaust pipe could, of course, be retrofitted to older engines. In addition, the 9.5in diameter diaphragm spring clutch was now standard.

Changes during 1967. In July the petrol engine-type of banjo bolt fixing the external oil pipe to cylinder block and cylinder head was introduced. This had a smaller jet size than the one it replaced. From August an improved rocker cover breather was introduced to reduce under-bonnet oiliness, and this could be retrofitted to older engines. November brought the availability of a sealed Lucas M45 starter motor with an improved solenoid mechanism; however, this was intended for replacement in cases of difficulty only.

Changes during 1968. The only change to Suffix H diesel engines in 1968 came in January when a semi-sealed cooling system with overflow bottle was introduced. This could be retrofitted to earlier vehicles.

Suffix J 271 Prefix Engines

It has not been possible to identify the special characteristics of the Suffix J engines. There may in fact have been no Suffix J engines at all.

Suffix K 271 Prefix Engines (March 1968–end of production, 1971)

There were several changes associated with the Suffix K engines. These had lip-type oil seals for the valve guides in place of O-rings to reduce oil consumption, a modification that could also be retrofitted. New compression piston rings had a chrome insert and these could also be retrofitted. A dustproof crankcase breather was another attempt to reduce under-bonnet oiliness and could be fitted to older engines. There was a new injection system with leak-off provision at the top rather than the side, and new flanged injectors replaced the clamped type. A new distributor pump permitted external timing and there was an improved reverse-flow fuel filter. The starter motor was also redesigned to reduce the ingress of foreign matter and improve reliability.

Changes during 1968. Shortly after the introduction of Suffix K engines, in March, improved glow plugs were introduced to give quieter running. They could be retrofitted in sets of four. In May dual-rate rubber engine mountings arrived, identifiable by their square outer plates with chamfered corners; these could be retrofitted in sets. Then in December the inlet manifold engine breather connection was moved to the rear of the manifold and a modified breather was introduced to make that component compatible with the one used on diesel engines in the Forward Control models.

Changes during 1970 and 1971. No production changes were recorded during 1969, but there were three during 1970. In April the pistons were modified to increase the tolerance of the piston-to-bore clearance. Modified manifold clamps arrived in June (and could be retrofitted). The third change came in September, when a five-bladed fan (from the 6-cylinder engine) and Morris-type radiator blocks were introduced as a temporary measure, supposedly to deal with an overheating problem. The first engine to be so fitted was number 271-60408K and the last was number 271-65959K, built in March 1971, when the four-bladed fan and standard radiator were reinstated.

2.6-litre NADA Petrol Engine

This engine was a distant relative of the 2-litre, 4-cylinder petrol engine, sharing its inlet-over-exhaust valve layout. Designed originally for Rover cars, it became available with a redesigned cylinder head incorporating modifications made by tuning specialist Harry Weslake in 1962. This high-compression 'Weslake-head' version of the engine was the one fitted to the special 109 Station Wagons built for the North American Dollar Area (NADA) in 1966–7. The NADA models were the first normal-control Land Rovers to have a 6-cylinder engine.

The engines had a swept volume of 2625cc (77.8mm bore×92.1mm stroke), a compression ratio of 8.8:1 and a single SU HD8 carburettor. They were visually distinguished by a large twin-intake paper-element air cleaner. These engines delivered 123bhp at 5,000rpm and 142lb ft of torque at 3,000rpm.

The identification number of the 6-cylinder NADA engines was stamped into the block just ahead of the exhaust manifold. All engines had a 343 prefix.

Production changes

The only recorded change to this engine was the introduction of a wax-type thermostat in September 1967, a modification that could be retrofitted to earlier engines.

2.6-litre Petrol Engine

A low-compression version of the 2.6-litre, 6-cylinder petrol engine had been used in the Forward Control Land Rovers from 1963. This same engine became an option for 109 normal-control models in May 1967 with a 7.8:1 compression as standard and a 7:1 compression option. The swept volume was 2625cc (77.8mm bore×92.1mm stroke) and the carburettor was initially an SU HD6, later replaced by a Zenith 175 CD-2S. The 7.8:1 compression engines had 85bhp at 4,500rpm and 132lb ft at 1,500rpm; the 7:1 engines had 81bhp at 4,500rpm and 128lb ft at 1,500rpm.

The identification number of the 6-cylinder engines was stamped into the block just ahead of the exhaust manifold. Prefix codes were:

345 with 7.8:1 compression ratio
346 with 7:1 compression ratio

These engines remained available for 109in Series III models after the Series IIAs had ceased production.

Suffix A Engines (May 1967–July 1971)

Changes during 1967. In August 1967, shortly after production of these engines had begun for the 109in Land Rovers, a Zenith 175 CD-2S, single horizontal dust-proof carburettor was introduced to replace the SU HD6 type. The new carburettor was fitted from engine number 350-00062A and was accompanied by a change to a closed breather system.

Changes during 1968. In March a new chainwheel was fitted. Its design was common to that of the 4-cylinder petrol engine's chainwheel, but the boss was thicker. This could be retrofitted to earlier engines. In May came a vacuum advance pipe with a push-on connection at the distributor end.

Changes during 1969. An engine tie rod became available as optional equipment in March and a heat shield was added to the distributor in October. The heat shield could be retrofitted.

Changes during 1970. A new ignition coil was introduced in April. This had one double male and one double female connector, to prevent incorrect LT connections. During July the dipstick guide tube was attached to the cylinder block instead of to the rocker cover.

Suffix B Engines (August–end of production, 1971)

The Suffix B engines seem to have been introduced in August 1971 at engine numbers 345-23298B and 346-00918B. They were characterized by a new body casting for the carburettor and a new air cleaner assembly.

THE COOLING SYSTEM

There were different radiators for the several engines. Thus 2-litre petrol, 2.25-litre petrol, 2-litre diesel and 2.25-litre diesel engines were all different. The 2.25-litre radiators were wider than the 2-litre types. Series II and early Series IIA 4-cylinder radiators had a flat top with ridges running front to back; from approximately the start of Suffix B production, Series IIA radiators had an angular top face with ridges running from side to side; then from Suffix G a dome-topped radiator was introduced. The 6-cylinder radiators had an angular top on Suffix A models but then changed to a dome-topped type. They also had a unique, two-piece, bottom hose.

There were 4lb pressure caps for 2-litre petrol engines, and either 9 or 10lb caps for the 2.25-litre types. On early models before the introduction of an overflow bottle the caps were chained to the filler neck. Each type of radiator also had its own fan cowl.

An overflow bottle was added to the cooling system in May 1967 and this was accompanied by a change from metal to plastic cowls. It was fitted to all the 6-cylinder models, which again each had their own radiator. All the 'overflow' radiators had a 9lb pressure cap.

THE EXHAUST SYSTEM

The 4-cylinder engines always had a three-piece exhaust system, consisting of a front downpipe, an intermediate pipe and a tail pipe incorporating a silencer. Over the years, several design rationalizations reduced the number of varieties, but there were different systems for 2-litre petrol, 2.25-litre petrol, 2-litre diesel and 2.25-litre diesel engines.

On 2-litre and early 2.25-litre engines the front exhaust pipe passed through a hole in the inner wing and then ran down behind the wheel; the 2-litre pipe was straight and the 2.25-litre had a swan-neck design. From October 1960 the exhaust manifold and pipe were redesigned so that the downpipe ran inside the engine bay.

Early front pipes had welded heat-shields, but in March 1959 bolt-on shields replaced these at chassis numbers 1419-01078, 1429-00562, 1449-00958, 1469-00891, 1479-00110, 1499-00148 (for 88s) and 1519-00383, 1529-01120, 1549-00576, 1569-00296, 1579-00180 and 1599-00076 (for 109s). Additional heat shields arrived on the exhaust manifold and pipe of petrol models in December 1960 to keep heat away from the left-hand toe box. There was always a heat shield on the toe box itself. This differed between RHD and LHD vehicles, and the ones used with engines from Suffix A to Suffix H differed from the ones used with Suffix J types.

Tail pipes were handed to suit RHD or LHD, so that the exhaust always emerged on the opposite side to the driver, and there were special versions for the 109 Station Wagons.

The 6-cylinder engines had a four-piece system, with a front downpipe, an intermediate pipe, an oval-section silencer and a tail pipe. There was a special tail pipe for Station Wagons. The tail pipe emerged on the left-hand side of the vehicle on both RHD and LHD models and was reshaped in April 1968 to prevent fumes from entering the rear of the vehicle. There was always a heat shield attached to the downpipe ahead of the left-hand toe box.

5

body and electrical

The bodies were sprayed as completed assemblies and the under-wing area remained unpainted except for small areas of overspray, as seen here.

This chapter looks at the body and superstructure of the Series II and IIA Land Rovers: the body (including paint colours) and canvas, the interior (including instruments and controls) and the electrical system.

THE BODY

The Land Rover body is built up around the bulkhead, which Land Rover often called the 'dash'. This changed only in minor details between 1958 and 1971. At Suffix D in May 1967 an indentation was added for the new Lucas wiper motor and the auxiliary panel in the centre disappeared to make room for the new flat heater. In April 1969 at Suffix G, the steady brackets moved inwards to make room for the new pedal-mounted brake servo.

There were also different types for the 4-cylinder and 6-cylinder models, and minor modifications resulted in a number of differences between diesel and 4-cylinder petrol types. From December 1968 the diesel and the 4-cylinder petrol bulkheads were made compatible, but the 6-cylinder type was not. The bulkhead ventilator flaps are bolted to their hinges on Series II models but spot-welded to them on Series IIAs; from Suffix G in April 1969, longer hinge brackets were used.

There are two basic types of front wing, in each case made of three panels with a splash shield at the rear. Series IIs and Series IIAs up to Suffix F have wings with a plain front panel (pierced for sidelights or sidelights and flashers as appropriate). Suffix G and later models have a headlamp cut-out in the front panel and piercings for sidelamps and flashers. There is a finisher panel around the headlamp on these wings, except on military models.

On 6-cylinder models the left-hand inner front wing has a removable panel to give access to the oil filter. The wings were secured to the bulkhead by captive nuts on 1958–9 models, but by spire nuts thereafter.

British-market models, and those for most developed countries, had a Britax driver's side wing mirror as standard from 1968. However, wing mirrors had been fitted as optional extras before then (*see* Chapter 6), and a passenger's side wing mirror became an option as well. The factory-issue mirrors had a circular metal mirror body, a cranked tubular arm and a black finish.

There were three types of bonnet. The standard or 'blade' type was used on all 88s except Station Wagons. The De Luxe type had a rolled leading edge and was fitted to all 109s and to 88 Station Wagons. The third type was a variant of the De Luxe type that was

Series II models have screw fixings for their bulkhead ventilator flaps. Screws, washers and hinges were sherardized. There is controversy over whether the screws and washers remained unpainted.

The bulkhead ventilator flaps are spot-welded to their hinges on Series IIA models.

optional on 109s, and had a recess with a mounting for the spare wheel. (There was also a fourth variant used on military 88s only, *see* Chapter 9. This had a spare wheel carrier on a blade-type panel.)

The bonnet hinges were always galvanized and not painted. They had a four-bolt fixing up to the end of Series IIA, Suffix C in May 1967 and a three-bolt fixing thereafter.

There were also three types of grille panel. The first suited models with bezelled headlamps and the second suited those with flat-lens lamps (*see* below). The third type had no cut-out for headlamps and was used on Suffix G and later models. The grille itself was changed only once, the earlier T-shaped type being used up to and including Suffix F and the later cross-shaped type on subsequent models.

All models had a Land Rover oval grille badge, but there were two types. The earlier one gave the company address as Birmingham, England, and the later one gave it as Solihull, England. The changeover was probably never exact, but the Solihull badges seem to have arrived during the 1959 model-year. Station Wagons have a 'Four Wheel Drive Station Wagon' badge mounted directly below the main badge, but the twelve-seater models for the British market did not have this badge; as far as the tax authorities were concerned, they were no longer Station Wagons but minibuses. There was also a special circular diesel badge on the grille for models with diesel engines. This plastic badge tended

The early type of windscreen fixing bolt had a large butterfly nut.

From Suffix D, bulkheads had a dished section behind the parcel shelf to accommodate the new wiper motor.

The strengthening ribs on the underside of the bonnet were always painted black. This is the blade-type bonnet on a Series II 88.

LEFT: Early bonnet hinges had a four-bolt fixing.

BELOW LEFT: The later bonnet hinges had only three fixing bolts.

ABOVE: The inspection cover on the gearbox tunnel changed over the years. This is the early type, on a Series II.

ABOVE LEFT: Early tailgates had a more substantial corner fillet than later types, and were secured by a stronger hinge with three bolts instead of the later two.

ABOVE: Door stay on a later IIA.

LEFT: The earliest Series II models had badges that read 'Birmingham, England' and were carried over from Series I Land Rovers.

BELOW LEFT: At some point in the 1959 model-year, the badges changed to read 'Solihull, Warwickshire'.

to degrade quite quickly and may not have been fitted to every diesel-engined Land Rover, but in theory it was used until the end of Series IIA production.

Series IIs and Series IIAs from Suffix A to Suffix F had a valance or apron panel between the front bumper and the grille panel. There were three types. The earliest was flat and was attached at its leading edge by domed rivets to a galvanized bar that bolted to the bumper. The second type, used from 1960–1, was also flat, but had no separate galvanized bar and was attached at each side by the two bumper bolts. The third type was curved. This was introduced with Series IIA Suffix B in March 1963 and left the bumper bolts exposed, belatedly making room for the lifting rings and double-bumpers of military models for the British armed forces.

The early sill panels were 125mm ($4\frac{15}{16}$in) deep. From December 1968, noticeably shallower panels with a 72mm depth ($2\frac{27}{32}$in) were introduced, but stocks of the early type were still being fitted to some vehicles as late as April 1969.

The side doors normally had detachable top sections containing the sliding window; these bolted through the tops of the lower door sections. The earliest type, used on Series II models, is distinguishable by a series of indentations along the top of the lower frame's inside edge. The sliding sections of both side windows had rectangular perspex knobs bonded to them. The early window catches were made of aluminium; later ones were made of plastic.

All models had tubular door stays bolted underneath the parcel shelf; these were bolted in place on Series IIs and welded on Series IIAs. Early Series II 109 truck cabs, hardtops and Station Wagons had single-piece doors; these same doors were also used on vehicles for Canada (*see* Chapter 10). However, two-piece doors were standardized on 1960 models or perhaps slightly earlier.

Locking door handles were standard on all 109s and on 88 Station Wagons. Up to Series IIA Suffix C the lock barrel was attached to the door handle itself and moved with it; from Suffix D onwards a fixed barrel-type lock was used.

ABOVE LEFT: Station Wagons had an additional semi-circular plate underneath the main badge.

ABOVE RIGHT: Diesel-engined models carried this 'Diakon' plastic grille badge, which rarely survives in good condition.

RIGHT: The earliest type of valance panel has a galvanized section at its leading edge.

BELOW: The later flat valance has no galvanized section and is attached by the bumper bolts.

The curved type of valance is seen here on a vehicle, with a flat one laid on the bumper for comparison.

The truck cab was always strictly an option, but was virtually standard on civilian pick-ups for most developed countries. It is a very simple structure consisting of a back panel and roof that bolt in place. The back panel has glass quarter-light windows and a two-piece sliding rear window made of perspex.

The back body or tub consists of a floor, two side or wing panels, a front panel and two tail panels on either side of the tailgate aperture. All 88s, including Station Wagons, used the same body tub (which is why the Station Wagons had redundant rope cleats on the body sides), and the tops of the panels were reinforced by galvanized cappings. On utility versions the spare wheel was bolted to the front panel, but on Station Wagons it was stowed outside the body on the back door.

The back body of the 109 utilities followed the same basic pattern and actually used the same tail panels as the 88. Its longer wheelboxes contained two cut-outs on each side, the rear two always designated as lockers. These had hinged lids with a turnbuckle fixing; the early turnbuckles had a circular base and later ones had a semi-circular base. The forward cut-out on the passenger side was used for the spare wheel stowage and was fitted with a circular recess. The other forward cut-out was covered with a closing plate.

There were different arrangements for the 109 Station Wagons. These had a unique back body section with an angled front edge to the wheelbox and a different floor panel with a front 'step'. There was only one locker, with the same choice of turnbuckles.

Tailboards were always mounted on two galvanized hinges and opened downwards. They had a sleeved safety chain on each side and were secured closed by a cotter arrangement. Early tailboards had a larger fillet in their lower corners than later ones, and their galvanized hinges were more substantial and attached by three bolts rather than the two used on the later hinges. The change probably took place in March 1963 with the arrival of Suffix B models. Station Wagons had a hinged door instead of a tailboard and this could be fitted as an option to hardtop models as well.

On models with canvas hoods there were removable hood sticks in locating sockets in the galvanized body cappings. The canvas hoods were either full-length (when the front was attached

Before December 1968, all models had this deep style of sill panel.

Later shallow sill.

to the windscreen header rail) or three-quarter-length (for truck cabs). Hardtop models had plain upper body side panels; early 109 hardtops (probably up to the end of Series II production) had two-piece panels but later ones were in a single piece. All Series II hardtops had windowless upper tail panels, but windows were added on Series IIAs. These were rubber-glazed, in contrast to the direct-glazed but similarly shaped windows on Station Wagons. On window hardtops the side windows were also rubber-glazed. The roof panel had a sloping section above the cab.

Station Wagons had upper rear body sides with a two-part sliding window, and 88s and 109s used the same window. Roofs on both 88 and 109 Station Wagons incorporated a single Alpine light on each side and had ventilators. In most cases a second-skin 'tropical' roof was attached above the main roof.

The rear number plate was usually fitted to the tail panel on the driver's side. A second oval badge, which duplicated that on the grille, was fitted on the tail panel opposite to the number plate, with the Station Wagon extension plate when appropriate.

Canvas

All the canvas elements of a Land Rover's body were options as far as the production lines were concerned, but to the customer they were simply part of a complete vehicle specification. Whether canvas was included in the specification varied from country to country, depending on local requirements.

Truck cab 88s and 109s were usually supplied with a canvas 'three-quarters' tilt, which covered the whole of the pick-up body. In Britain this had plain sides but there were also tilts with plastic windows in the sides for export territories. The fully open models (not normally seen in Britain except as military vehicles) came with a 'full' canvas tilt, which also covered the cab area. Again, there were versions of these tilts with side windows for export territories. In both 'full' and 'three-quarter' forms, the export 'window soft-top' tilts had one window in each side on 88s and two windows in each side on 109s.

Canvas was green or blue on Series IIs; khaki or blue on Series IIAs.

Body Colours

Series II Models (1958–61)

There were seven standard colours:

	Bergers code	*ICI code and remarks*
Beige*	SB2033	
Bronze Green	SA4225	2651
Dark Grey	SB2035	
Light Green	SB2031	3185
Light Grey	SB2032	
Marine Blue	SB2034	3184
Poppy Red	SA4568	fire engines only

* Beige was initially known as Fawn.

The roof, upper side and upper rear panels of hardtop bodies were painted in Off-white with all body colours. On Station Wagons the Tropical Roof was painted in Off-white with all body colours, but the main roof panel was in the body colour. Wheels were painted in the body colour on Bronze Green and Red vehicles; on all other factory-painted models they were painted Off-white (Bergers SB2029).

Series IIA Models (1961–8)

There were seven standard colours:

	Bergers code	*ICI code and remarks*
Bronze Green	SA4225	2651
Dark Grey	SB2035	extra-cost option in all markets
Light Green	SB2031	3185
Marine Blue	SB2034	3184
Mid Grey		3181
Red		extra-cost option in all markets
Sand		3182 for export; extra-cost option on home market

Vehicles supplied for finishing elsewhere (for example, by conversion specialists) left the factory with the body panels painted in Mist Coat Grey. The roof, upper side and upper rear panels of hardtop bodies were painted in Off-white with all body colours. On Station Wagons the Tropical Roof was painted in Off-white with all body colours, but the main roof panel was in the body colour. Wheels were painted in the body colour on Bronze Green and Red vehicles; on all other factory-painted models they were painted Off-white.

Series IIA Models (1969–71)

There were seven standard colours:

	Bergers code	*ICI code and remarks*
Bronze Green	SA4225	2651
Light Green	SB2031	3185
Limestone		3307
Marine Blue	SB2034	3184
Mid Grey		3181
Red		extra-cost option in all markets
Sand		3182 for export; extra-cost option on home market

Vehicles supplied for finishing elsewhere (for example, by conversion specialists) left the factory with the body panels painted in Mist Coat White. The roof, upper side and upper rear panels of hardtop bodies were painted in Limestone with all body colours. On Station Wagons, the Tropical Roof and main roof panel were painted in Limestone with all body colours. Wheels were painted in the body colour on Bronze Green and Red vehicles; on all other factory-painted models they were painted Limestone. On vehicles supplied in Mist Coat White the wheels were finished in Primer. Some authorities believe that Limestone wheels became available with Bronze Green bodies at this stage.

THE INTERIOR

Seats

There were normally three separate front or 'cab' seats, although the middle one would be omitted when a centre PTO was fitted in order to give access to its controls. Cushions and squabs differed from one type to the next: 88s and utility 109s shared passenger and centre seats, but 109 Station Wagons had their own variety of each. All forward-facing Station Wagon seats had trimmed backs, but seats for the utilities had no trimming on their rear panels. The driver's seat was fixed on 88s but had an adjustable cushion on 109s and was

Three-abreast seating in an early Series II truck cab. This is the grey 'elephant hide' upholstery.

There was a pair of inward-facing folding seats on each side in the rear of 88 Station Wagons.

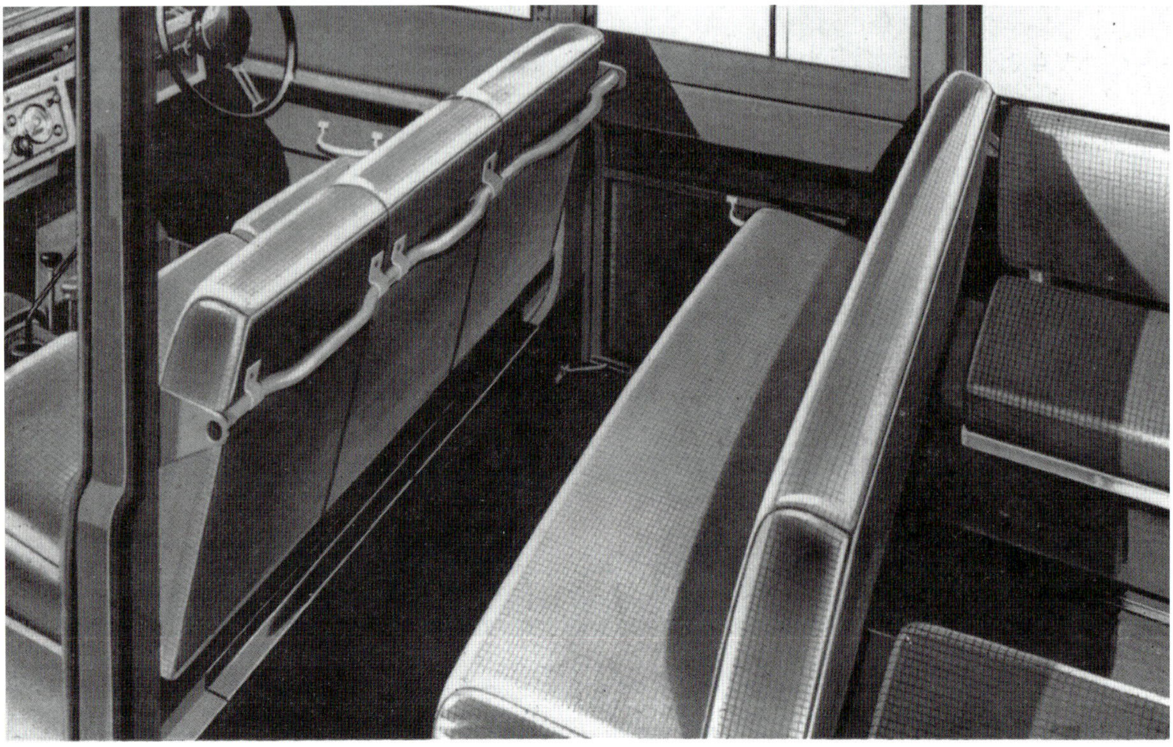

The 10-seater Station Wagons had a bench seat for the middle row. This picture shows an upholstery type not used in production.

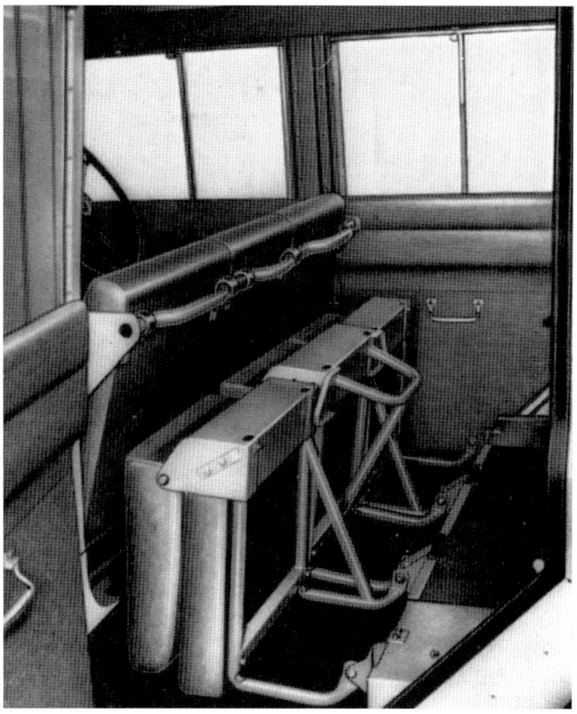

again different on 109 Station Wagons. In August 1960 an authorized service modification was introduced to allow the driver's seat on 88s to be reclined.

On 'utility' models it was possible to fit inward-facing bench seats on top of the wheelboxes in the rear. This option was largely seen on models for non-British territories.

The 88 Station Wagons were always seven-seaters, with three separate front seats and two pairs of inward-facing, individual seats in the rear. These rear seats could be folded upwards against the body sides to give more cargo space in the back.

The 109 Station Wagons were normally built as ten-seaters, but to avoid tax penalties in Britain they were configured as twelve-seaters for that market from early 1962. The ten-seaters had a front row of three separate seats, a 'middle' bench designed to seat three more and inward-facing bench seats in the rear to accommodate two more passengers each. The back of the 'middle' bench folded down, and the cushions of the two inward-facing benches could be folded up to create more load space.

The twelve-seaters had a different configuration. The three front seats were the same, but the 'middle' row consisted of three separate seats that folded over and tipped forwards – ostensibly to allow access into the back through the side doors. The inward-facing benches were longer (supposedly so that they could seat three each) and were fixed in place.

ABOVE LEFT: The 12-seat Station Wagons on 109 chassis had three individual seats in the middle row.

ABOVE RIGHT: The middle row of seats could be folded forwards on 12-seaters, either all together or individually.

RIGHT: The 12-seater Station Wagons had longer inward-facing rear seats than the 10-seaters.

Early seats had spring interiors, but from April 1965 the cushions and backs had foam interiors. The sprung seat backs had rubber buffers on their reverse side, but with the foam type these buffers were fitted to the body cappings instead. From June 1969 the metal protective cappings on all seats were replaced by plastic ones, which could also be retrofitted to earlier seats.

Seats were upholstered in grey 'elephant hide' with plain facings before October 1968, and after that in black with fluted centres and plain sides. From October 1967 there was a De Luxe front seat option, in black PVC trim with a backrest taller by 75mm (3in). Adjustable driver's and outer passenger's seats also became available for all models. A black seat cover was made available in March 1968 as an optional extra for the driver's and the outboard passenger's seats.

Land Rovers supplied from the factory as fire engines normally had red upholstery. This appears to have been discontinued at about the same time as black upholstery replaced grey on standard vehicles.

Seat belts and anchorage points became available as optional extras in 1962, initially only for 88s (except truck cab models) in October and then for the remaining models in November. They could be retrofitted to Series II models. They then became part of the standard specification with Suffix D models in May 1967, but were standard only on home market models, remaining optional on export types.

Other Interior Trim

Doors were normally supplied without interior trims, although Station Wagons had such trims as standard and they could also be ordered as part of a De Luxe trim option for truck cabs. When fitted, the door trims came in two sections and a grab handle was bolted through them. Trims were in grey with grey upholstery or in black with black upholstery. The tail door of Station Wagons had a single-piece trim and a grab handle or a longer grab rail were alternative fittings. Station Wagons also had trim panels covering the rear lights and these were also in grey or black to suit the upholstery.

Station Wagons always had a white vinyl roof lining. This came in two sections on 88s and in three sections on 109s. It was held in place with a variety of brackets and there were padded side rails above the doors in grey or black to suit the upholstery. White vinyl trim for the window area (but not the roof) was part of the De Luxe trim option on truck cab models.

Station Wagons also had additional felt soundproofing pads glued into the front footwells and around the transmission tunnel. They had a black rubber tunnel cover and black rubber front footwell mats as standard. There was black ribbed flooring for the rear footwell area on 109s, and both 88s and 109s had black ribbed flooring in the rear. The rear mat on 88s and 109s and the 'centre' mat on 109s were both held in place by metal finishers.

The door pull was bolted directly to the door on utility models.

Instruments

The main instrument panel in the middle of the dashboard was painted to match the body until the end of Suffix C production in May 1967. With the change to Suffix D and a negative-earth electrical system, the panel was always finished in black; this panel was also used on the NADA 109 Station Wagons from 1966.

On the earlier panels (up to and including Series IIA Suffix C) the three segments of the combined instruments dial on the left contained an ammeter, the fuel gauge and a main beam warning light. The speedometer dial – always on the right, even on left-hand drive models – had no warning lights, and all warning lights were on the panel itself. The red ignition light (initially in the centre above the lighting switch) and the green oil light (initially at the left-hand lower corner of the panel) changed places in October 1960, and the oil light also gained the word 'OIL' on its lens.

There were three different types of speedometer: for 88s, 109s and 88s with

Early catches for the sliding windows in the cab doors differed from later types. This one is on a 1959 model.

Early bulkhead ventilators were operated by a knurled handle like this one. On later models, a lever moved up and down in a rack.

ABOVE: *Early instrument panels were painted to match the body. The small yellow light between the switches on the right of this one was not standard.*

RIGHT: *The ignition switch on a late 1959 petrol 88. Note how the warning light lenses have already changed from the type fitted on the 1959 models.*

7.50 tyres, and 6-cylinder 109s; each type was available marked in miles or kilometres per hour to suit its intended market.

The switches were push-pull types. Between the dials the combined ignition and lights switch had a knurled outer ring for the lights on Series IIs, and an outer ring with a projecting lever on Series IIAs. The starter button was always mounted separately, below the dash.

Series II and Series IIA Suffix A diesels shared their key-operated electrical services switch on the dash panel with petrol models, but they had a separate key-operated starter and glow plug switch under the dash where petrols had a starter button. From Series IIA Suffix B, the electrical services switch was deleted and was combined with a starter and glow-plug switch under the dash.

Diesel models destined for export to hot climates were fitted as standard with a combined water temperature and oil pressure gauge from January 1961, at the same time as these models took on the new wax-filled thermostat. (The same gauge later became optional on other models.)

On the later panels (from Suffix D) the combined instruments dial had segments for water temperature, fuel and a battery charging light; the fuel and water temperature gauges were now damped. The speedometer contained three warning lights – for the main beam, oil and choke ('cold start'), and there were again different types to suit different vehicles and markets. All the switches were now toggle types and the main lighting switch was no longer combined with the ignition switch. Redundant holes in the panel were blanked off with black plastic plugs. Diesel models had a different ignition switch with chromed 'ears' and no separate starter button under the dash; this new switch incorporated a glow plug switch with improved waterproofing after September 1968.

From January 1968 the water temperature gauge was recalibrated to improve its accuracy.

Steering Wheel and Controls

Series II models and Suffix A and B Series IIAs had a spring-spoke steering wheel. From October 1960 the wheel had a central horn push and was mounted on a slightly longer steering column ($29\frac{3}{16}$in/741mm long instead of $28\frac{3}{16}$in/716mm). From Suffix C in August 1965 the steering wheel had three black plastic spokes.

On Series IIs built before October 1960 the horn push was mounted on an arm attached to the right-hand side of the steering column.

Turn indicators were an optional extra before the introduction of Series IIA Suffix F models in January 1969, and very early examples were operated by a white plastic switch mounted to an auxiliary panel on the dashboard. From May 1961 a conversion kit was made available to suit 1961 Series II models; this had a stalk switch on the right of the steering

On early models, the horn button was always on an arm mounted to the steering column. This is a 1958 Series II 88, with the spring-spoke steering wheel.

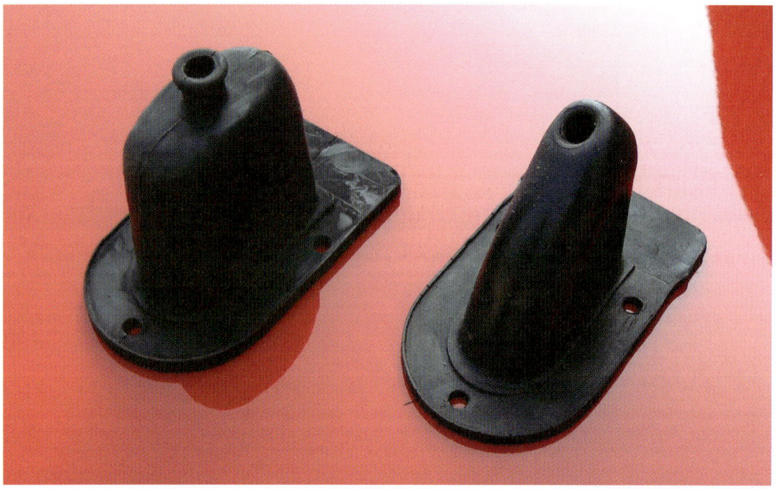

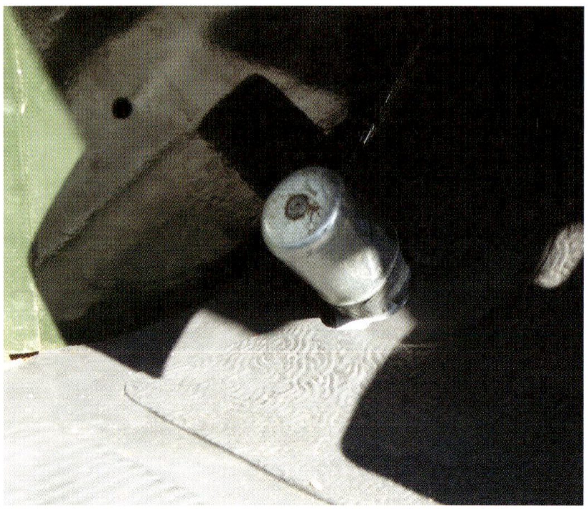

ABOVE: The rubber gaiter for the transfer lever was changed early on. The early type is on the right in this picture.

LEFT: This is the early type of dipswitch, mounted through the floor. The later type was the same as in Rover cars.

column. A Flashing Indicator Kit for Series IIA models was introduced in January 1962.

The accelerator and clutch pedals were painted black when new and remained essentially unchanged throughout the Series II and IIA period. The accelerator pedal restrictor spring, which was initially an option on 88s (*see* Chapter 6), was made standard in late 1959 at chassis numbers 1410-01495, 1420-00991 and 1440-02770. There were, of course, different clutch pedals for RHD and LHD models and from April 1968 the pedal trunnion was hardened and a washer was welded on either side of the lever to give a greater trunnion bearing area. Brake pedals changed at Suffix F to suit a new mechanical brake light switch; 88s and 109s had different brake pedals and 6-cylinder 109s had a different one again.

There were three types of floor-mounted dipswitch. On early Series IIs it was mounted through the floor, but from October 1960 a Rover car-type switch was bolted to the floor. There were then two alternative types, a Lucas 21SA and a Lucas 103SA.

The first type of handbrake lever was a simple cylindrical type.

The longer handbrake was introduced so that a driver wearing a static safety belt could reach it.

Up to and including Series IIA Suffix C the handbrake was a straight cylindrical type with a release button in the end; a variant used on some models, probably beginning with Suffix B, had a cranked lever. The Suffix D and later models had an extended lever, which was much more easily accessible to a driver wearing a safety belt.

The main gear lever always had a flat-topped black knob. On 4-cylinder models it was cranked and on 6-cylinders it was straight; there were RHD and LHD versions of each so that the lever was always angled slightly towards the driver. From July 1961 a Vulkollan O-ring was inserted into the ball end of the lever to prevent rattles; this change occurred at chassis numbers 1411-00981, 1421-00516, 1441-01022, 1461-00410, 1471-00061 and 1491-00116 (88s), and at 1511-00400, 1521-01074, 1541-00421, 1561-00264, 1571-00124 and 1591-00099 (109s), and the O-ring could be fitted to earlier vehicles. However, a worn O-ring allowed the gear lever to rattle and so in May 1971 polyurethane was bonded to the ball to improve longevity.

The transfer box lever with its red knob was changed once when a cranked stem was introduced with the Suffix F models. It was mounted further back on 6-cylinder models than on 4-cylinder types. The four-wheel-drive selector with its yellow knob also remained unchanged, but its rubber gaiter was modified at Suffix C to reduce wear through tearing.

The bulkhead ventilator controls were originally operated by a knurled knob acting on a screw adjuster. From September 1960 these were replaced by lever-type controls.

Tools

A tool roll was always standard equipment and consisted of hand tools in a black hessian roll with pouches. It was supplied in a variety of locations, probably depending on where the dealer chose to put it during the vehicle's pre-delivery inspection. Also supplied with every Land Rover (and normally located

Small hand tools were contained in a hessian tool roll …

… which rolled up like this.

loosely behind the front seats) were a starting handle, a wheelbrace, an oil gun and a jack with separate operating handle. On ten-seater Station Wagons the starting handle was located in clips under the middle row of seats, but on twelve-seater models it was in clips on the rear wheelarch, with the jack handle in clips on the opposite wheelarch.

THE ELECTRICAL SYSTEM

The electrical system was always a 12V type (except on some military models, *see* Chapter 9), with a positive earth up to Series IIA Suffix C and a negative earth from Suffix D. Petrol models had a single 12V battery; on Series II models, the battery was under the bonnet, but on Series IIAs it was relocated under the left-hand seat box to give clearance for the larger radiator. The diesel models always had twin 6V batteries. On Series II models these were mounted under the bonnet on opposite sides of the engine, but later diesels had one battery under the bonnet and one under the left-hand front seat. Early batteries always had single-cell filling, but the OE fit changed to a manifold-fill type in March 1968.

On Series IIA models the battery rested on a polystyrene pad. This was deleted on diesel and 6-cylinder models in June 1969, when the battery tray gained a shield to protect it from exhaust heat. This change took place on 88s at chassis numbers 271-10795F, 272-01913F, 274-06764F, 320-00023F, 321-00091F, 323-00966F, and on 109s at 276-01935F, 277-05268F, 279-05715F, 281-00861F, 282-01044F, 284-02294F, 345-01129F, 346-00277F, 348-00675F, 350-00744F, 351-00374F and 353-00595F.

The wiring harness always had a woven fabric sheath, which was covered by plastic tape from some time in the late 1960s. It differed between models, and extension sections were used for some optional equipment. In January 1960 some colour changes were made to the wiring to suit the introduction of a standardized five-pin trailer socket, and in October 1960 the engine harness was changed to give clearance for the modified exhaust down-pipe.

Several electrical items were mounted on the engine side of the bulkhead. These were the voltage regulator, the fuse box, the glow plug resistor (on diesels) and the starter solenoid. The voltage regulator was on the right-hand side of the vehicle (the left when looking into the engine bay). 4-cylinder petrol models always had an RB106-2 regulator, mounted upside-down on a board up to Series IIA Suffix C but the right way up and direct to the bulkhead on negative-earth models. The 6-cylinder types had an RB340 regulator. Diesel models had three different types. The early one was a Lucas RB310 type with an aluminium casing, which was rerated from 22 to 25A in July 1959 at chassis numbers 1469-01120, 1479-00122, 1499-00214, 1569-00667, 1579-00307, 1599-00167, 1669-00001, 1679-00004 and 1699-00023. This in turn was later replaced by an RB340, probably when the Suffix D chassis brought a negative-earth system in May 1967.

The fuse box, also attached to the bulkhead on the engine side, always contained just two 35A fuses. Only one was actually used unless the vehicle was fitted with an interior light, which would be covered by the second fuse. Additional electrical equipment, such as a radio, would be protected by additional wiring with a separate fused connector that was normally located just above the fuse box.

The glow plug resistor on diesel models was on the engine side of the bulkhead, more or less in the middle. Suffix D (negative earth) and later models had a remote starter solenoid; on 4-cylinder models, this was on the engine side of the bulkhead, just above the flywheel

Most common on the 2.25-litre engines was a Lucas C40 dynamo, seen here on a petrol variant.

Four-cylinder petrol models had an RB106-2 regulator. This one is on a 1959 Series II, and was mounted upside down and on a board.

With the negative-earth system at Suffix D came a new wiring loom, and the RB106-2 regulator was now mounted the right way up and directly to the bulkhead.

The RB340 regulator box used with the 6-cylinder engine was rectangular in shape.

housing, but on 6-cylinders it was in the seat box next to the battery. From April 1968 an improved 4ST type was used for both four- and 6-cylinder petrol engines; this could be retrofitted to earlier models with the negative-earth system.

Starter Motor

Starter motors were always made by Lucas. There was an M418G for the 2-litre and 2.25-litre petrol engines and an M45G type for the diesel engines; a fully sealed version of the M45G became optional for the diesels in November 1967, but was originally intended as a replacement in cases of difficulty only The 6-cylinder engines had an M418G motor.

Charging System

A Lucas dynamo was always standard equipment, although alternators were available to special order after March 1960 and there was a special generator for 24V military models (*see* Chapter 9). The 2-litre petrol models initially had a C39 19A dynamo. The 2.25-litre petrol models had a C40 PV5 22A type, but some early 2.25-litre models may have had the earlier C39. A sealed-bearing C-40T become optional on later 2.25-litre models.

The 2-litre diesel models initially had a C40 PV5 dynamo, but changed in July 1959 to a 25A C40 PV6 at chassis numbers 1469-01534 and 1569-01019. The

On the negative-earth 4-cylinder petrol models, the starter solenoid was mounted to the bulkhead just above the flywheel housing. The rubber boots would normally cover the cable fixing nuts.

2.25-litre diesels had the same C40 as petrol engines of the same size, with the sealed-bearing C40-T as an option later on; 6-cylinder models had a C42 dynamo.

Coil, Distributor and HT Leads

The coil was mounted on the left-hand side of the bulkhead with its nose downwards on 4-cylinder models; on 6-cylinders it was mounted on the right-hand side with its nose pointing upwards. From March 1968, the 4-cylinder models had a new type with a snap-in connection for the HT lead, which could, of course, be retrofitted as well. In May 1968 the coil changed again to suit the new Hypalon HT leads with angled connectors. In April 1970 another change was made, bringing in a coil with one double male and one double female connector; the aim was to prevent incorrect LT wire connections.

There were several varieties of distributor cap. This is the earliest 4-cylinder type, with screw-in top entry.

On 4-cylinder engines, the distributor was initially a Lucas DM2 type. This was replaced in December 1963 by a 25 D4 type at engine number 251-59746. The 6-cylinder engines had a 25 D6 distributor. In May 1968 they took on a new vacuum advance pipe with a push-on connection at the distributor end.

The plug leads were waterproofed from January 1959 at engine number 1519-05713 by adding rubber boots at each end, and at the same time the spark plugs gained new combined suppressors and covers. The suppressors were changed again in September 1959 when Lodge M90X types were fitted at engine number 1519-19650; these could also be retrofitted to earlier engines.

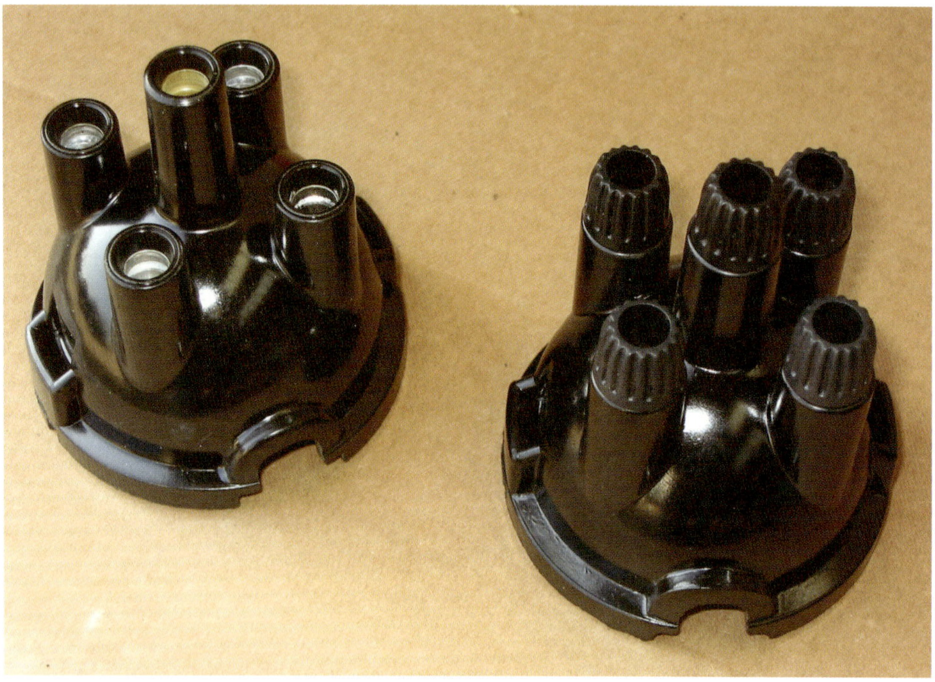

LEFT: Later screw-in distributor caps had taller projections (right). On the left is the later type with push-fit connections.

BELOW LEFT: There were also two types of side-entry distributor caps. This is the earlier one …

BELOW RIGHT: … and this is the later one.

The 6-cylinder distributor cap always had push-fit connections.

The early wiper motor drove only a single wiper, and only that on the driver's side was standard. These early motors normally had a silver casing.

From May 1968, the HT leads on 2.25-litre petrol engines were fitted with angled connectors, and there were changes to the distributor and coil to suit. The ignition wire carrier and its associated clips were also deleted. All these changes could be retrofitted. New Hypalon ignition leads with push-in connections on the distributor cap were introduced in May 1971 to improve the waterproofing at engines 241-40826A, 253-55094K, 325-00687B; they could be retrofitted in tandem with a new distributor cap.

Some later single-wiper motors had a gold paint finish. Also visible here is the later lever-type bulkhead ventilator control.

Windscreen Wiper Motor and Arms

All the positive-earth models had a single Lucas wiper motor as standard, attached to the base of the windscreen on the driver's side and operated by a lever on the body. A second wiper was optional on most models, but standard on Station Wagons and with the De Luxe cab option. There was a blanking plate in the windscreen frame when it was not fitted. With the switch to a negative-earth system in 1967 at Suffix D there also came a single Lucas DR3A motor with a cable drive, operating wipers on both halves of the windscreen. This motor was mounted behind a concealing plate on the left-hand side of the dashboard and controlled by a switch on the instrument panel. With Suffix F in January 1969

The redundant wiper motor fixing holes were covered by a blanking plate on the passenger's side.

there was a change to a permanent-magnet motor with an improved rack tube to give quieter running.

There were three distinct types of wiper arm. The earliest ones were made of chromed mild steel and attached to the wiper blade supports by a black rubber peg. By the time of the Series IIA, a second type with a 'spoon'-type fixing was in use; again, the metalwork was in chromed mild steel. From March 1968 a third type was introduced, with a cranked arm and a push-fit with sprung locking peg for the blade support. The metalwork changed to stainless steel at this point. Rover service literature records a further minor change in April 1969 as Suffix G replaced Suffix F, but the details are again not clear.

Windscreen Washer

Windscreen washers did not become standard in British and most other developed-country markets until 1968. They were available as an option before then (*see* Chapter 6). The standardized type had a tubular aluminium body and a black end-cap containing the washer jets. A plastic washer reservoir (made by Lucas) was normally fitted to the left-hand inner wing. From April 1970 the cap of this reservoir was modified to incorporate a keyway slot next to the positive Lucar blade terminal, to prevent incorrect polarity connections.

Horn

There was a single electric horn, initially mounted in a recess in the left-hand inner front wing. From September 1960 it was repositioned at the front, a change that could also be made on earlier vehicles. The relocated horn was always mounted on a projecting plate that was designed to prevent it dropping into the steering if it became loose and fell off.

On positive-earth models (up to Series IIA, Suffix C), Lucas and Mixo horns were used interchangeably. On the negative-earth models from Suffix D there were Lucas, Mixo and Clearhooter types. French-market vehicles are listed as having two horns, one for town use and one for the country.

Turn Indicators

Flashing direction indicators were optional up to and including Series IIA, Suffix E (*see* Chapter 6) and became standard with Suffix F. From Suffix G in April 1969, a new Lucas 8FL flasher unit replaced the original type.

LEFT: On early models, the horn was tucked away in a recess in the left-hand inner wing.

BELOW: This typical Series II front light combination pairs a Lucas 488 sidelight with a Lucas L639 turn indicator.

A Sparto front flasher was also used on Series II models.

The Lucas L638 was another early sidelight option.

ABOVE: The Lucas 488 with red lens was sometimes found on Series IIs as a stop-and-tail lamp.
RIGHT: This Series II headlamp by Lucas has a domed lens and a chromed bezel.

Another typical Series II arrangement, this time with a Sparto 57101 stop-and-tail lamp and a Sparto 57103 flasher lamp.

Series II and IIA Lights

The Series II and IIA Land Rovers were fitted with a wide variety of different lights and reflectors. In some cases Rover sourced lights from more than one manufacturer to avoid shortages on the assembly lines, and these different types were fitted interchangeably (but in matching sets) to new vehicles.

After Series IIA production ended a common design of sidelamp and flasher made by LE Perei was used as a service replacement for all Series IIA models from Suffix A to Suffix H. These lamps have an 'LEP' logo on the lens, which is otherwise similar to the type supplied by Lucas for Series III Land Rovers.

Series II (1958–61) and Series IIA, Suffix A (1961–3), except North America		
Headlights	Lucas 7in with separate bulb	Chromed bezel and domed lens
Sidelights	Lucas L638	Separate chromed bezel
	Sparto 5835	Separate chromed bezel
*Front flashers**	Lucas L639	Separate chromed bezel
	Sparto	Cone-shaped amber lens and separate chromed bezel
Stop/tail lights	Lucas L581	
	Sparto 57101	Central reflector and outer concentric rings
*Rear flashers**	Lucas L637	
	Sparto 57103	Amber lens with concentric ring design
Number-plate lamp	Lucas LU53876	Always fitted to the tail panel on the driver's side

** when fitted*

Series IIA, Suffix B to F (1963–9), except North America		
Headlights	Lucas F700 sealed-beam	Flat lens and no bezel. LHD models sold in Europe had lamps with a separate bulb
Sidelights	Lucas L760	
	Sparto 62402	Lens with concentric ring design
	Wipac WP840	Lens marked Series 169
*Front and rear flashers**	Lucas L760	Amber lens; not for Switzerland at rear
	Sparto 62406	Amber lens with concentric ring design; not for Switzerland at rear
	Wipac WP843	Amber lens marked Series 169; not for Switzerland at rear
Stop/tail lights	Lucas L761	Clear sector for number plate illumination; not for Switzerland
	Sparto 62401	Clear sector for number plate illumination; not for Switzerland
	Wipac WP842	Lens marked Wipac and 5170. Clear sector for number plate illumination; not for Switzerland
	Sparto 62401/A	All-red lens; for Switzerland
Number-plate lamp	Not fitted; clear sector in tail-lamp illuminated number plate	Lucas LU53876 available as an option and for Switzerland; always fitted to the tail panel on the driver's side

** when fitted*

LEFT: The separate number-plate lamp is seen here on a 1958 Series II.

The Perei front indicator and side lamps used as service replacements had the same design as those made by Lucas for Series III models.

Another typical Series IIA combination, this time a Perei rear flasher with a Sparto stop-and-tail lamp incorporating a clear section to illuminate the number plate.

The Lucas L691 was commonly seen as a rear flasher on Series IIAs.

Sparto's 62406 became available for both front and rear flashers on Series IIA Suffix B models.

The Lucas F700 headlamp without bezel is seen here on a mid-1960s model.

The Wipac WP843 was another alternative for front and rear flashers from Suffix B on.

Series II and IIA Lights

Series IIA, Suffix G to H (1969–71), except North America		
Headlights	Lucas F700 sealed-beam	Flat lens, no bezel. Separate bulb type for France and Italy
Sidelights	Lucas L760	Type L594 for France and Germany
	Sparto 62402	Lens with concentric ring design
	Wipac WP840	Lens marked Series 169
Front and rear flashers	Lucas L760	Type L691 for Germany; type L794 on front for France
Stop/tail lights	Lucas L761	Clear sector for number plate illumination
Rear reflector	Lucas RER22	Rectangular; for France and Germany only
Number-plate lamp	Lucas L467/2	Type L467 for France and Germany

ABOVE LEFT: The all-red Lucas L581 was used on Suffix B models.

ABOVE: The Sparto 62401 incorporated a clear panel for number plate illumination.

LEFT: The Lucas L692 was used on North American Series IIAs.

BELOW: The Sparto 57101 was an all-red tail lamp used on Series IIA Suffix A models.

BELOW LEFT: The all-red Sparto 62401/A was used on Suffix B and later models exported to Switzerland, where a separate number plate lamp was required.

OPPOSITE PAGE:

TOP LEFT: This style of Sparto sidelamp was used on some later Series IIAs.

TOP RIGHT: Headlamps in the wings and a typical combination of Sparto indicator and side lamps are seen on this 1969 model.

MIDDLE LEFT: The Wipac alternative stop-and-tail lamp with a clear panel for number plate illumination was the WP842.

BOTTOM: When German lighting regulations changed in the early 1970s, a very different layout was needed at the rear.

OXC
597J
LAND ROVER

6 optional extras

The bonnet mount for the spare wheel is seen here on a De Luxe bonnet.

The Land Rover had always been intended as a basic platform to which a variety of options could be added to give maximum flexibility. Everything that was not part of the core specification was considered to be an option on the assembly line, and most of these items could also be bought and added to the vehicle at a later date.

The options fitted to early Series IIs built for the British market were limited by regulations that restricted the overall weight of a 109 to 3,360lb (1,525kg); any extra weight would mean that it was classified as a commercial vehicle and subject to Purchase Tax. However, certain optional extras were not counted in that weight and therefore could be added without incurring tax. These were the rear and centre pulley units, the chaff guard, the UJ covers, the heavy-duty pintle hook, the engine speed governor, the combined water temperature and oil pressure gauge, the centre and rear PTOs, the hand throttle control, towing equipment, lifting and towing rings, the capstan winch, the oil cooler and the trailer socket plug and leads. For customers whose vehicles were getting close to the limit, Rover advised that an extra 30lb (13.6kg) could be shaved off the weight by fitting 7.00×16 tyres instead of the standard 7.50×16s.

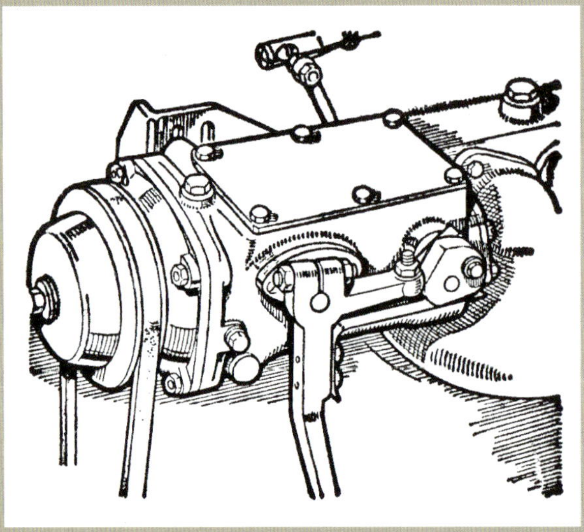

The optional engine speed governor was made by Iso-Speedic.

BODY OPTIONS

The truck cab, hardtop, three-quarter tilt and full tilt were all technically 'options' on the Land Rover. The windowed hardtops and soft tops were also options, reserved for export. So were tropical roofs for the truck cab and hardtop (although a tropical roof was standard on Station Wagons). On hardtops a Station Wagon-type tail door was an option in place of the customary lifting top tailgate with standard lower tailgate.

A curtain was available to divide the driving compartment from the load area on 88s with the full tilt, and retaining straps for the hood side curtains became available around April 1959.

The body panels and canvas options are covered in more detail in Chapter 5.

CHASSIS AND MECHANICAL OPTIONS

Chamois leather *ball swivel gaiters* could be fitted. They were attached to the swivel pin housing and secured to the end of the axle casing by a large Jubilee clip.

Brake mudshields could be riveted to the back of the brake anchor plates to prevent mud causing excessive wear to the linings. A Girling Powerstop *brake servo* could be fitted to the left-hand front inner wing. This was introduced in December 1961 and was intended for the 109 models.

There were two types of *freewheeling front hubs*. First on the market, probably in 1965 or early 1966, was the MAP (Mayflower) type, made by Mayflower Automotive Products of Tavistock in Devon. This seems to have been the most common type used on Series IIA models. From July 1966 (according to Rover service literature) Winquard Dualmatic B80 hubs were made available as an alternative option.

There was also a *heavy-duty suspension* option. On Series II 88s with the 2-litre petrol engine, there were special front springs (handed, as always), but on all other models there were different springs for the rear axle only. There were three types, to suit petrol 88s, diesel 88s and 109, and each one came as a driver's side- or passenger's side-type. Both front and rear dampers differed from standard with all heavy-duty suspension fits.

Twin *horns* could be fitted instead of the standard single horn. This option may have been intended only for US Federal models.

The front axle could be fitted with a *hydraulic steering damper*, which was placed between the steering drag link and a bracket on the chassis. This option

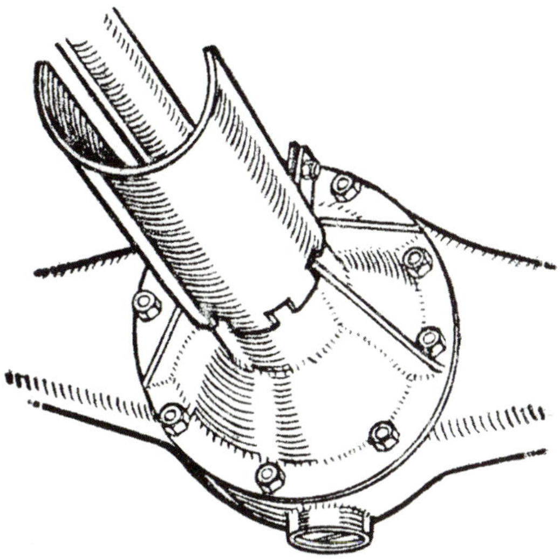

The early type of UJ cover was shaped to fit the front face of the differential.

BELOW: The later type had a different shape to suit the later flat-nosed differential.

The cab curtain was an option on 88s with the full tilt.

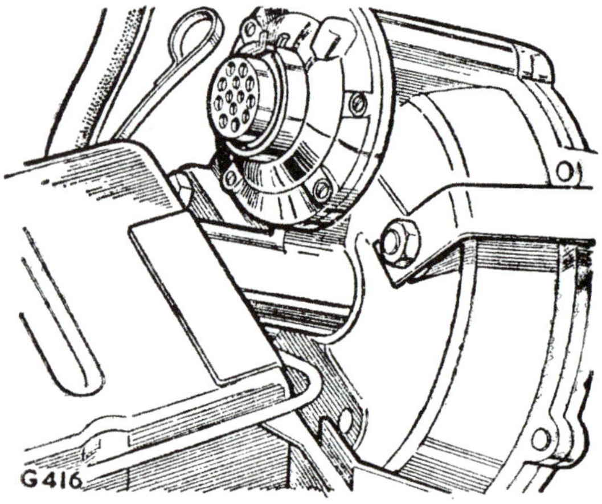

The early Powerstop brake servo was mounted remotely.

was introduced in August 1962 but could not be fitted to vehicles with a hydraulic or capstan winch at the front.

A Powr-Lok *limited-slip differential* for the rear axle only became available in June 1965 with the 242- and 252-series axles, but this proved troublesome in service and was withdrawn from the options list in August 1969.

A *reinforced axle casing* could be ordered for the front axle, and was recognizable by the additional welding along its front face.

Split-rim road wheels were available for 88 models, together with a wheelbrace for the special nuts securing the two sections of wheel together.

There were several *tyre options*, as follows:

88 models

- 6.00×16 Dunlop T28
- 6.50×16 Dunlop RK3 or Dunlop T29A
- 7.00×16 Avon TM, Dunlop Fort, Dunlop RK3, Dunlop Road Trak Major, Dunlop 'tractor tread' or Dunlop T29A
- 7.50×16 (on 109 wheels) Avon TM, Dunlop RK3 or Michelin XY (from approximately October 1959)
- 8.20×15 Dunlop sand tyres (with circumferential tread)
- 9.00×15 Dunlop sand tyres (with block tread)
- 7.00×16 sand tyres (late models, maker not known)

LEFT: The most common freewheeling hub was by MAP.

BELOW LEFT: The optional steering damper.

BELOW RIGHT: The reinforced front axle casing.

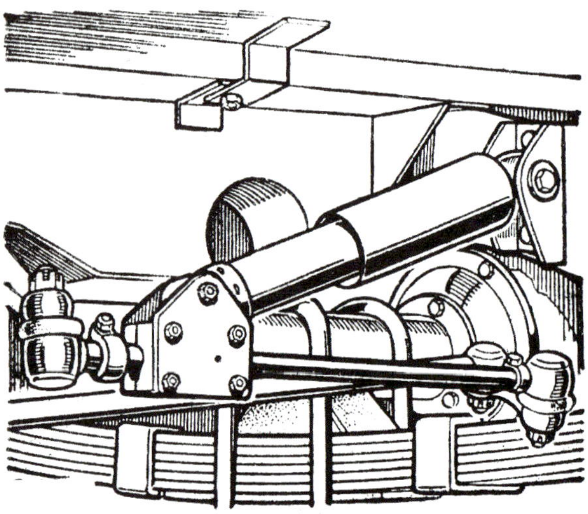

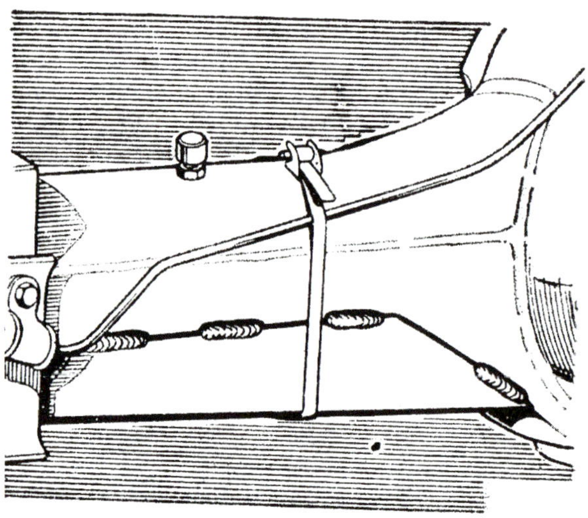

109 models

- 7.50×16 Avon TM, Dunlop Fort, Dunlop Gold Seal Heavy Duty, Dunlop RK3, Dunlop Road Trak Major (6-ply or 8-ply), Dunlop T29A or Michelin XY (from approximately October 1959)
- 8.20×15 Dunlop sand tyres (with circumferential tread)
- 8.90×15 sand tyres (maker not known)
- 9.00×15 Dunlop sand tyres (with block tread)
- 7.50×16 Michelin X Sahara sand tyres

Universal joint covers were intended to prevent grass or other vegetation from becoming entangled in the UJs during cross-country use. There were half-cylindrical covers under the front and rear differential joints and a plate secured under the transfer box to protect the front output shaft joint. These covers were suitable only for Rover-type axles.

ABOVE: Michelin XS tyre.
RIGHT: Michelin XY tyre.
BELOW: Dunlop tyres: left to right, RK3, T29A, T28, Gold Seal Heavy Duty, 8.20x15 Sand Tyre.

ENGINE, ENGINE ANCILLARY, FUEL SYSTEM AND TRANSMISSION OPTIONS

An *alternator* (usually described as a 12V AC/DC generator) was available from March 1960, but could be fitted only to petrol-engined models. Manufactured by AC, it gave a 50–60A output at low engine speeds and was designed to balance the load of extra electrical equipment on the vehicle. From November 1965 a Prestolite alternator kit was made available, but it was a negative-earth system and required a change of vehicle polarity. A Lucas 11AC alternator became optional on 6-cylinder models from January 1968 instead of the Prestolite type, and from January 1969 the Lucas type became available for 4-cylinder models as well.

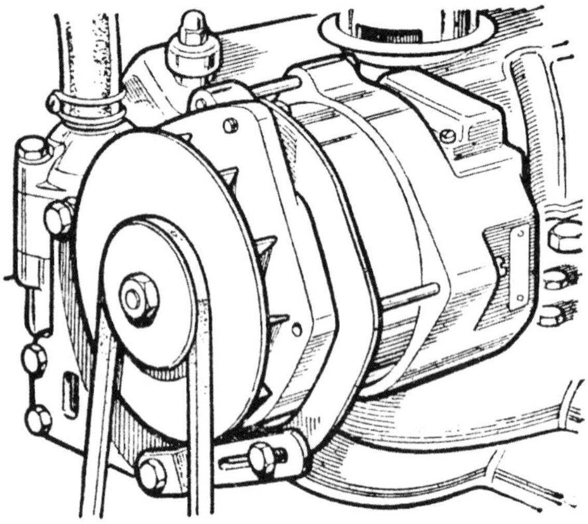

The alternator was quite rare.

An *altitude corrector* could be fitted to the Solex carburettor on 4-cylinder engines in place of the main jet and main jet carrier.

A *carburettor heater* for petrol models was available in kit form. It was fitted to the carburettor starter unit to prevent icing up. For cold climates, a *cylinder block immersion heater* could be permanently plugged into the cylinder block where it heated the coolant in the water jacket. An extension cable ran back to a socket on the dashboard and a removable plug could then be connected through a cable to the mains supply. There were two types available, one for 100 to 125V, 400W mains, and one for 200 to 250V, 250W mains.

The 2.25-litre petrol engines could be fitted with a *dust-proofed breather* in

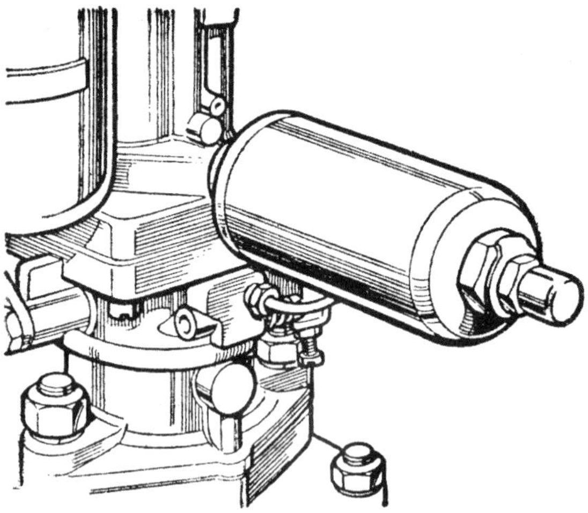

The altitude corrector was another rarity.

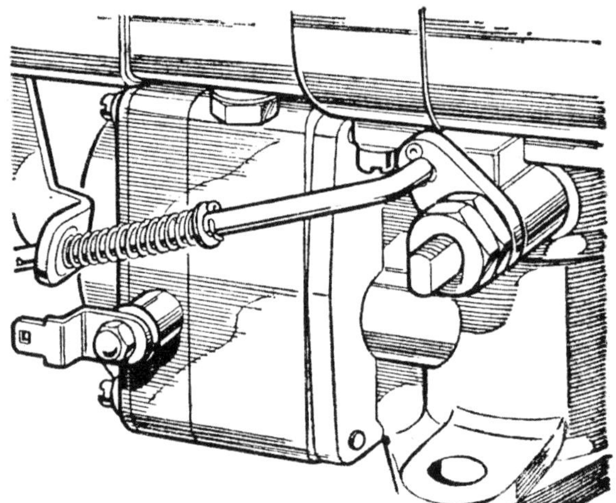

The carburettor heater was for cold climates.

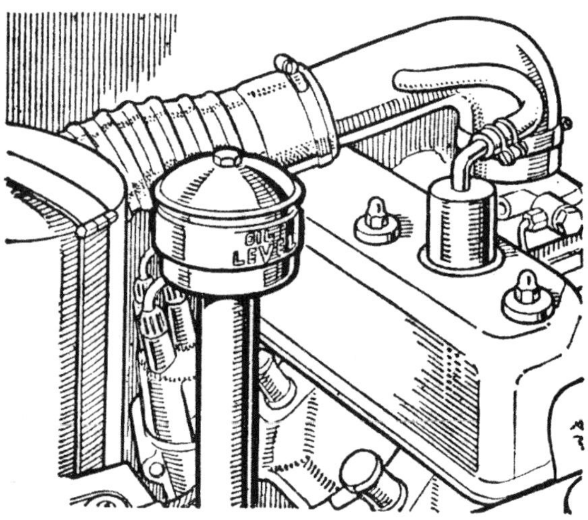

The dust-proofed breather suited certain types of terrain.

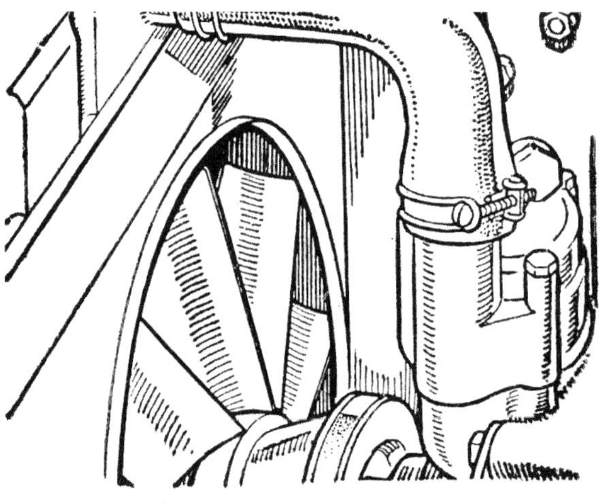

The eight-blade fan was intended for hot climates.

place of the normal filler cap. The breather was filled with oil but had to be changed frequently.

An *eight-blade fan* was available for both petrol and diesel 4-cylinder engines from about April 1959. The fan was always fitted with twin belts and there were dual-belt pulleys on the crankshaft, water pump and dynamo. In addition, a tie rod was fitted between the bell housing and chassis to prevent excessive fore and aft movement. The fan alone was also listed as an option for 2.25-litre petrol engines.

An *electric fuel pump* made by SU was available for 2.25-litre petrol models. It was normally fitted on the dashboard, next to the dash vent aperture.

Petrol-engined models could have an *engine speed governor*, which was used particularly with the PTOs. The governor was made by Iso-Speedic of Warwick, who had made a different type for Series I models. It was connected to a twelve-position quadrant lever on the dashboard. (For details of the associated hand throttle control *see* Interior Controls and Instrument Options).

Diesel models could be fitted with an *extra fuel filter*. A second 10gal *fuel tank* could also be fitted under the left-hand side of the seat box, with a changeover tap on the front of the seat box.

From June 1965 there was a *heavy-duty clutch* option. This was the 9.5in diameter, diaphragm-spring type already used on the Forward Control models.

An *oil cooler* was recommended for vehicles used to drive stationary equipment. It consisted of four wound coils in a frame and was fitted in front of the radiator. The oil cooler was always accompanied by an oil-temperature gauge on the dashboard.

Radio interference suppressors were offered, with different types for early Series II 88s with the 2-litre petrol engine, diesels and 2.25-litre petrol models.

The 2.25-litre petrol models could have a *raised air intake*, which could not be used without the dust-proofed breather described above. The breather on the top rocker cover was connected to an elbow between carburettor and air cleaner, and a pipe was mounted to the right-hand side of the windscreen frame. A domed, centrifugal air cleaner was fitted on top of the pipe, just above roof height.

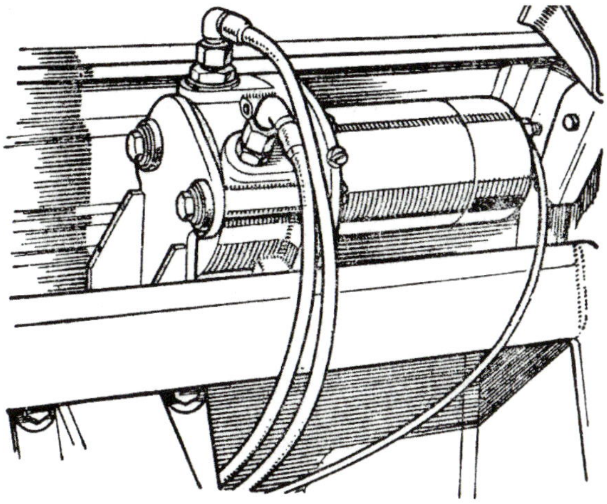
The elecric fuel pump was fitted to the parcel shelf.

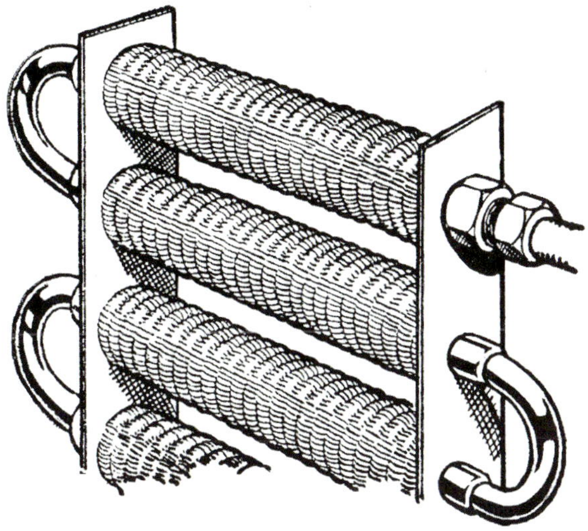
The oil cooler normally sat ahead of the radiator.

BELOW: The oil tank used with a CPTO was fitted into the wheelbox.

A *split-charge system* first appeared in June 1962, but at that stage it could be fitted only on production with the optional 12V AC/DC generator. A split-charging conversion kit was made available in October 1962. When the later Lucas alternator was fitted to a vehicle with a split-charge system an ammeter was also added to the auxiliary charging circuit.

The raised air intake was always accompanied by the dust-proofed breather.

EXTERIOR OPTIONS

The optional *bonnet lock* was a simple metal hasp bolted to the underside of the bonnet that slipped over a turnbuckle attached to the grille panel. There were different types for standard and de luxe bonnets. Customers had to supply their own padlock for the turnbuckle.

A fine-mesh *chaff guard* could be fitted in front of the radiator grille, using the grille's own fixings. It was designed to prevent the radiator from becoming clogged when the Land Rover was used for farm work. There were different types for models with headlamps in the grille panel (up to Series IIA, Suffix F) and for those with headlamps in the wings (from Suffix G).

Flashing turn indicator lamps were initially an option and were later standardized in most markets. The lamps themselves had amber lenses for both front and rear positions. When fitted by the factory or by dealers the front lamps were always fitted into the original sidelamp positions and new inboard drillings were made to relocate the sidelamps.

There was a self-cancelling switch for the interior. On early models this was

LEFT: The bonnet lock was a simple hasp. BELOW: The spare mount on a standard 'blade' bonnet.

a vacuum-operated type with a white pendant lever and was fitted to an additional panel bolted to the dashboard. From 1961 a stalk control was bolted to the steering column, with a warning light incorporated in its base. A flashing indicator conversion kit to suit Series IIA models only was introduced in January 1962.

A *foglamp* kit was made available in August 1966; the lamp itself was a Lucas SFT 576, with chrome centre button in the lens.

Folding steps could be bolted to the chassis frame under each side door, or to the rear cross-member if required for a tail door. The Series II type was rectangular; the Series IIA type had a less angular shape. On 88 Station Wagons the rear step could not be folded up if a towing jaw were fitted, and the jaw itself had to be bolted direct to the cross-member because its attachment bracket could not be fitted with a step.

A *fuel filler lock* was available, consisting of a hinged bracket that fitted over the lower 'ear' of the filler cap to prevent it from being turned. The bracket was attached to the body by the fuel filler screws, and a padlock (not supplied by Rover) could be fitted through the hole drilled as standard in the cap's 'ear'.

The optional spare wheel lock: a padlock could be put through the hole in the peg.

RIGHT: Early type of chaff guard.
BELOW: Later type of chaff guard.

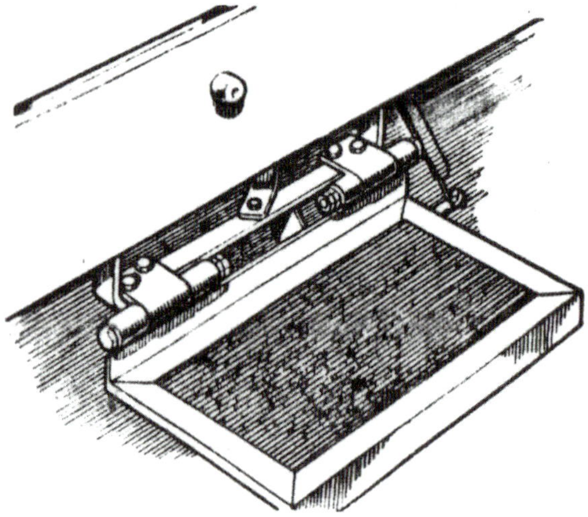

The early type of folding step was rectangular.

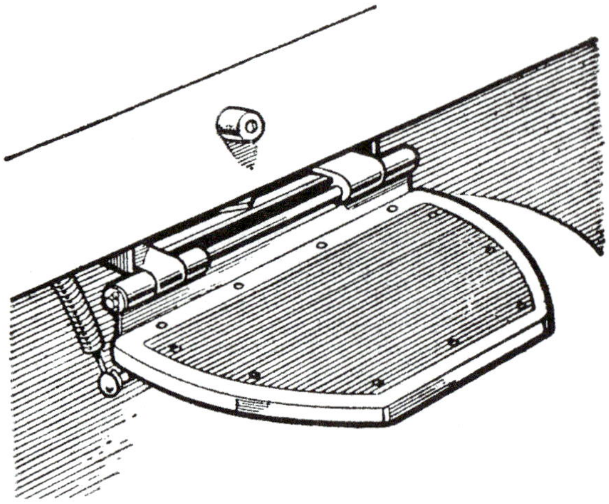

The later type of folding step had curved sides.

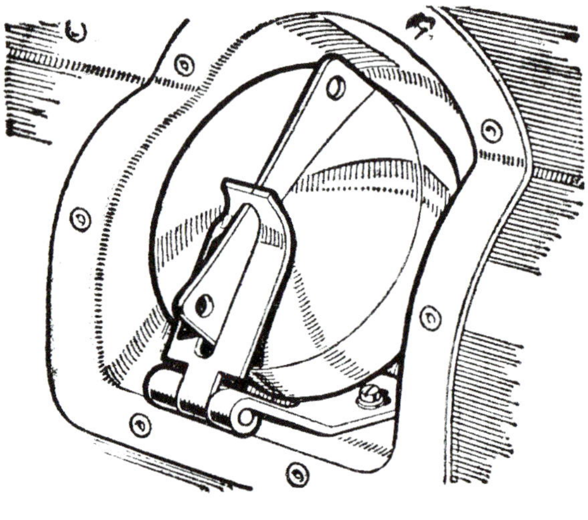

ABOVE: The folding step could also be fitted to the rear cross-member.
LEFT: The fuel filler lock needed a padlock supplied by the owner.

The *full-length doors* standard on early Series II 109 truck cabs, hardtops and Station Wagons could be ordered for 88s in place of doors with detachable tops. Conversely, half-doors for the 109 were an option in these early years, and their top sections were then a further option. From the start of the 1960 season or slightly earlier, two-piece (or half-) doors were standard on all models.

A *heated windscreen* conversion kit became available in July 1966.

Jerrycan holders seem never to have been on the published options lists, but were certainly fitted to several vehicles before Suffix G prepared at Land Rover and were also seen on some camper conversions. They were fitted on the front bumper directly in front of the wings and were therefore not available for Suffix G and later models (when the headlamps were moved to the wing fronts). Blanking plates were fitted over the holes for side and turn indicator lamps, these were relocated on the wing tops. The indicators were mounted in special aluminium housings and the sidelights were replaced by chromed 'torpedo' units, similar to those used on Rover saloons in the mid 1950s.

A *laminated glass windscreen* was available for all models.

Lifting and towing rings could be bolted on either side of the front bumper, using the bumper's own securing bolts.

The *locking door handles* that were standard on Station Wagons and all 109 models could also be fitted to 88s. A locking catch could be fitted to the lock on the inside of the passenger's side front door and all sliding windows could also be secured by locking attachments.

Rubber *mudflaps* were available for both front and rear. The early types had an oval logo printed in white, but these were rare. About 1965, they were replaced by mudflaps with the Land Rover name indented into the rubber and picked out in white.

Jerrycan holder.

An early mudflap.

A late mudflap.

ABOVE: These are the wingtop lights used when jerrycan holders were fitted. The larger light normally had an amber lens.
RIGHT: Lifting and towing ring.

RIGHT: On the early type of locking handle, the lock moved with the handle; on later types, it was fixed. FAR RIGHT: Swivel pin gaiter.

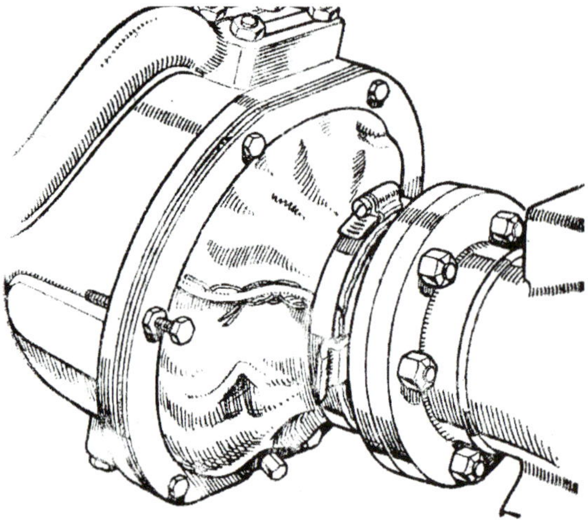

BELOW: This early tow hitch is pictured on a 1958 Series II 88.

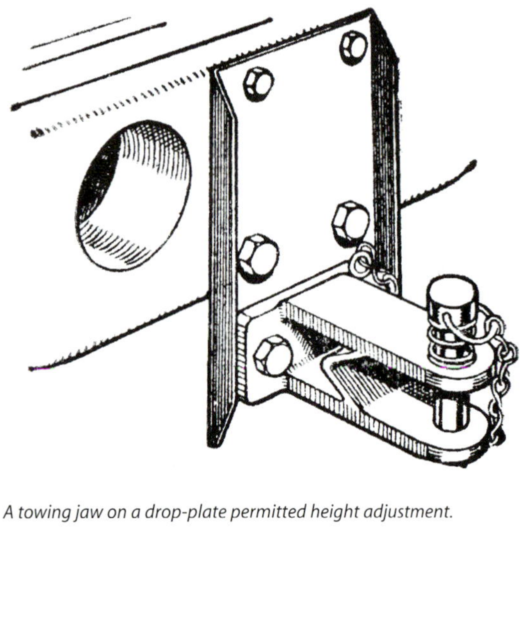

A towing jaw on a drop-plate permitted height adjustment.

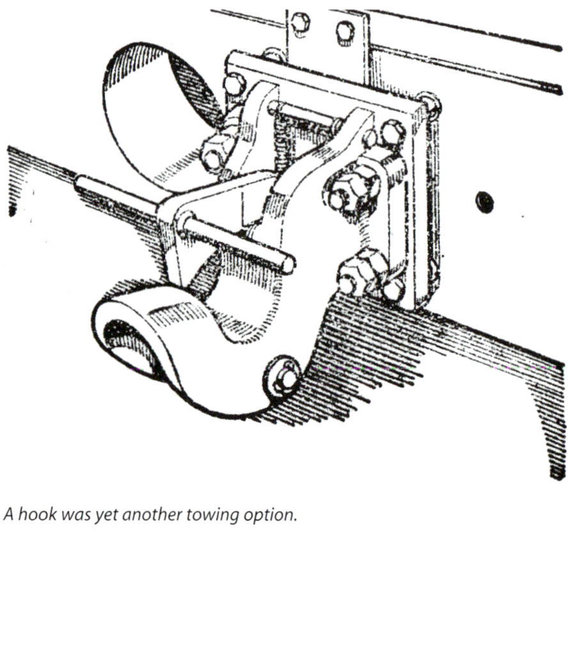

A hook was yet another towing option.

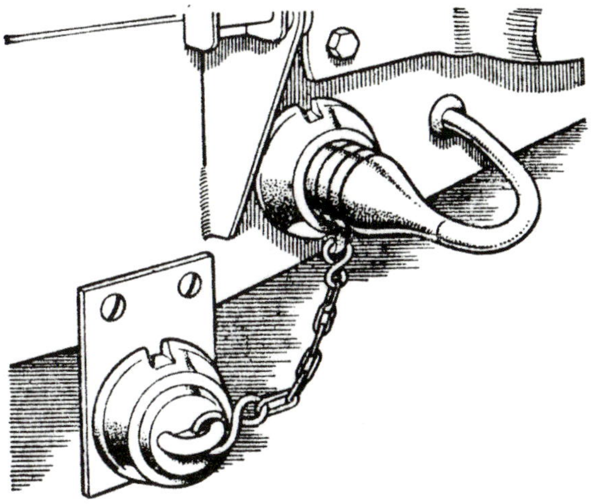

The early five-pin trailer socket.

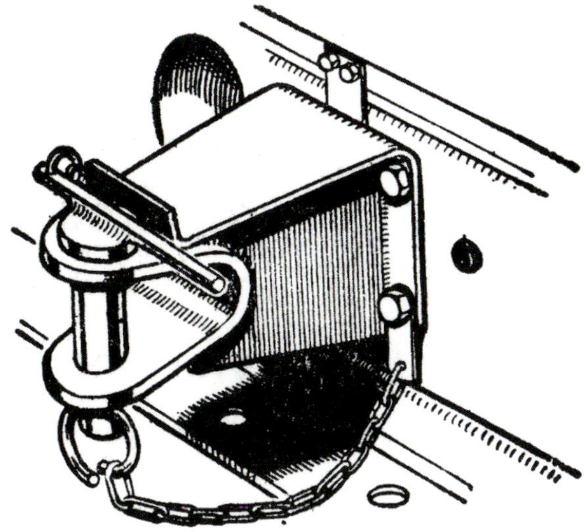

A heavy-duty towing pintle was also available.

A *reversing lamp kit* arrived in February 1966; it consisted of two rectangular lamps, an illuminated push-pull switch for the dashboard and the appropriate wiring.

A *roof rack* was available for hardtop and Station Wagon models, but on vehicles with a tropical roof it was necessary to drill the panel to provide an aperture for the feet. The front feet rested over the first or second strengthening rib on the roof and the rack was secured to the gutter by four adjustable arms.

The *spare wheel carrier* was normally inside the body, but special bonnets

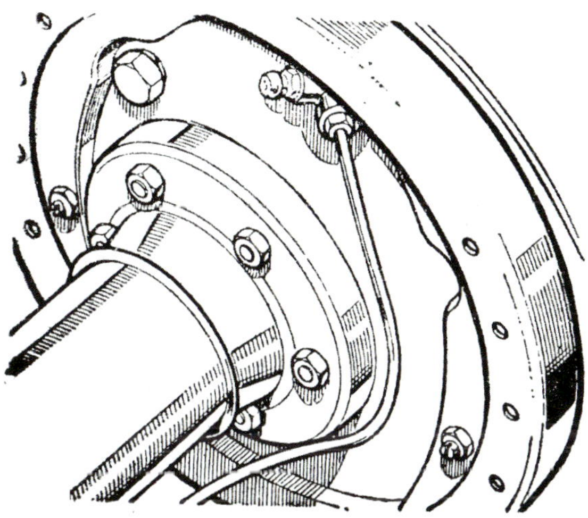

RIGHT: Mud shield in place.

BELOW LEFT: Mudshield rear face.

BELOW RIGHT: Mudshield front face.

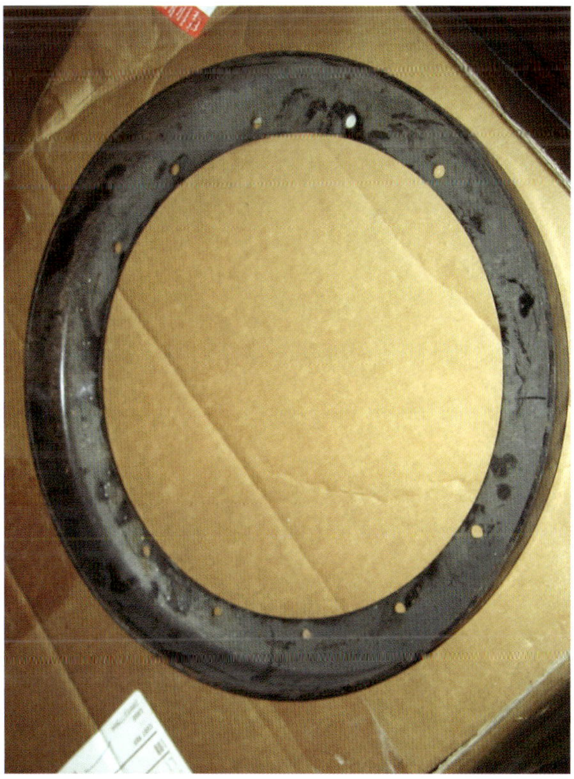

The roof rack: note the off-white enamel finish.

The passenger's side wiper motor was the same as the driver's side type.

were available with alternative carriers. The carrier consisted of a central mounting plate with four rubber support blocks positioned under the tyre wall to ensure even weight distribution. These blocks were initially rectangular and later round. There were versions of both the standard and the de luxe bonnet with wheel carriers.

As a separate option, a lockable spare wheel carrier was available. In this case a peg was fitted through the central mounting plate. This protruded through one of the wheel stud holes and was drilled to take a padlock. Customers had to supply their own padlock.

A *spotlamp* kit was made available in August 1966; the lamp itself was a Lucas SLR 576.

The *windscreen washer* option appeared in June 1961. It consisted of a jet attached to the wiper arm on the driver's side (or on both sides) and fed by a plastic hose.

The standard *wing mirrors* were black (*see* Chapter 5), and a passenger's side mirror was available to match the driver's side mirror standard in some markets. By 1964, hinge-mounted mirrors were also available (*see* Chapter 9), as were car-type, chromium-plated 'boomerang' trapezoid wing mirrors. The chromed mirrors had probably been discontinued by about 1968.

INTERIOR, CONTROLS AND INSTRUMENT OPTIONS

An *accelerator pedal restrictor* was available for Series II and IIA 88s with the 2.25-litre petrol engine. It consisted of an

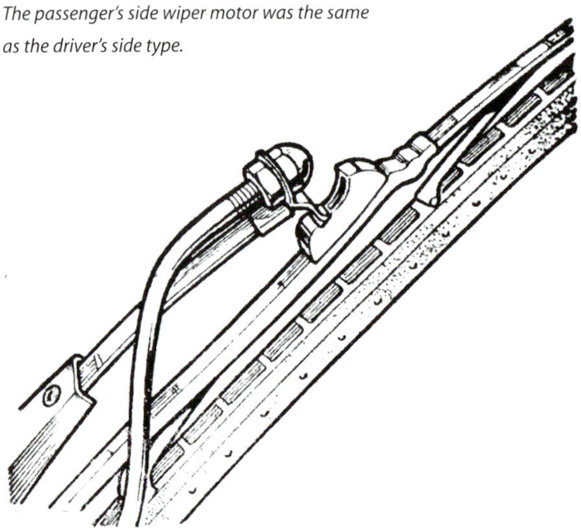

Early windscreen washers were attached to the wiper arms.

A passenger's side wing mirror was available to match the driver's mirror.

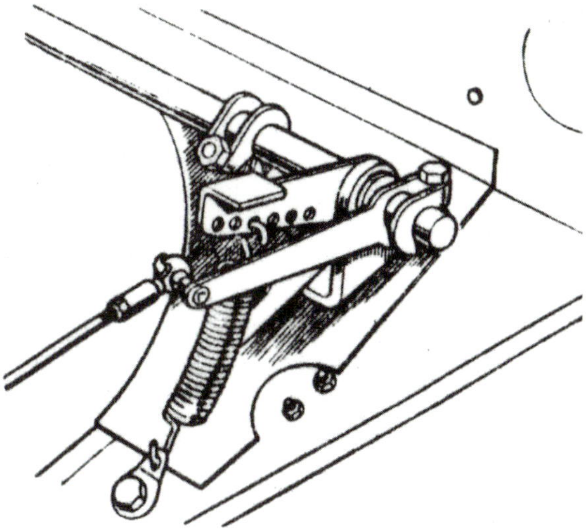

ABOVE: *The accelerator pedal restrictor.*
RIGHT: *The combined water and oil gauge.*

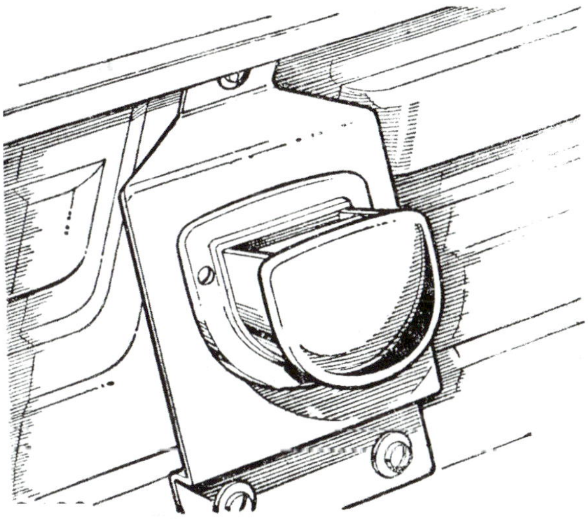

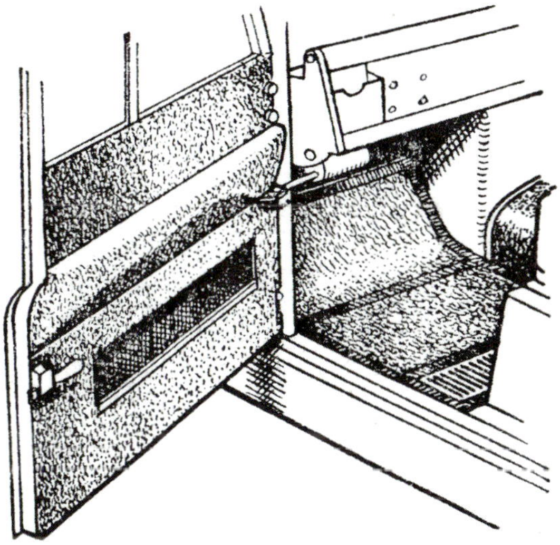

ABOVE: *The ashtray was a Rover car item.*
ABOVE RIGHT: *De luxe trim included full door panels.*

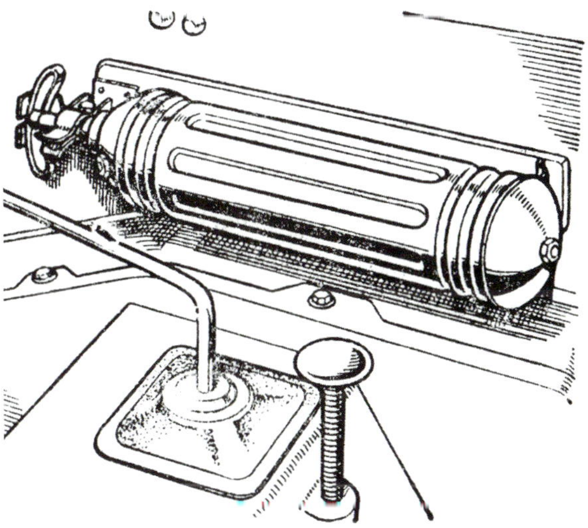

ABOVE: *The recommended position for the fire extinguisher was above the gearbox tunnel …*
RIGHT: *… but it was often mounted elsewhere.*

Flyscreens could be fitted behind the vent panels.

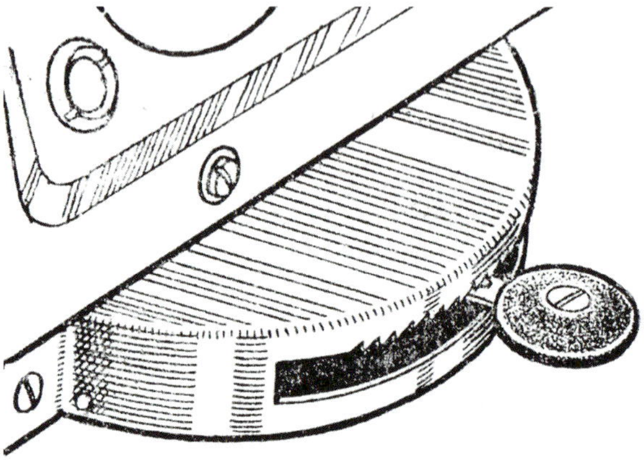

ABOVE: The early hand throttle worked in a horizontal plane.
RIGHT: Heated windscreen switches.

additional strong spring in the linkage, which made use of full throttle uncomfortable.

An *ashtray* could be fitted to the dashboard. This was the pull-out unit used in Rover saloons during the early 1960s and had a plastic, mock-wood finish. It was fitted in a purpose-designed bracket that bolted to the dashboard.

A *combined water temperature and oil pressure gauge* became optional in June 1961. It was fitted on an extra panel bolted alongside the main instrument panel, usually on the passenger's side. The water temperature gauge was connected to the cylinder head by an adaptor, and the oil pressure gauge had a feed teed into the oil pressure switch feed pipe.

De-luxe interior trim was available for all models. This consisted of black rubber floor coverings and door panels with armrests, trimmed to match the seats. On truck cab models the de luxe trim option also included a headlining (*see* below).

A *fire extinguisher* could be carried in a bracket bolted to the bulkhead just in front of the gear lever (where it obscured the chassis number and transmission control instruction plate). The bracket was normally painted black and the extinguisher had a bright chrome finish.

The dash vents below the windscreen could be fitted with fine gauze *flyscreens* over their openings.

The *hand throttle control* was standard on diesel models but could be fitted to petrol types for use with the PTOs. Models up to and including Series IIA, Suffix E had the quadrant mounted horizontally under the dashboard; from Suffix F it was mounted vertically to clear the larger optional heater.

Hardtop 88s could have a *headlining* for the cab area from approximately April 1959. Like the headlining in other models, this was made of perforated, white, plastic cloth.

A *heater-demister* was always an optional extra, and the first kits for Series IIs became available in August 1958. The heater was a large, black, circular box mounted in the passenger's footwell, with piping running through the bulkhead to plumb into the engine cooling system and with flaps in the front face for air distribution. There was a tap in the engine bay to isolate the heater from the cooling system in warm weather. Plastic trunking ducted air from the heater body to demister outlets bolted to the lower windscreen frame. The early demisters were straight and were mounted alongside the wiper motor; later a C-shaped type was introduced, which fitted around the wiper motor. The heater was rated at 2.5kW and was made by Smith's. Its blower fan was controlled by a rheostat switch. There was a different type of heater for the 6-cylinder models. This had a rectangular casing, a two-speed fan and was rated at 3.5kW. A version of this heater (which differed mainly in its fixings and pipework) became available in January 1969 for the 4-cylinder models, beginning with Series IIA Suffix F. This 'flat' heater could also be retrofitted to earlier models if the associated cranked transfer box lever and vertical hand throttle (where fitted) were also used to give enough clearance. There was also a very rare rear heater option, mainly intended for Station Wagons. This used a version of the round Smith's front heater used before 1969 and had to be plumbed into the front heater. It appears not to have been possible to use it with the later, rectangular, front heater.

Rubber *pedal pads* were available for the brake and clutch pedals. They were secured by two metal tags that bent over the sides of the pedals and behind them. These pads were not recommended for use in wet or muddy conditions because they became slippery. The pedal pad 'kit' originally included a rubber pad for the accelerator pedal as well, but this had been deleted by 1964.

A *radio* was introduced as an extra in January 1960. It was mounted in a bracket that bolted to the upper flange of the dashboard, outboard of the driver. Its aerial was normally attached to a bracket on the windscreen frame and a speaker would be mounted to the front

The early, round heater made by Smith's.

Heaters could be turned off at a tap on the engine.

This 'flat' heater was available for the 6-cylinder models.

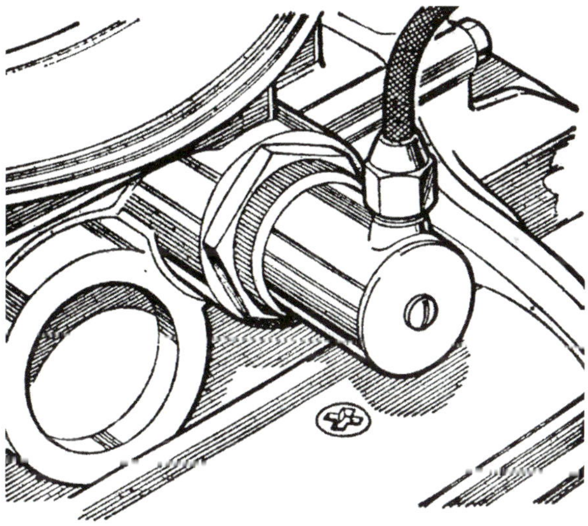

The cylinder block immersion heater.

The early straight demister vent on a 1959 model.

Pedal rubbers came as a set.

The later demister vents were C-shaped.

parcel shelf. In the beginning, the set was made by Pye, and in Britain it was either an MW/SW or an MW/LW type.

Inward-facing *rear seats* were available and were bolted to the rear body and wheel arch. Their detachable cushions could be hinged up when not in use, to give maximum carrying space. Each seat was designed to accommodate two passengers; 88s could have one seat unit on each side, while 109s could have two on each side.

A *rear view mirror* was standard on Station Wagons, Truck Cab and Hardtop models, but was an optional extra on models with the full-length hood. The mirror used was the same as that on those models which had one as standard.

From 1965 *safety belts* were added to the options list. Each harness consisted of a short strap bolted to the transmission tunnel and carrying the tongue section of the buckle, and a long, diagonal shoulder strap bolted to the top of the

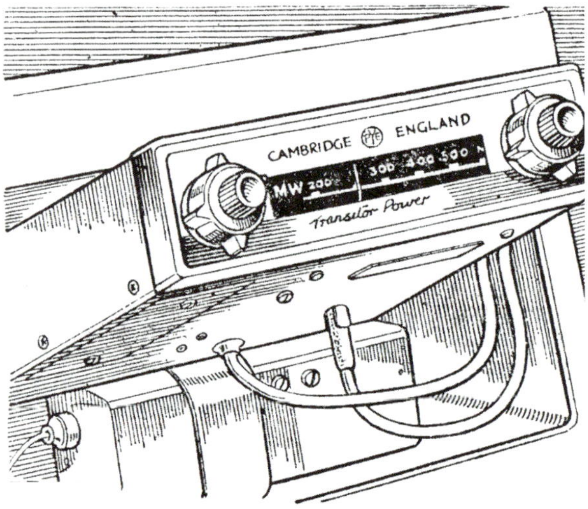

Early radios were Pye sets.

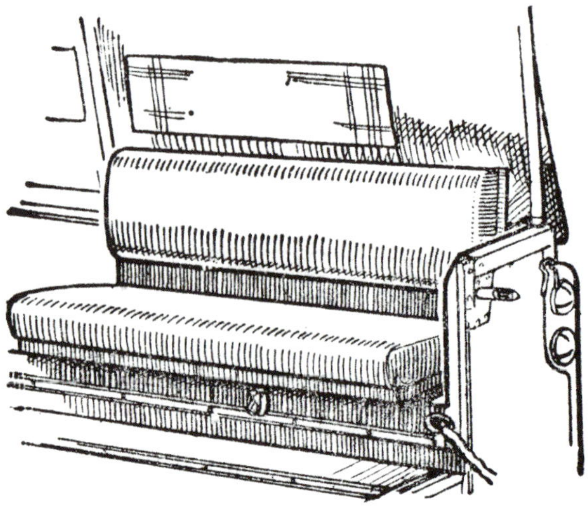

The rear seats faced inwards.

The rear-view mirror bolted to the windscreen frame.

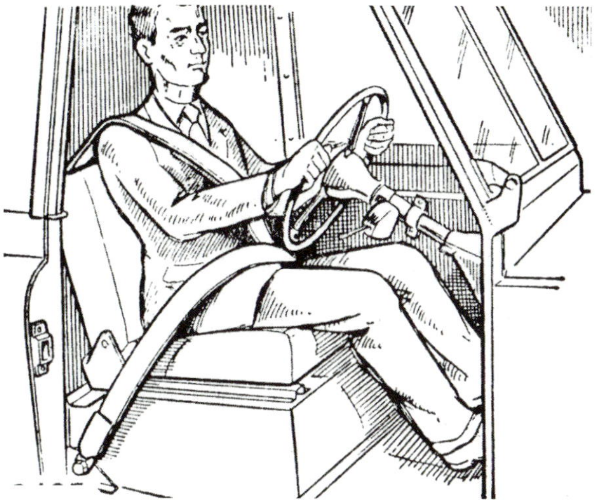

Safety belts gradually became more common.

A reinforcing gusset fitted with safety belts.

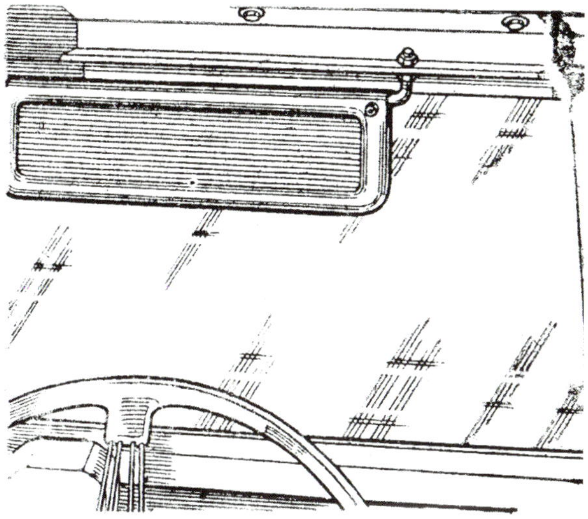

Sun visors also bolted to the windscreen frame.

back body's front panel and carrying the mating buckle. On chassis-cab models supplied with a truck cab, there was a spreader bar for the belt fixings behind the bulkhead; on models with a rear 'tub' there were also two triangular gussets that braced the back body's front panel to the rear floor. (Belts became a standard fit for the British market in 1967.) Seat base insulation was available from around April 1959 for 88 hardtops.

A *sun visor* could be bolted to the windscreen top rail on the driver's side, the passenger's side or both. These visors were introduced around April 1959.

The standard speedometer had no trip function, but a *trip speedometer* was available. There were versions with mph and kph markings. Up to Series A Suffix C, the trip reset button operated direct on the casing; from Suffix D it was on the end of a short, black, flexible cable.

When a passenger's side *windscreen wiper* was fitted as an option on pre-Suffix D models, it used the same Lucas motor as the driver's side item.

RIGHT: *The trip speedometer was available in both mph and kph forms.*

POWER TAKE-OFFS

There were four optional power take-off positions on Series II and Series IIA Land Rovers. At the front, power could be taken from the engine crankshaft. In the centre, power could be taken from a unit mounted on the rear of the transfer box. There was also a 'bottom PTO' in the centre of the vehicle, when an auxiliary gearbox was mounted under the transfer box and driven from its intermediate gears. The rear PTO took its drive from the back of the gearbox through a propshaft to a dedicated gearbox mounted outside the rear cross-member.

The crankshaft PTO was normally used with a capstan winch. A short propshaft ran from the centre of the crankshaft pulley to the winch drive and could be engaged or disengaged from the starter dog clutch on the pulley by a lever mounted in front of the grille panel.

The centre PTO was mainly used to power equipment mounted on the Land Rover and was rated to deliver 20–25bhp. Typically, it would be fitted with a multi-belt pulley, with a shaft to drive machinery mounted on the vehicle or with a shaft that led to a more accessible position on an outrigger. However, a hydraulic pump was also available, rated at 6.5gpm at 1,500rpm and a maximum of 2,000lb/sq.in. This hydraulic pump was manufactured by the Tooley Electro Mechanical Co. Ltd of Earl Shilton, near Leicester.

The centre PTO's drive was taken through a dog clutch on the rear of the gearbox mainshaft and normally had a Hardy Spicer 1300 Series flange at its drive end. It was engaged by a lever in the heelboard under the seat. The centre PTO was available for both 88 and 109 models and there was a special variant for the 109 One Ton types. It could not be fitted to 109 Station Wagons.

The bottom PTO was bolted to the underside of the transfer box in place of the transfer box cover plate. Its main function was to offer an additional PTO position when the other PTOs were already in use, but it was rarely fitted. It gave a mechanical drive when fitted with the drive unit normally used for the rear PTO, or a hydraulic drive if fitted with a reverse-running version of the pump that was available for the centre PTO.

Drive to the rear PTO was taken through a dog-clutch on the rear of the gearbox mainshaft. An auxiliary propshaft ending in a standard SAE six-spline output took drive to the rear of the vehicle and emerged through a circular cut-out in the rear cross-member. This splined output was invariably fitted with a shaped metal guard. If the guard were removed an optional pulley unit could be fitted over the output splines and bolted in its place. This 8in pulley was designed to transmit up to 20bhp.

There were three versions of the rear PTO: to suit 88s, 4-cylinder 109s and 6-cylinder 109s. It was not possible to fit a rear PTO to 109 Station Wagons because of their rear-mounted fuel tank.

TOWING OPTIONS

The 'standard' towing jaw was suitable for maximum towed weights up to 4,480lb (2,032kg). It could be used on Station Wagons or on other models with a Station Wagon-type tail door if the spare wheel was first removed from its tail-door mounting.

The jaw could be bolted to the centre of the rear chassis cross-member (and had to be so fitted on 88 Station Wagons) or could be mounted on a bracket which set the towing jaw lower down, below the bottom of the cross-member. This

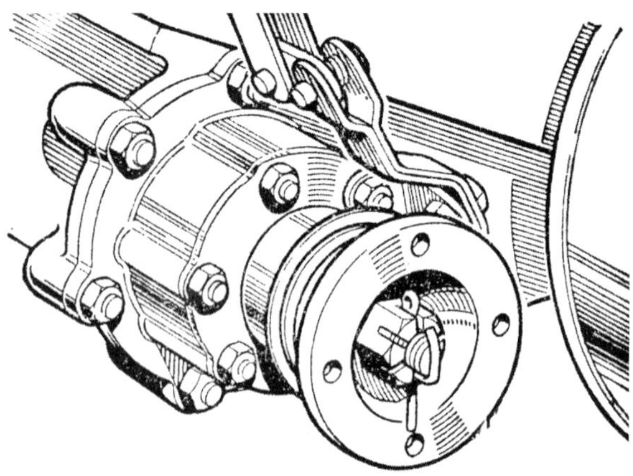

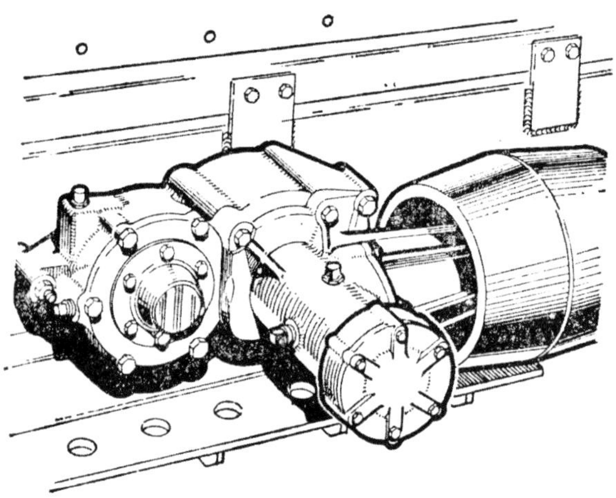

ABOVE: A mechanical drive on the bottom PTO.
RIGHT: A pulley unit on the rear PTO.

A splined shaft drive on the rear PTO.

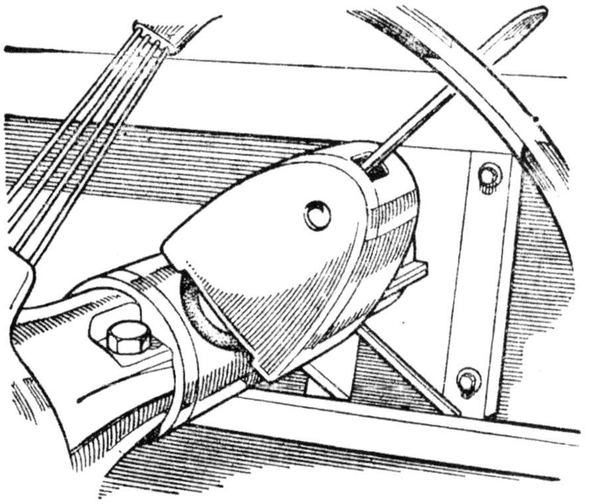

A later type of flasher switch.

was the normal fitting on 109 Station Wagons. The bracket could not be used on 88 Station Wagons with a rear folding step or on models with a rear power take-off.

The rear PTO was supplied with a draw plate and extension, and these items could also be bought separately. They allowed the towing jaw to be used with the rear PTO in position, but were not suitable for the 109 Station Wagon.

The heavy-duty towing pintle was for trailers with an oversize towing eye and for towed weights greater than 4,480lb (2,032kg). It could be used on 88 Station Wagons or 88 hardtops with a Station Wagon tail door only if the spare wheel was removed from its door mounting. The pintle could be fitted to 109 Station Wagons, but access to the four bolts securing it to the rear cross-member could be achieved only by dropping the fuel tank. It could not be used in conjunction with a rear power take-off.

The towing hook was again for heavy-duty applications and had to be fitted to the rear cross-member with an adaptor plate.

The early type of trailer socket had five pins and was fitted to the rear cross-member. When no trailer was attached the flasher plug on the vehicle had to be reconnected to the socket. When a trailer was attached the flasher plug on the vehicle had to be inserted into a dummy socket carried on a bracket bolted to the rear cross-member. The dummy socket and five-pin flasher plug option included the trailer socket pin and leads, which were also available separately.

When regulations changed in Britain the trailer electrics changed. From August 1966 there was a new trailer flasher kit, and then in September 1967 a seven-pin trailer socket arrived. From September 1970 a new seven-pin plug and socket with improved weatherproofing were introduced.

WINCHES

A front-mounted capstan winch manufactured by Fairey delivered a maximum pull of 2,500lb (1,135kg). It was mounted on the front bumper and driven direct from the engine crankshaft, and had a rope speed of 12.75ft/min at the recommended engine speed of 600rpm. An operating knob on the winch casing engaged or disengaged the drive, and provision was incorporated to apply the starting-handle at the front of the winch instead of at the dog on the crankshaft.

A hydraulic winch was also available. This was a drum type, driven by a hydraulic pump fitted to the centre or bottom PTO. A control valve was mounted on the heelboard, and a hydraulic oil supply tank in the rear wheel arch. Early examples had a tubular fairlead, later ones had a 'letter-box' type.

TOP: Early Fairey capstan winch. The operating knob should have a flat rather than a ball-type knob.

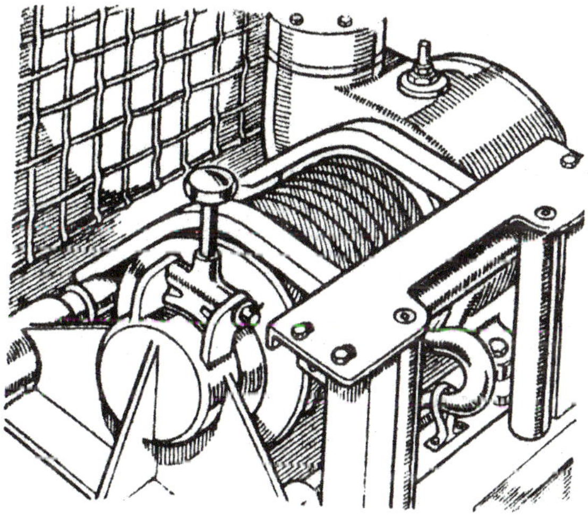

RIGHT: A hydraulic winch with the early type of fairlead.

BELOW: The later type of fairlead is seen on this hydraulic winch.

7 major conversions

The Land Rover was advertised as 'the world's most versatile vehicle', and this group of conversions from the Special Projects Department was intended to prove the claim.

The versatility of the Land Rover encouraged specialist manufacturers to build their own conversions of it. This raised warranty issues, and the Land Rover Special Projects Department was established in 1957 to examine these conversions and to determine whether they would adversely affect the base vehicle's operability or durability. Those conversions which met the necessary criteria were granted Land Rover Approval, which meant that Solihull would honour its standard Land Rover warranty and would also promote the conversions through its own dealer network and at exhibitions and shows.

Some conversions involved quite radical alterations to the body or running gear of the Land Rover, and those are the subject of this chapter. Others were simply items of equipment that could be driven by the Land Rover's PTOs or otherwise attached to the vehicle; those are covered in Chapter 8.

Worth noting is that the major conversions were usually made on chassis numbered as 'export' types, even for the home market. The Rover Company operated a similar system for its saloon cars when a special order was going down the lines, and it seems likely that special features – whether for a special order, a conversion or an overseas requirement – were all most easily accommodated under the broad heading of 'export specification'.

AIRCRAFT LOADERS

Precision Engineering Products (Suffolk) Ltd of Bury St Edmunds produced the Moy Conveyor, which, in its low-level form and mounted on an 88in Land Rover, was specifically intended as an aircraft loader. It was named after its inventor Peter Moy, and there was a companion Conveyor on the 109in wheelbase chassis, which shared some of the aircraft loader's components.

The basic vehicle was an open 88in model fitted with a centre PTO. The steering position was offset to the right and a fabricated support section allowed the seat cushion to extend beyond the side of the vehicle. The spare wheel was relocated on a mounting just behind the left-hand front wheel, and the main boom of the conveyor rested on the body next to the driver. The conveyor's support frame was bolted through the floor of the load bay to a steel sub-frame that was secured to the chassis by U-bolts. The two booms of the conveyor pivoted

The Moy 88 aircraft loader.

from the top of this frame, the short rearward one swinging down to about axle height to act as a pick-up while the longer main boom could be swung up to a height of 13ft 6in (4.1m) to reach the hold of an aircraft. The elevating mechanism for the booms and the drive for the single rubber conveyor belt that passed over both of them were powered by a PTO-driven Dowty hydraulic pump.

This conversion was sometimes known as the SPALE, which stood for Self-Propelled Aircraft Loading Equipment. By July 1964 its manufacture had been taken over by H.W. Edghill (Equipment) Ltd of Hook, Hampshire. This company specialized in aircraft servicing equipment and loading ramps and marketed the conversion as the Edghill-Moy Aircraft Loader.

AIRFIELD CRASH TENDERS

All three major builders of Land Rover fire appliances (*see* Fire Appliances) adapted their designs to create airfield crash rescue tenders. In the later 1960s Pyrene also adapted the Sun Engineering fire tender designs as crash tenders and developed an additional model.

Fire Armour

The earliest airfield crash tender seems to have come from Fire Armour Ltd of London and to have been available by November 1959. This was a truck-cab model with custom-built open back body on the 109in chassis. It is not clear whether this ever carried the Firefly name used for the company's fire appliances. Fire Armour Ltd was bought out by George Angus & Co. Ltd, makers of fire-fighting equipment, in the early 1960s and under the Angus Group from 1963 its fire and crash rescue designs were handed over to HCB-Angus.

The RU type of crash tender from HCB-Angus.

The Firefly brand was originally owned by Fire Armour but later passed to HCB-Angus. This 1961 fire engine was new for the Snowy Mountains Hydro-Electric Authority in Australia.

HCB-Angus

HCB-Angus did use the Firefly name for their airfield rescue tender. This had the standard Firefly back body design (*see* Fire Appliances) but carried no water or fire pump. Instead it had a PTO-driven generator to power twin 500W floodlights and cutting equipment, and carried dry-powder units with high-pressure delivery hoses.

Carmichael

The several fire tender conversions offered by Carmichael & Sons (Worcester) Ltd could also be configured as airfield crash tenders, but probably not before about 1961 (*see* Fire Appliances).

Pyrene

The Pyrene Company Ltd, whose Fire Engineering Division was at Sunbury-on-Thames in Middlesex, took over the Sun Engineering fire tender designs and developed the BLR1 into a dry-chemical airfield crash tender as the BLR3. This carried floodlights, a ladder and a number of portable extinguishers in the pick-up bed. The company also developed the BLR4 as a cheaper model for use at small airfields. This was similar to the BLR3 but lacked the floodlights and ladder.

The Pilchers standard ambulance was based on a truck cab 109.

The Pilchers two-stretcher ambulance was coachbuilt.

The Pilchers four-stretcher ambulance was intended for military use.

AMBULANCES

There were seven ambulance designs with the Land Rover Approval, from three specialist converters. All were built on the 109in chassis and most were probably sold outside Britain.

Pilchers

The earliest approved conversions were by Pilchers, who had already been building ambulances and mobile dispensaries on long-wheelbase, Series I chassis. Originally based in the south-west London suburb of Merton, the company moved to new premises at Burgess Hill in Sussex some time in the early 1960s and took on the name of Pilchers (Merton) Ltd. The basic Pilchers ambulance consisted of a tall, hardtop-type body mounted on a 109 truck cab. This usually came with sliding side windows and there were several interior configurations. However, from the start of Series II production, Pilchers also offered their Land Rover Cross-Country Ambulance, which had an elegant and distinctive coach-built body made from aluminium. This was fully insulated to suit tropical use and was available with three interior configurations: two stretchers plus an attendant's seat, one stretcher and three seats for sitting patients, or six seats for sitting patients. In all cases there were lockers for medical equipment and a built-in wash basin with its own water supply.

By 1964 a Four Stretcher Ambulance had been added, and the company promoted this third design for military use. Slightly taller than the coach-built type, it retained standard Land Rover cab doors and did not have the distinctive body side pressings of the coach-built model. A single sliding window on each side replaced the coach-built model's two.

It was probably during the first half of 1967 that Pilchers gave their conversions identifying numbers. The hardtop-bodied ambulance became the Series 7428/S2 and was available with two stretchers as a standard or a de luxe model. The coach-built ambulance, now with just two interior configurations, became a Series 7428/S3. And the 'standard ambulance' or four-stretcher 'military' type (now available with the option of just two stretchers as well) became a Series 7489/S3. All these designs continued through to the Series III period.

Lomas

Herbert Lomas Ltd, of Handforth near Wilmslow in Cheshire, introduced three ambulance bodies in late 1964 or 1965. Cheapest was the J/C type, with aluminium panels on a wooden frame, aimed at the British and north European markets and featuring a single-pane windscreen. Second cheapest was the metal-framed J/M type, again with aluminium panels but this time with a two-pane windscreen and twin windows on each side of the body. The most expensive was the F/M type, with a body of aluminium panels on a metal frame, a heating and ventilating system for the rear body and

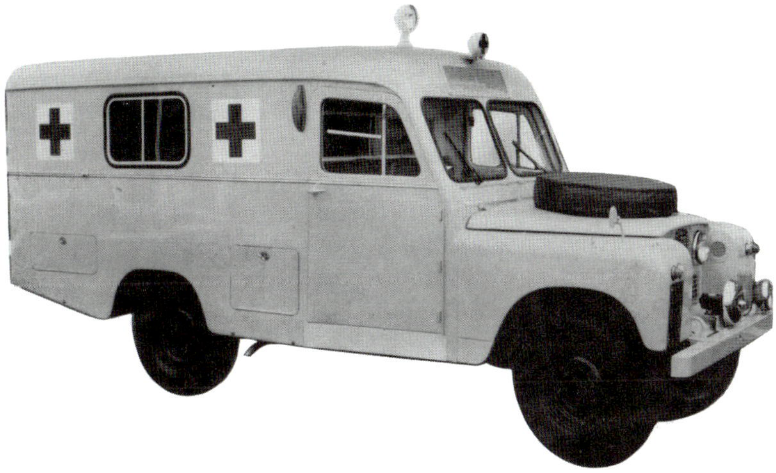

TOP RIGHT: *Pilchers 7489/S3 ambulance.*
ABOVE RIGHT: *Lomas F/M ambulance.*
RIGHT: *Lomas J/C ambulance.*
BELOW: *The Lomas maker's plate.*

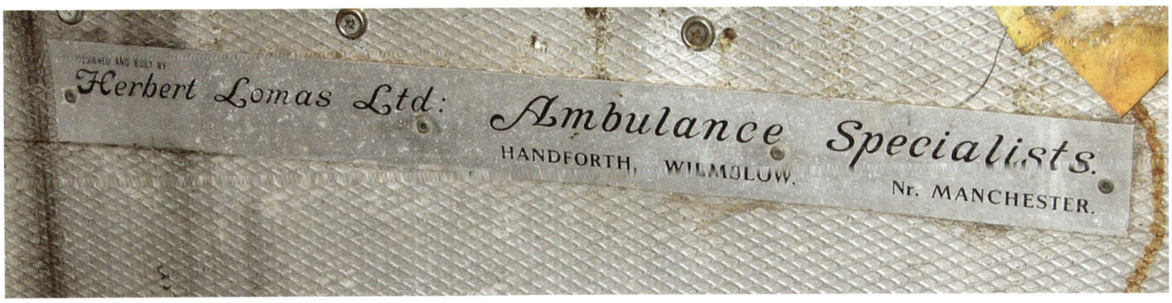

a two-way radio as standard. These special-bodied ambulances were expensive, and by June 1966 the J/C and F/M types seem to have been dropped. This left the J/M body at the top of the range, while a simple hardtop conversion filled the middle range and the entry-level model had a canvas hood.

Invercarron

Invercarron (Stonehaven) Ltd had a budget ambulance conversion available by mid 1966, consisting of a special hardtop fitted to a 109 truck cab and an interior kitted out with stretchers and seats according to the customer's wishes.

The Lomas J/M ambulance had a metal-framed body.

ARMOURED PATROL CAR

The original design for an armoured car on the 109in chassis was drawn up in the workshops of the Royal Ulster Constabulary in Belfast in 1962–3. The design was then handed over to Short Brothers & Harland Ltd of Belfast, who started production in July 1965 and marketed the conversion under the name of the Shorland. The original Mark 1 types had the 2.25-litre petrol engine; Mark 2 types had the later high-compression type to deliver much-needed extra power; and Mark 3 types, introduced in about 1969, had the 2.6-litre, 6-cylinder engine. These vehicles were fitted with the low-ratio transfer box from the Forward Control models and with heavy-duty axles.

BACKHOES

Late in the Series IIA period, Airdrive Ltd of High Wycombe developed a backhoe digger for the 109 Land Rover, which they branded the Harrier. This was a small excavator mounted on the back of the vehicle, and Land Rover hoped that it would find a market with local councils looking for an affordable and versatile grave-digging machine. Unfortunately, sales did not live up to expectations.

BREAKDOWN RECOVERY VEHICLES

There were two suppliers of light recovery equipment for Land Rovers. These were Mann Egerton & Co. Ltd of Norwich and Harvey Frost of Bishop's Stortford in Hertfordshire. Mann Egerton were taken over by the Westinghouse Brake and Signal Co Ltd by 1964 but continued

ABOVE: Shorland armoured patrol car.
RIGHT: A Series IIA Harrier backhoe.

to market the recovery equipment under their own name.

Harvey Frost

The Harvey Frost Pick-Up Crane was slightly cheaper than the Mann Egerton equipment and had been available for Series I models since around 1956. It consisted of a tubular jib with a crane rated at 30cwt. A lifting sling was available as an extra-cost option, as were rear supporting jacks. The crane could be fitted to either 88in or 109in Land Rovers (the jibs were of different lengths), but heavy-duty suspension was recommended in both cases.

Mann Egerton

The Mann Egerton Light Recovery Equipment conversion was on sale by November 1959. It was also available as a retro-fit for Series I models and may have been available during their production lifetime. It had gone from the Land Rover accessories lists by June 1968. It consisted of a 2-ton crane with a tubular frame that could be mounted in the load-bed of either 88s or 109s. Early examples had the hand-operated winch mounted against the cab bulkhead, but later examples had it on the framework of the crane. There were also chassis jacks at the rear to stabilize the vehicle during lifting operations, and two varieties of two-wheel ambulance were available; these were carried on a special bracket mounted between the front dumb irons. The Mann Egerton conversion was initially sold as a complete package, but by mid-1964 the components could all be bought separately. A windowed canopy behind the truck cab was often fitted as part of the conversion.

ABOVE LEFT: Harvey Frost breakdown recovery crane.
ABOVE RIGHT: Breakdown recovery vehicles often had an extended cab or canopy, as on this November 1963 Series IIA fitted with a Harvey Frost crane.
RIGHT: Mann Egerton light recovery vehicle.

The Mann Egerton ME MkII also had a canopy extension.

CAMPERS AND CARAVANS

Two companies offered approved mobile caravan conversions on the Series IIA models, and at least two more offered conversions that did not have the Land Rover Approval. The approved converters were Martin Walter Ltd of Folkestone (whose conversion was always known as the Dormobile), and R.J. Searle Ltd of Sunbury-on-Thames. The others were Hall Park Garage, who made the Park Ranger conversion, and X-Panda-Cab, who were based in the USA and sold their conversions only in North America.

Martin Walter

Martin Walter Ltd had first marketed Dormobile conversions on other chassis in the middle 1950s, and the Land Rover Dormobile seems to have been announced in 1961. The conversion was always based on a 109 Station Wagon, and its most recognizable feature was a GRP roof with a striped PVC canopy. This roof was hinged on one side and, when raised, gave standing room in the body of the vehicle and also clearance above a pair of optional roll-out bunks attached to the cantrails. The Dormobile featured special Dormatic seats, which folded flat to make a bed, and the rear load area was fitted out with cooking and washing equipment, plus a small wardrobe. Dormobiles sold quite strongly and seem to have been popular with Land Rover buyers in the USA.

ABOVE: Martin Walter Dormobile.

LEFT: Inside the Searle Safari Sleeper.

BELOW: A Park Ranger conversion.

Searle

Searle seem to have built their campers to order from a menu of options, and so there were several varieties. Both 88 and 109 models were converted, in each case either from a hardtop or a Station Wagon. The basic conversion during the Series IIA period was called the Safari Sleeper. This was on the 88in chassis and was probably available by about 1966, although it did not receive Land Rover Approval until 1968. The centre and passenger seats were modified to fold down into a double bed in conjunction with a specially designed, inward-facing rear seat. Jerry cans mounted on the front wings were a standard feature until the Land Rover's headlamps were moved to that position in 1968, and a free-standing mahogany-veneered picnic table was also supplied. Searle later marketed their conversions under the Carawagon name.

Park Ranger

The Park Ranger was made by Hall Park Garage of Berkhamstead in Hertfordshire and was probably introduced around 1966–7. It was based on a 109 hardtop with special side windows. With its roof panel divided longitudinally, each section hinged at cantrail height, so that when open it gave good headroom across the full width of the vehicle. The typical interior layout provided a double-bed at seat level plus two roll-out bunks at cantrail height, together with cooking, washing and wardrobe and cupboard stowage in the load area. This conversion seems to have been very rare. Hall Park Garage promised a conversion on the 88in chassis as well, but it is doubtful whether this ever materialized.

X-Panda-Cab

The X-Panda-Cab was made in Grand Junction, Colorado, and was probably introduced in 1966. The conversion was designed for an 88 window hardtop, although at least one example was built on a 109in model. The roof panel was hinged at the rear and removable plywood panels then formed a platform at cantrail height, which supported a double futon. The back body contained a table, a cooking stove and some wooden storage units. The company seems not to have survived long, and these conversions were rare.

CONVEYORS

The Moy Conveyor system used for aircraft loaders (*see* above) was also available on the 109 models, when it was known as the 'standard' conveyor. In this case, the whole system was mounted in the load bay of a truck cab model with its spare wheel mounted on the bonnet, and was claimed to be demountable in 10min. In travelling position, the forward boom passed over the cab roof and rested on a support mounted to the front bumper. As it passed above the driver and did not take space in the cab, the standard steering position was retained. The Moy Conveyor could lift materials to a maximum height of 16ft 2in (4.9m) above the ground. Different types of belt were available to allow the conveyor to handle loose materials. It is not clear whether this conversion remained available after H.W. Edghill Ltd took over the manufacture of the aircraft loader that used the Moy Conveyor system.

FERTILIZER DISTRIBUTORS

Kenwall Engineers Ltd of Newport, Monmouthshire introduced a fertilizer distributor in the early 1960s; it was not available by January 1960 but was intended for the Series II models, which suggests an introduction date of 1960 or early 1961. Land Rover no longer listed this conversion by June 1966.

The basic vehicle was a 109 chassis cab with a 15cwt hopper fitted on a frame above the rear chassis; the distributor was driven from the centre PTO through oil bath gearboxes. Both petrol and diesel models had to have a bonnet-mounted spare wheel and Dunlop Trakgrip T29A 7.50×16 tyres. Petrol-engined models also had to be fitted with an engine speed governor.

FIFTH-WHEEL CONVERSION

B. Dixon-Bate Ltd of Chester were makers of trailers and towing equipment, and in about February 1960 they introduced a fifth-wheel conversion for the 88in Land Rover. They offered a wide variety of swan-neck trailers to go with this and by June 1964 were also marketing a detachable, all-steel pick-up body, which allowed the Land Rover to be used as a load-carrier when it was not towing its semi-trailer.

FIRE APPLIANCES

The earliest manufacturer of Series II fire appliances was probably Carmichael & Sons (Worcester) Ltd. This company equipped both 88 and 109 chassis from some time in 1958, and it looks as if these conversions (broadly similar to the later FT/1 and FT/2 types) were initially marketed as Land Rover Fire Tenders, as if Rover themselves had manufactured them, in the same way as had occurred during Series I days.

By November 1959 Fire Armour Ltd of London had also become an approved

The prototype of the Moy standard conveyor.

The Kenwall fertilizer distributor.

The Dixon-Bate fifth-wheel conversion was pictured here with a horsebox semi-trailer.

supplier. After Fire Armour passed into the ownership of the Angus Group in 1963, its fire and crash rescue designs were handed over to HCB-Angus Ltd who retained the Land Rover Approval and developed the designs further. From about 1965 Sun Engineering of Richmond in Surrey were appointed as a third approved converter, but their products were less common than those of the other two companies. Pyrene took over the Sun designs in the later 1960s. The majority of conversions by all these companies were exported.

Carmichael

The Carmichael models were marketed under the Redwing brand name, although it is not clear whether Redwing branding was used on the early models marketed as Land Rover Fire Tenders. There was a single model on the 88 chassis and three different models on the 109 chassis: a fully open appliance, a similar model with enclosed truck cab and a two-door, van-body model with fibreglass roof. All were designed to carry a crew of five and all featured a PTO-driven fire pump mounted amidships (customers could choose from KSB or Coventry Climax types), a 75gal first-aid water tank, a hose reel with delivery hose and an extension ladder. Each model could also be configured as an airfield crash tender.

As the Series IIAs came on-stream, Carmichael's expanded their range to six models. The Redwing brand name was retained, but the individual models now had type names as well: the 88in model was the FT/1; the FT/2 was a truck cab 109; the FT/3 was an open 109,

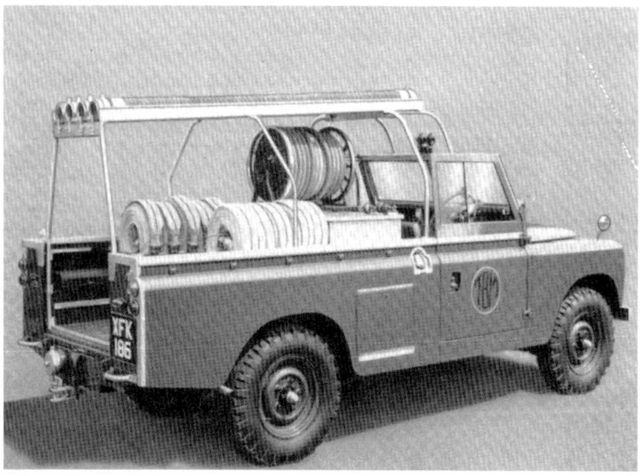

Carmichael fire tenders. Clockwise from top left: FT/1, FT/2, FT/4 and FT/3 conversions.

mainly intended as a pump appliance and hose carrier; the FT/4 was a truck cab 109 with a ladder and equipment rack carried above the body, while the FT/5 had an enclosed body with lockers in the upper body sides and a ladder rack on the special GRP roof. The sixth model, the FT/6, was a special forward-control conversion announced in 1961 and available the following year. It was based on a standard 109 chassis to which Carmichael's added a front extension. The driving cab was relocated here, alongside and slightly ahead of the engine, and the original bulkhead formed a strengthening member in the middle of the new body, ahead of the rear seating compartment. The vehicle was designed to carry a crew of five, and its enclosed body combined standard and modified Land Rover body panels with specially-made GRP panels.

The Carmichael FT/5 had a special enclosed body.

Carmichael's FT/6 was a Forward Control conversion.

Fire Armour

The original Fire Armour Firefly conversion had earned Land Rover Approval by November 1959. The 'standard' Firefly was a 109 with truck cab and a back body made of aluminium over a jig-built, steel frame. This body had high sides with gently curving rear quarters into which were built several lockers, while the pump was mounted at the rear – although an optional, front-mounted pump freed more space for equipment stowage in the back. The size of the amidships-mounted water tank (and therefore its weight when full) depended on the weight of other equipment on the vehicle. There was a first-aid hose reel and (usually) a ladder rack resting on the cab roof. Fire Armour was absorbed by the George Angus Group and briefly became Angus Fire Armour before merging with HCB Engineering in 1963 to become HCB-Angus (the HCB initials had originally stood for Hampshire Car Bodies).

HCB-Angus

HCB-Angus retained the Firefly name, developing the brand to include appliances on the 88in wheelbase and also some on the Forward Control chassis. However, production of Land Rover fire appliances was limited before about 1965, perhaps because the company focused initially on its larger fire appliance conversions. The 'standard' Firefly design with its coach-built back body on the 109in chassis was retained, but from 1965 (and possibly earlier) there were also cheaper vehicles based on 88

The HCB-Angus DEL hardtop conversion.

The HCB-Angus HP Hi-Fog had a special back body.

The HCB-Angus REL was based on an 88.

The HCB-Angus PK was for rural first-aid fire duties.

HCB-Angus continued production of the original Firefly design.

This HCB-Angus conversion was a variant of the DEL type.

and 109 truck cab models, with a water tank and lockers built into the pick-up body, a first-aid hose reel above them and a ladder-rack supported above this and on the cab roof. These normally had rear-mounted Coventry Climax fire pumps, but a front-mounted pump seems to have been available to special order. The truck cab 109 was also the basis of a Rural First Aid Fire Engine, which carried a portable fire pump in its load-bed. Above this was a canopy roof, and the rear of the body was permanently open, while flaps hinged from the canopy gave access from the side. HCB also offered a fire engine based on the 109 hardtop, with lockers cut into the upper body sides and the fire pump mounted amidships on the left. The water tank and first-aid hose reel were enclosed within the hardtop body, and the rack for ladders and hoses was fitted on the roof. Lastly, there was the Hi-Fog appliance, based on a 109 truck cab and bearing twin first-aid hose reels fitted with Angus Fire Armour Super Fog Gun nozzles and a suitably rated pump.

Sun

Sun Engineering, based in Feltham, Middlesex, offered the BLR1 and BLR2 conversions, although the literature promised 'specific designs in accordance with requirements' and illustrated a pair with special bodies apparently built for a Caernarvonshire brigade. The BLR1 was based on a 109 truck cab and had a distinctive, square-rigged ladder rack, while first-aid tank, lockers and hose reel were all carried in the pick-up bed. The Sun fire pump was rear-mounted. The BLR2 had a specially built rear body behind the standard truck cab, looked rather like a cut-down version of the 'standard' HCB-Angus Firefly and employed the same construction method of alloy panels on a steel frame.

Pyrene

Already well-known as a manufacturer of fire extinguishers and other fire-fighting equipment, the Pyrene Company Ltd took over Sun Engineering's fire tender designs in the later 1960s. The BLR1 and BLR2 models remained available, and the BLR1 was developed further as an airfield crash tender (*see* Airfield Crash Tenders). The BLR5 was a new model based on the 109 One Ton chassis and fitted with a 135gal pre-mix tank designed for the latest 'light water' foam. In other respects it was similar to the BLR1 design. The BLR5 was also offered on the standard 109 chassis with 4-cylinder engine, when the pre-mix tank capacity was reduced to 100gal.

HYDRAULIC PLATFORMS

There were two types of hydraulic platform – the 'cherry-picker', as many people call them – with Land Rover Approval. The earlier and heavier-duty type was made by Simon Engineering Ltd of Dudley, and the later one came from Western Engineering (Delabole) Ltd, who were based in Cornwall.

Simon Engineering

Simon Engineering offered their L25 hydraulic platform for fitting to a 109in Land Rover. This was new to the Approved Conversions list in January 1960. If fitted to a truck cab model with standard pick-up bed it was suitable for road use only; customers who wanted it for cross-country work as well had to order a chassis-cab, when the Simon platform would be fitted direct to the rear chassis frame. The hydraulic pump that raised and lowered the booms was driven from the centre PTO. All models had to be ordered with Land Rover's own heavy-duty rear springs, and with heavy-duty front and rear dampers. Petrol models needed a hand throttle. Simon fitted their own rear spring lock-out jacks, and from July 1964 (and possibly earlier) they also modified the handbrake. Most examples probably had brake line safety locks with a warning light on the dashboard. The L25 platform was still listed in June 1968 and was presumably available after that as well.

Western Engineering

By July 1964 Western Engineering had gained Land Rover Approval for a simpler and cheaper platform that extended to a height of only 15ft (4.6m) but was demountable and could be fitted to an 88in Land Rover as well as a 109in model. In the beginning, this was driven by a hydraulic centre PTO, but from June 1966 the Land Rover lists showed it being supplied with a 119cc BSA petrol engine.

Both 88 and 109 models needed heavy-duty suspension for this conversion, and 88s had to have their spare wheels mounted on the bonnet to leave enough room for the platform in the back body. The Land Rover hand throttle for petrol-engined models was an optional fit in 1964, but was probably not needed on later platforms supplied with the BSA petrol engine. The Western Engineering platform was still listed in June 1968 and was presumably available after that as well, but according to

ABOVE: *The Sun BLR1 fire tender.*
LEFT: *A Simon hydraulic platform.*
RIGHT: *The Western Engineering 'cherry-picker' was a lightweight design.*

The Ibbett Eezion low loader was designed as a car transporter.

George Mackie of the Special Projects Department, writing in Ken and Julie Slavin's *Land Rover, the Unbeatable 4×4*, the conversion was not a success. Mackie also notes that it had started life as a device for lifting bales of hay and had been converted for its later use.

LOW-LOADERS

Ibbett Engineering of Bedford created a striking low-loader conversion by attaching their Eezion low-loader unit to the front end and cab of a Land Rover. For loading, the rear suspension units rotated to bring the tail end of the low-loader down to ground level. Several examples were delivered to the Automobile Association in 1971 to meet a need for a vehicle to transport immobilized cars quickly off motorways. These were based either on 109 One Ton models or on chassis fitted with heavy-duty suspension and 9.00×16 tyres; the track of the low-loader section was wider than that of the Land Rover. There were also some narrow-track versions, where the rear wheels had the same track as the front ones, and these were used as cable-layers by a public utility company in Britain.

MOBILE CINEMAS

Two companies were approved to provide Land Rovers fitted out as mobile cinemas; these were probably sold mainly to aid agencies in developing countries for showing health and other educational films. The two companies were Cintec Ltd and British Films Ltd, both based in London, and the conversions they offered were similar to one another.

Cintec

The Cintec Cineroma conversion was available by November 1959. The base Land Rover was a 109 Station Wagon stripped of all its seats except the front row. It had to be ordered from Solihull with a centre PTO, radio-interference suppressors, an engine speed governor, an oil cooler, water temperature and oil pressure gauges, a dry battery, a de luxe

The Cintec mobile cinema was based on a 109 Station Wagon.

bonnet with spare wheel carrier and wheel lock, a fuel filler lock, an additional fuel tank under the driver's seat, equal settings for nearside and offside springs, and heavy-duty rear suspension. Cintec added an alloy platform on the roof with an access treadplate on the front section, a mounting assembly for the screen and loudspeaker assemblies, a 3kVA alternator driven from the centre PTO, power wiring in flexible metallic conduit, an automatic accelerator stop, a dustproof stowage cabinet, stowage facilities for equipment and a built-in cable drum. The projection equipment consisted of a Bell & Howell 8399 projector with cabinet loudspeaker, a Bellmont high-level projector stand, two large bell-shaped speakers, an 8ft×6ft (2.4m×1.8m) roller screen, a floodlight and mounting assembly, a microphone and stand, microphone matching unit, a rewinder and splicer, a power supply redistribution box, a set of ancillary cables and various spares and instruction manuals. Optional extras were a Model 8302 projector, a tape recorder, a record player, a PA amplifier, a filmstrip and slide projector and a tripod screen. Land Rover still listed this conversion in June 1968.

British Films

The British Films Filmobile conversion was available by July 1964 and was still listed in June 1968. Later versions were known as the FR/640/15A model. Like the Cintec conversion, this was based on a 109 Station Wagon with only the front row of three seats. The vehicle had to be ordered with radio interference suppressors, an engine speed governor, water temperature and oil pressure gauges, an oil cooler, a centre PTO and laminated windscreen glass. Later conversions required driver's springs all round. An extra 11gal fuel tank was fitted under the driver's seat and a corrugated alloy platform with mounting brackets and a treadplate forward section with grab handle was added to the roof. There was a PTO-driven 3kVA alternator with control panel, a built-in cable drum and a dustproof stowage cabinet on shockproof mountings for the projection equipment. Additional stowage was fitted for the screen, loudspeakers, screen and speaker mounting assembly, floodlight, projector stand, rewinder and splicer, and microphone stand. The projector was a Bell & Howell 8399A (later a Bell & Howell 640) with a cabinet speaker and high-level projector stand. There was a 1.2kVA transformer, an 8ft×6ft (2.4m×1.8m) roll-up screen, two bell-shaped loudspeakers, a record player (a tape recorder was an optional alternative later), rewinder, splicer, microphone with floor stand, microphone matching unit, Vitavox hand microphone, 150W floodlight and stand, 15W PA system with dual mains or battery feed, a set of ancillary cables, a distribution box and a set of spares and instruction books.

MOBILE DISPENSARIES

By 1964 Pilchers (Merton) Ltd were offering a Mobile Dispensary based on a 109 truck cab. It shared the basic structure of its tall hardtop body with the entry-level ambulance conversion from the same makers (*see* above), but had twin fixed windows on each side instead of the ambulance's single sliding unit, and was obviously supplied with different equipment. Most of these conversions were probably sold outside Britain. Like the ambulances from Pilchers, the mobile dispensary later acquired a type number, and from some time probably in the first half of 1967 it was known as

The BFL Filmobile mobile cinema was also based on a 109 Station Wagon.

The Pilchers mobile dispensary was based on a 109 truck cab.

a Series 7427/S2. Both standard and de luxe versions were available.

MOBILE WORKSHOPS

Long-wheelbase Land Rovers could be converted into mobile workshops by the Tooley Electro Mechanical Co. Ltd of Earl Shilton, near Leicester. These conversions were available by July 1964 and were still catalogued in June 1968. The base 109 had to be equipped with a centre PTO and, if it had a petrol engine, with an engine speed governor as well. Some of these mobile workshops incorporated the Tooley generators that were available separately (*see* Generators, p.108). Workshop equipment included tool lockers, tailboard benches, drills, vices and fire extinguishers, grinders, power drills, floodlights, air compressors and welding transformers. The company also offered a range of welders separately (*see* Welders).

PLANT MAINTENANCE UNITS

Two approved conversions turned the Land Rover into a mobile servicing plant that could be used for plant and machinery operating remotely from its own depot. The earlier one was by C.C. Wakefield & Co. of London (who were subsequently bought out by Castrol Ltd, also of London) and the later one by Tecalemit (Engineering) Ltd of Plymouth.

Wakefield/Castrol

The Wakefield Lubrequipment conversion probably obtained Land Rover Approval before the Series II models entered production. It consisted of a frame mounted in the back of a long-wheelbase model, to which were fitted a series of fluid containers and delivery hoses. Each vehicle was custom-designed to suit its customer, but there were typically five containers and hose reels; an air supply could also be fitted. The base 109 had to be equipped with heavy-duty springs. By July 1964 Wakefield had been bought by Castrol Ltd and the conversion was listed as a Castrol Lubrequipment 4389V. However, it was no longer catalogued by June 1966.

Tecalemit

A broadly similar conversion by Tecalemit (Engineering) Ltd of Plymouth was introduced probably in late 1964. This one had the advantage of being demountable and did not require any modification to the basic 109in Land Rover. The Tecalemit TSU (Transportable Service Unit) could also be mounted to a Brockhouse trailer (although this was not the 15cwt type specially designed for the Land Rover) or on a free-standing platform. This approved conversion was still listed in Land Rover literature in June 1968.

POST-HOLE DIGGERS

By November 1959 there was an approved post-hole digger attachment made by Transplanters (Robot) Ltd. This had disappeared from Land Rover listings by July 1964. The attachment could be fitted to any 88 or 109 fitted with a three-point linkage and a rear

A Tooley workshop; note the rear awning.

The Castrol plant maintenance unit was taken over from Wakefield.

PTO. Petrol-engined models needed an engine speed governor as well. The Land Rover's tailboard was removed and the digger was bolted into the aperture. A variety of augers was on offer to suit different diameters of post hole.

A Tecalemit plant maintenance unit.

The post-hole digger from Transplanters (Robot).

REFUSE COLLECTORS

By July 1964 the Eagle Engineering Co. Ltd of Warwick had obtained Land Rover Approval for a 3cu.yd (2.3cu.m) refuse collection conversion. This was mounted on a 109 chassis-cab equipped with heavy-duty suspension and a bonnet-mounted spare wheel. The body had twin side hopper-type doors and a tail door for tipping. It could be raised for tipping by a hand-operated screw attachment. The conversion remained available into the Series III era.

SEWER AND DRAIN CLEANER

An 88 or 109 Land Rover could be converted into a sewer and drain cleaner by Metering Pumps Ltd, of Ealing Broadway in London, who used the trade name of Atumat. The conversion was first listed in June 1967 and was still available in June 1968. The Land Rover had to be ordered with heavy-duty suspension and a rear PTO less its gear box; petrol models also needed an engine speed governor. MPL fitted a special gearbox to drive the 22gal/min (100ltr/min) pump that was fitted in the tailgate aperture, together with a large hose reel in the load bed. The hose had a patented Atumat cleaning head.

SNOW BLOWERS

Although demountable snowploughs were available (*see* Chapter 8), there was also a more elaborate snow-clearing conversion from Rolba Ltd of London, who offered a trailer-mounted, rotary snow blower. This seems to have been available as early as June 1963 but was not listed after June 1966.

For transportation, the trailer ran on two removable wheels with pneumatic tyres. The towing 88in truck cab Land Rover required major modifications. The base vehicle was expected to be petrol-powered, with heavy-duty suspension, an oil cooler, engine speed governor, a trailer socket and flashing indicators. Hydraulic equipment and a hydrostatic transmission were installed in the floor of the load bed under a metal cover, and were driven from the centre PTO. The cab was equipped with reversible seats and a second steering wheel mounted on the rear bulkhead; this had a chain and sprocket drive and allowed the vehicle to be driven in reverse, pushing its snowplough. The rear cab window, normally a sliding

RIGHT: The Eagle tipping refuse collector.
FAR RIGHT: An Atumat sewer and drain cleaner.

LEFT: *Rolba snow blower.*

ABOVE: *Second steering wheel in the Rolba cab.*

perspex type, was replaced with a single pane of Triplex Safety Glass and the fuel tank was replaced by two 20gal (91ltr) tanks, one mounted on each wheelbox in the rear.

STAKE BODIES

P.D. Stevens & Sons Ltd, of Market Drayton in Shropshire, gained Land Rover Approval for their stake-side body during 1965. This was designed as a livestock carrier and consisted of a platform body mounted to a 109 chassis-cab, with demountable wooden stake sides. The base vehicle had to have heavy-duty rear springs and heavy-duty dampers all round, plus flashing indicators. Normal tyre equipment was 7.50×16s, but the heavy-duty suspension allowed room for 9.00×16 tyres if required. This conversion remained available into the Series III era.

The Stevens stake body on a 109 chassis.

The Stevens tipper was a late arrival.

TIPPING BODIES

P.D. Stevens & Sons Ltd, makers of the stake-body conversion, also gained Land Rover Approval for a tipping body on the 109 chassis. This seems to have been introduced around 1970 and remained available into the Series III era. The body itself was made of aluminium alloy, with drop-sides and a hydraulic tipping mechanism that was probably powered from the centre PTO.

TRACKS AND TRACTOR TYRES

Two companies gained Land Rover Approval for conversions that gave the vehicle additional rough-terrain capability. James A. Cuthbertson Ltd of Biggar developed a set of tracks to give the vehicle swamp-wading capability and also to minimize its ground pressure, while Roadless Traction Ltd of Hounslow in Middlesex fitted large tractor wheels and tyres to improve the Land Rover's ground clearance.

Cuthbertson

The Cuthbertson tracked conversion was probably introduced in 1961, but was no longer listed in Land Rover literature by July 1964. It consisted of four tracked units, one for each wheel station, with a toothed driving wheel bolted in place of the standard road wheel and twin road wheels which ran on the tracks. The steering was power-assisted. Cuthbertson's offered mud wings for road work, but it is probable that their prototype was the only example to have them. The conversion was available to suit both 88 and 109 models, but remained rare. The RAF took a small quantity of 88s for ordnance clearance work at Orford Ness and elsewhere. In theory, the track units could be removed and the vehicle turned back into a standard Land Rover.

A Cuthbertson tracked conversion on the 109 chassis.

The Roadless 109 used tractor wheels and tyres.

Roadless

The Roadless 109 had its origins in a Forestry Commission requirement for a vehicle that could cross deep ditches and climb over fallen logs. The Commission built and tested its own experimental prototype and then handed the design over to Roadless Traction Ltd. who specialized in tracked systems and 4×4 conversions for tractors. After further development, Roadless announced it as a Land Rover-approved conversion in September 1961. The last of around eight examples was probably built in 1966, and the conversion was no longer listed by June that year. Roadless retained the standard Land Rover transmission, but geared it down through hub reduction units to suit the large tractor wheels with 10×28 tyres. The axles were US military-surplus units, probably from a Studebaker truck, modified by Kirkstall Forge Engineering in Leeds. At the front, the Land Rover steering swivels were simply bolted to the axle ends, which gave the vehicle a track that was 14in (36cm) wider at the front than at the rear and consequently a much tighter turning circle than would otherwise have been the case.

WELDERS

Three companies offered Land Rover approved welders. These were the Lincoln Electric Co. Ltd of Welwyn Garden City in Hertfordshire, Tooley Electro-Mechanical Co. Ltd of Earl Shilton, near

ABOVE: A Lincoln LR150 welder in action.
LEFT: The Hayter welder. Inset: the alternator was mounted in the cab.

Leicester and Hayters Ltd of Bishop's Stortford, also in Hertfordshire.

Lincoln

Lincoln had been making welder conversions for the Land Rover since 1948, and in this period they offered the LR150 with 150A generator and the LR 200 with a 200A type. These were mounted in the rear body of the Land Rover and driven from the rear PTO. The basic model, either an 88 or an 109, had to have a rear PTO and the associated engine speed governor if it was petrol-engined. Conversions destined for tropical climates required an oil cooler. The 200A generator (usually known as an SA 200 type) was available from the beginning, but the less powerful SA 150 became available some time between 1960 and 1964. Both types were still listed in June 1968.

Tooley

By July 1964 Tooley listed a range of welders. Most were available only for 109s, but there were also some installations for 88s. The base vehicle required a centre PTO and an oil cooler, and petrol-engined types also needed an engine speed governor. The welding generator was normally installed on a sliding frame that was bolted to the floor of the Land Rover's back body. However, there was also a Medium Frequency Welding Unit called the R/P200W in Tooley's Rovpak range of tailboard-mounted equipment.

Hayters

Rather bizarrely, Hayters advertised their welder as an Alternator Attachment for the Land Rover, but sold it complete with welding gear. The alternator that developed the welding current of 250A was mounted between the two front seats of an 88 or a 109, and was driven by a vee-belt from the centre PTO. It was made to be demountable. The basic Land Rover had to have a centre PTO and oil pressure and water temperature gauges. Petrol-engined models also needed an engine speed governor, and Hayters recommended the fitting of an oil cooler as well on conversions intended for use in hot climates. This conversion was first listed in June 1967 and was still available in June 1968.

8 attachments and equipment

The BEN air compressor and a selection of air-operated tools.

The Special Projects Department approved not only major body conversions for the Land Rover but also all kinds of equipment that could be driven by its PTOs or otherwise attached to the vehicle. This chapter covers the attachments and equipment for the Series II and Series IIA models. Some items that did not receive Land Rover Approval but are known to have been available are also listed here.

AIR COMPRESSORS

Five different makes of air compressor were granted the Land Rover Approval during the Series II and IIA era.

Atlas Copco

Atlas Copco (Great Britain) Ltd manufactured the Overlander NT series air compressor, a high-speed two-stage, vee-type compressor designed as a permanent fixture in the load bay of a Land Rover and driven from the centre PTO. By November 1959 both the NT7LR delivering 63cu.ft/min (1.8cu.m/min) at 100lb/sq.in and the NT9LR with 110cu.ft/min (3.1cu.m/min) at 100lb/sq.in were on offer. The larger model was available only for 109in Land

Atlas Copco air compressor in a 109 truck cab.

Rovers (and was sometimes advertised as the Overlander One-Ten conversion), but the smaller one could be fitted to either 88 or 109 models. According to its makers, this conversion was 'particularly suitable for attending to repairs to underground public supply services and other kinds of emergency maintenance work'. It was normally fitted to a truck cab model that had to have an engine oil cooler, centre PTO, engine speed governor (on petrol models), a bonnet-mounted spare wheel and a three-quarter tilt with roll-up sides. By July 1964, it was no longer listed as a Land Rover approved accessory.

BEN Patents

The first BEN portable air compressor delivered 41cu.ft/min (1.2cu.m/min) at 100lb/sq.in and was designed to power small tools such as drills, sanders, wire brushes and sprayers. The attachment was fitted in a demountable frame that fitted into the tailgate aperture, was belt-driven from the rear PTO and was available by November 1959. By July 1964 (and probably as early as December 1963), BEN Patents Ltd had become a division of Broom & Wade (*see* below) and were offering a 52cu.ft/min (1.5cu.m/min) twin-cylinder reciprocating compressor, but the company was no longer listed in Land Rover sales material by June 1968.

Broom & Wade

Broom & Wade Ltd were based at High Wycombe in Buckinghamshire and their products carried the Broomwade name. The Broomwade WR100 Whirlwind Uniflo compressor installation for the Land Rover was probably introduced some time around July 1962 and was still listed by June 1968. The WR100 could be installed only in a 109in Land Rover that had a specially modified rear chassis and heavy-duty suspension. The usual base vehicle was a truck cab model. The compressor was fitted at the rear of the chassis under the load floor, so that the standard pick-up body could still be used to the full for load-carrying. The compressor was an oil-cooled rotary type, driven from the PTO, and delivered 100cu.ft/min (2.8cu.m/min) at 100lb/sq.in, which was claimed to be enough to operate two medium-duty concrete breakers. There was an automatic governor, which reduced engine speed when the compressor reached the required maximum pressure and raised engine speed to a maximum of 2,300rpm if the pressure dropped.

ABOVE: A Broomwade air compressor.

ABOVE: The Edwards air compressor.

RIGHT: A Hymatic air compressor on an 88.

Edwards

Lawrence Edwards & Co. (Engineers) Ltd were based in Kidderminster, Worcestershire and offered a small compressor that developed 3cu.ft/min (0.08cu.m/min) at pressures of up to 200lb/sq.in. It was designed to power small tools such as tyre inflators and spray guns. The Edwards compressor could be fitted to the rear PTO, when it was easily detachable, or to the centre PTO, when it would normally be left in place. Drive attachments differed between the two applications, and the rear PTO version came with a support bar that could be fitted to the Land Rover's towing plate. Both versions were available by November 1959 (although not listed by Land Rover in January 1960) and were still listed in June 1968.

Hymatic

The Hymatic Engineering Company were at Glover Street in Redditch, Worcestershire. Their Hydrovane 72LR compressor was mounted to a demountable frame that fitted into the tailgate aperture of an 88 or 109 Land Rover. No additional body or chassis strengthening was needed. The compressor was driven by the rear PTO. Additional Land Rover extras required were an engine oil cooler and, on petrol models, an engine speed governor. There were two varieties of Hydrovane compressor, type 72LR-P for petrol-engined models and type 72LR-D for diesel models. Both were oil-cooled rotary types which delivered 72cu.ft/min (2cu.m/min) at 100lb/sq.in – enough, claimed their sales literature, to run a heavy concrete breaker continuously at full power. Engine speed was adjusted automatically to balance air demand. The Hydrovane compressor was available by 1962, was still listed in July 1964 but was no longer by June 1968.

AIR-CONDITIONING SYSTEM

Just one manufacturer of air-conditioning systems was granted Land Rover Approval during the Series II and Series IIA era. This was Normalair, whose address was Hyde Road, Hayes, in Middlesex. The conversion appears to have been introduced around 1962. By June 1968 Normalair had become a division of Westland Aircraft Ltd, and the conversion was still on offer. The system could be fitted to any standard normal-control Land Rover with a petrol engine. Most of its components were installed in the engine bay, and the visible items were a compressor unit driven off the engine and a large air box mounted to the bulkhead. Inside, two adjustable outlet grilles were mounted above the dashboard and a panel of four press-button controls was fitted alongside the instrument panel. A coolant radiator was installed behind the grille panel, and the headlamps were relocated on the wing fronts in order to give maximum airflow.

The Normalair air conditioner under the bonnet of a 109.

BULLDOZERS

The Dale bull-angledozer was available as an approved conversion by November 1959 from J.B. Howie Ltd of Salford Priors, near Evesham in Worcestershire. The blade was normally angled at 25 degrees to the vehicle and was mounted on a frame bolted to the front bumper. There was a hydraulic ram to raise and lower the blade; this could be operated from a hand pump inside the Land Rover's cab or by an electro-hydraulic pack. A snowplough blade was also available from Howie's (*see* Snowploughs), and was interchangeable with the bulldozer blade. In some cases, both were supplied. The Howie company was taken over by Atkinson's of Clitheroe in the early 1960s, and the Dale name for these conversions was dropped; they were then known as Howie conversions.

The Howie bulldozer blade was raised and lowered hydraulically.

CONCRETE MIXERS

F.W. McConnel Ltd offered a concrete mixer among the attachments for their Power Arm conversion, which had originally been developed to suit tractors. The Land Rover version of the Power Arm, known as a Type U, was available by January 1960 and could also be

The McConnel concrete mixer on the company's Power Arm attachment.

used to drive a sawbench and a mower (*see* below). The Power Arm was attached to a three-point linkage approved for the Land Rover. It had an adjustable leg to support a small concrete mixer attachment. This was then driven from the Land Rover's rear PTO.

FIRE PUMPS

The Coventry-based engine specialists Coventry Climax Engines Ltd were also manufacturers of fire pumps, and their ACP type was approved for front mounting on Land Rovers. It was a single-stage, centrifugal pump with its own oil cooler, driven from the Land Rover's crankshaft and had a maximum delivery rate of 500gal/min (2,275ltr/min). The ACP pump could be supplied separately from fire appliances that had the Land Rover Approval. It was available by July 1964 but was no longer listed in Land Rover catalogues by June 1966.

A Coventry Climax ACP fire pump.

ABOVE: The Silorators forage harvester was driven from the rear PTO.
BELOW LEFT: The English Electric generator.
BELOW RIGHT: The Tooley generator.

FORAGE HARVESTERS

By November 1959 Silorators Ltd of London were offering a forage harvester that could be towed behind a Land Rover. There were versions with a short chute and with a long chute. The Land Rover was not modified in any way but needed a rear PTO to drive the forage harvester. This conversion appears to have been short-lived and was no longer listed in Land Rover catalogues by July 1964.

GENERATORS

Two conversions were made available to make the Land Rover into a mobile generator. These were by the Tooley Electro-Mechanical Co. Ltd of Earl Shilton, near Leicester, and by the Special Products Group of the English Electric Company Ltd, based in Bradford, Yorkshire.

Tooley

The Tooley generator (alternator) conversions were available by July 1964. The base vehicle had to be fitted with a centre PTO and a governor as well if the engine were a petrol type. Smaller generators could be fitted to either 88 or 109 models, but generators of 10kVA and above were for 109s only. An oil cooler was needed if the generator had an output of 6kVA or more. The Tooley generators ranged in output from 1.5 up to 14kVA. There were 1.5kVA and 3kVA types that could be fitted under the nearside seat; one 3kVA type could also be fitted behind the cab, and all larger-output types were also fitted behind the cab. In addition, Tooley had a range of Rovpak tailboard generators, which were designed to be fitted in place of the tailboard and driven from the rear PTO. Petrol-engined base vehicles had to have an engine speed governor.

English Electric

By June 1967 English Electric was offering a 15kVA generating system as a mobile power source for installation in either 88 or 109 Land Rovers. The generator was mounted in the centre of the vehicle and was driven from the centre PTO; petrol-engined vehicles had to have a speed governor fitted.

GRASS CUTTERS AND MOWERS

Land Rover gave their approval to gang mowers made by F. Mitchell (Nottingham) Ltd, a rotary grass cutter made by Hayters (Sales) Ltd of Bishop's Stortford and a mower attachment for the Power Arm made by F.W. McConnel Ltd.

McConnel

A grass mower with a 5ft (1.5m) cut was one of the three attachments available for the Power Arm made by McConnel as early as 1960; the others were a concrete mixer and a sawbench (q.v.). The cutter was driven from the Land Rover's rear PTO by a vee-belt. By June 1967 Land Rover no longer listed this attachment for the Power Arm.

Mitchell

The Mitchell Dreadnought range of gang mowers was on offer by November 1959 but was no longer listed in Land Rover literature by June 1967. Initially only a five-gang set was available, but later on a three-gang set was also offered. Both types could be bought with either pneumatic or steel tyres. The Land Rover served only as a towing vehicle and needed no modification.

Hayters

The rotary grass cutters offered by Hayters appear to have been available as early as July 1958. The towing Land Rover had to be fitted with a rear PTO, a tow plate and, if intended for tropical climates, an oil cooler. The grass cutter was known as the 6/14 type, a name derived from the width of its cut. The central unit with a 6ft (1.8m) cutting width was towed immediately behind the Land Rover and was driven by its rear PTO. An additional transfer box then took the drive to demountable 'wing' cutters on each side, each of 4ft (1.2m) width. This allowed cutting widths of 6ft (1.8m), 10ft (3m) or 14ft (4.3m). The cutters themselves ran on small wheels, and there were two alternative wheel heights to suit the terrain. By 1968, the Hayter grass cutter was listed by Land Rover as a 6ft rotary type, although it is probable that the three-element configuration had not changed.

GROUND ANCHORS

Mayflower Automotive Products of Tavistock in Devon gained Land Rover Approval for their bumper-mounted winch (*see* Winches), and by June 1967

The McConnel mower again depended on a Power Arm attachment.

A Mitchell five-gang mower.

The Hayters rotary mower was driven from the rear PTO.

ABOVE: MAP ground anchors. LEFT: A Bunce Tintern gully emptier.

they were offering ground anchors as an accessory to go with this. These anchors were finished in grey stove enamel and had a chain to secure them to the front bumper when in use. They folded flat for stowage. Mayflower also offered a heavy-duty front bumper made of ¼in (6.4mm) steel to go with its winch and ground anchors. This was otherwise identical to the standard Land Rover bumper.

GULLY EMPTIER

William Bunce & Son of Ashbury, near Swindon in Wiltshire, obtained the Land Rover Approval for their Tintern towed gully emptier. This was a large tank on a single axle, and its pump had to be driven from the rear PTO of the towing Land Rover. Petrol-engined models had to have an engine speed governor as well. The gully emptier was, in fact, made by Alan Fuller Ltd of Chepstow in Monmouthshire (*see* Manure and sludge trailer tanks), but William Bunce were the sole concessionaires. The Tintern gully emptier appears to have been approved in the early 1960s; by July 1964 it had been joined by a cheaper Cess Pit Emptier, but neither was listed by Land Rover in June 1966.

HEDGE CUTTERS

New in the January 1960 lists published by the Land Rover Special Projects Department were hedge cutters and trimmers made by R.M. Marples & Son Ltd of Parkstone in Dorset, who made similar implements for use with farm tractors. These were presumably driven from the rear PTO. In 1960, there were two types of Shearomajor hedge cutter, one with a short-saw knife and one with a long-saw knife. There were also two types of Shearomatic trimmer, one with a standard blade and one with a long blade. By July 1964 the two types of trimmer were still listed but by then there was just one type of Shearomajor hedge cutter, described as a heavy-duty type. By June 1966 neither trimmers nor hedge cutters were listed in Land Rover publications.

HF RADIO

Pye Telecommunications Ltd of Cambridge offered an HF two-way radio set with a range of 30 miles (48km) for installation in Land Rovers. The radio set was Pye's C12 type, and could be configured to suit either a 12 or a 24V electrical system. The only Land Rover extra required was heavy-duty battery charging equipment. The C12 probably gained Land Rover Approval before the Series II models came on-stream, and was still listed in June 1966. By June 1967 an approved telecommunications fit was still available from Pye, but it is not clear whether this was the C12 or another type.

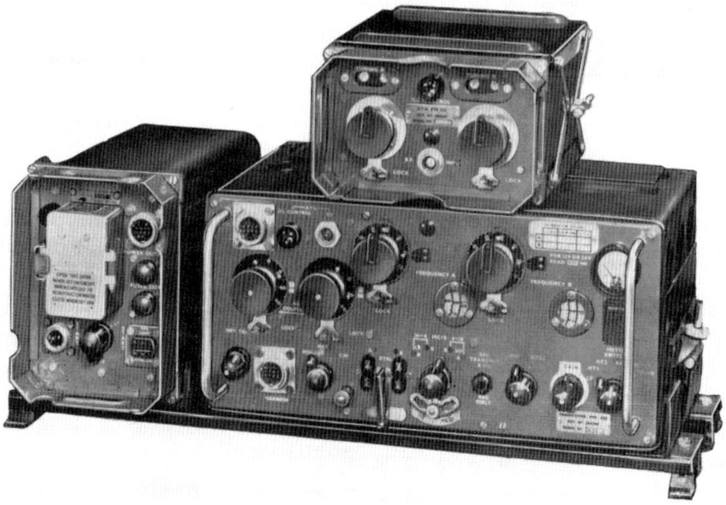

The Pye C12 radio was normally mounted in the Land Rover's back body.

HIGH-PRESSURE HOSES AND COUPLINGS

Oil Feed Engineering Ltd of London gained Land Rover Approval for their Hi-Flex range of hydraulic high-pressure hoses and couplings, which were suitable for use with hydraulic attachments provided for the Land Rover by other specialist companies. These were listed in Land Rover catalogues by July 1964 but had disappeared by June 1966.

LAND-RECLAMATION MACHINERY

Land Rover granted approval to towed bracken and weed breakers made by the Holt Weed Breaker Company of Kirbymoorside, near York, and to a towed slashing machine from the Wolseley Engineering Co. Ltd of Witton in Birmingham.

Wolseley

The Wolseley machine was called the Super Swipe. It was towed behind a Land Rover and driven from its rear PTO. Towing vehicles used in tropical climates were recommended to have an oil cooler. The Wolseley Super Swipe was available by January 1960 but was last listed by Land Rover in June 1966.

Holt

The Holt Weed bracken and weed breakers were three-gang units attached to a tubular baulk that in turn was attached to the Land Rover's tow hitch. The bracken breaker was known as a Mark IV type and the weed breaker as a Mark VI type. These breakers were available by January 1960 but were last listed by Land Rover in June 1966.

MANURE AND SLUDGE TRAILER TANKS

Allan Fuller Ltd of Chepstow in Monmouthshire probably secured Land Rover Approval for their manure and sludge trailer tanks before the Series II became available. There were initially two sizes, one with a 420gal (1,890ltr) capacity and one with a 300gal (1,350ltr) capacity, but by July 1964 only the smaller size was listed. By June 1966 the trailer tank could be equipped at extra cost with Bramber Flexitor suspension, but by June 1967 the tanks were no longer listed in Land Rover material. The towing Land Rover had to be equipped with a towing plate, a rear and a centre PTO (to power the trailer's pumps), and with a hand throttle.

MANURE SPREADERS

SKH & Son of Whitchurch in Shropshire seem to have been among the first companies to gain Land Rover Approval in the Series II era. They were makers of

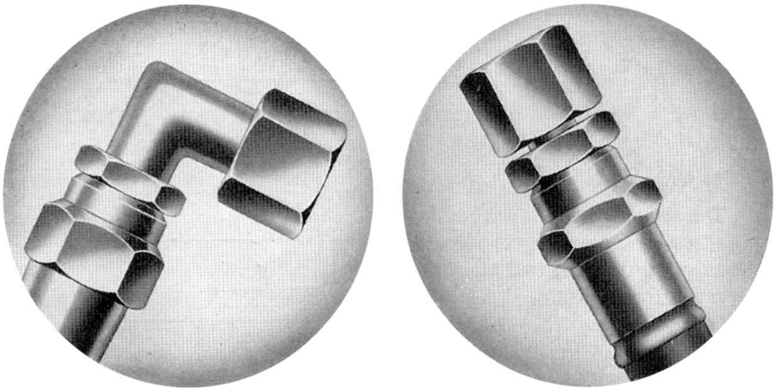

Hydraulic couplings by Oil Feed Engineering.

The Wolseley Super Swipe was towed behind the Land Rover.

A bracken and weed breaker from the Holt Weed Breaker Co.

LEFT: A Fuller sludge and manure spreader.

BELOW: The Evenspreader manure spreader.

BOTTOM: The Quikspreader manure spreader.

agricultural equipment who used the Salopian trade name, and from some time in the mid 1960s appear to have expanded their name to Salopian-Kenneth Hudson Ltd. From around April 1958 they were offering two types of towed manure spreader. The Quick-spreader needed no separate power source, but the more expensive Even-spreader had to be driven from the rear PTO of the towing Land Rover. The Salopian manure spreaders were no longer listed in Land Rover literature by June 1968.

PNEUMATIC SAWS

Pneumatic saws with 16in (406mm) and 23in (584mm) blades were on offer from chain saw specialists Danarm Ltd of Stroud by July 1964, but had disappeared from Land Rover lists by June 1966. It is not clear how these were operated from the Land Rover.

PUMPS

Two companies were granted Land Rover Approval for pumps. These were Autometric Pumps Ltd of Maidstone and Dowty Hydraulic Units Ltd of Ashchurch in Gloucestershire.

Autometric

The Autometric pumps were listed by January 1960 and were last catalogued in June 1966. All three types were shaft-driven from a rear PTO. They were the RS50/HV nylon roller vane type, the HA7502 turbine pump and the C150/OA centrifugal pump.

RIGHT: *An Autometric RS50/HV rollervane pump.*

Dowty

Dowty offered a hydraulic pump driven from the Land Rover's centre PTO. The installation consisted of three elements: the pump, a control valve in the cab, and a motor that could be mounted at the front or rear of the vehicle. The base Land Rover needed a centre PTO, but a hand throttle and engine speed governor were optional requirements on petrol-engined models. These pumps were available by January 1960 and were last listed in June 1966.

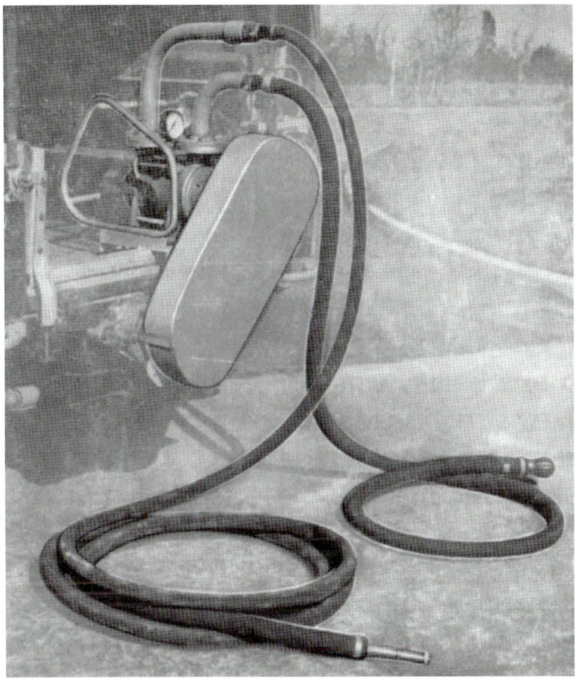

ABOVE: *An Autometric 150/OA centrifugal pump.*
LEFT: *An Autometric HA7502 turbine pump.*
BELOW: *The Dowty pump and details of its installation.*

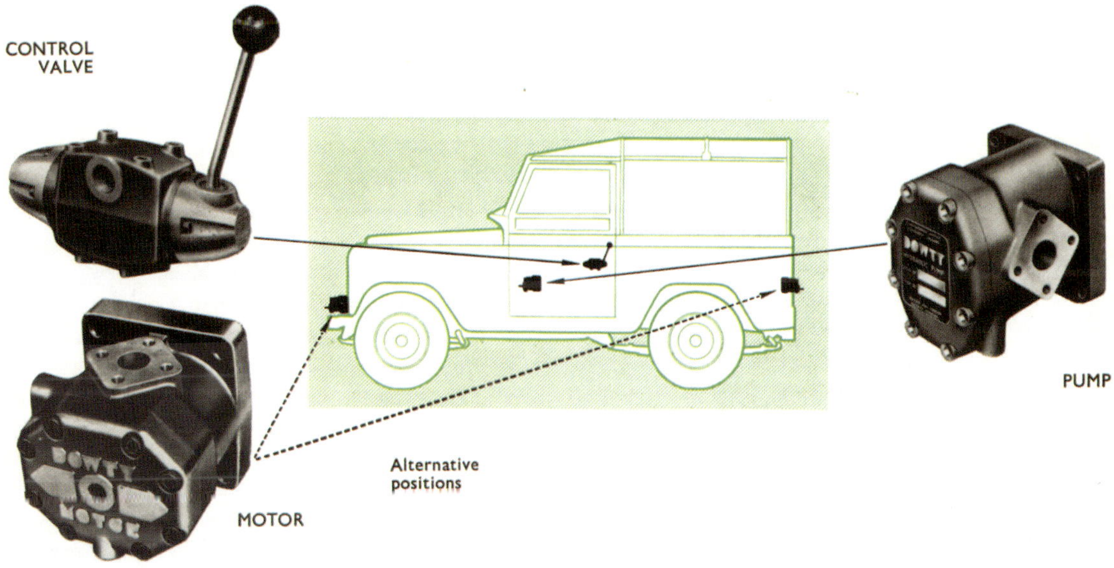

The Iso-Speedic road speed governor.

The Lawrence Edwards rotary tiller.

The McConnel sawbench with the company's Power Arm attachment.

ROAD-SPEED GOVERNOR

The Iso-Speedic Co. Ltd of Warwick gained Land Rover Approval for a road-speed governor system that limited a vehicle's speed. This was available by July 1964 and still listed in June 1968, but was suitable only for use with the 2.25-litre petrol engine. The basic Land Rover needed no extras. The governor consisted of a centrifugal switch mounted on the speedometer cable and a throttle control linked to it, which acted on the carburettor butterfly. Different control springs were available to alter the speed at which the device operated.

ROTARY TILLER

Lawrence Edwards & Co. (Engineers) Ltd of Kidderminster in Worcestershire had their Mark 4R rotary tiller on offer by January 1960. This cultivator was driven from the rear PTO on the Land Rover and was attached by a three-point linkage. It was no longer listed by July 1964.

SAWBENCH

A sawbench with a 30in (760mm) diameter circular saw blade was one of three attachments for the Power Arm made by F.W. McConnel Ltd; the others were a concrete mixer and a mower (qqv).

The bench itself was made of steel and measured 31.5in×48in (800mm×1,220mm), and was marketed as the All-Work type. The saw was driven by a belt from the Land Rover's rear PTO. This attachment remained available longer than the other two and was still listed by Land Rover in June 1968.

SHEEP SHEARERS

R.A. Lister & Co. Ltd of Dursley in Gloucestershire gained approval for their sheep shearers early in the life of the Series II, probably in May 1958. Land Rover no longer listed them by June 1966. A frame mounted to the Land Rover's towing plate supported a gearbox that was driven from the rear PTO. There were cable drives leading to two handpieces, which evolved over the years. Early examples were Lister's Ace type, by September 1962 they were the Super-Ace type and by February 1964 they were the Tallygrip type.

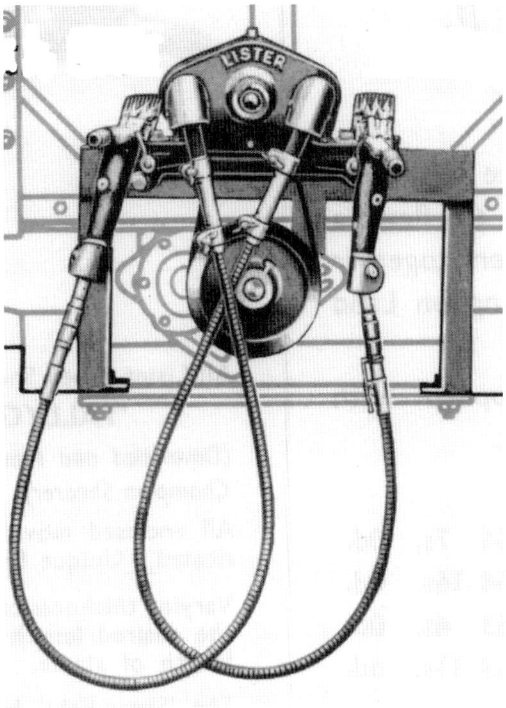

ABOVE: *The Bostrom Manufacturing shock-absorbing seat.*

LEFT: *The Lister sheep shearer was driven from the rear PTO.*

BELOW: *A Cuthbertson vee-blade snowplough.*

SHOCK-ABSORBING SEATS

The American truck seat specialists Bostrom Manufacturing Ltd gained approval for their Saxon Thinline shock-absorbing seats and Land Rover first listed these in June 1967. The seats could be upholstered to match the latest black upholstery of the period and remained available in 1968.

SNOWPLOUGHS

Four snowplough manufacturers had Land Rover Approval for their products during the Series II and IIA period. These were J.A. Cuthbertson of Biggar in Scotland, J.B. Howie Ltd of Clitheroe in Lancashire, Snowclear Ltd of Thorpe Bay in Essex and Rolba Ltd of London. Snowclear and Rolba both offered American-made Meyer snowploughs and these were available under their own brand name for Land Rovers in the USA.

Cuthbertson

The Cuthbertson vee-blade snowplough attachment appears to have gained Land Rover Approval during 1961 and was still listed in June 1968. It consisted of a 78in (1,980mm) wide vee-blade that was attached to the front dumb-irons and bumper of a Land Rover. The base vehicle needed no modification.

Howie

Howie's were a subsidiary of Atkinson's of Clitheroe (they had earlier been based at Salford Priors in Worcestershire), and some of the later snowploughs were probably labelled as Atkinson products. Howie made two types of 'approved' snowplough attachment. One was a vee-blade and the other a straight blade that could be used as an alternative to their bulldozer blade (*see* Bulldozers). The straight blade appears to have been available as early as 1960, but the vee-blade may not have been available until mid 1964. Both types were bolted to the front bumper of the Land Rover on a small frame. The straight-bladed type ran on small rubber-tyred wheels and was spring-loaded to enable it to 'trip' over obstructions; the vee-blade ran on three replaceable metal skids. The blades were raised and lowered hydraulically by a hand-operated pump mounted in the Land Rover's cab. An electro-hydraulic pack was available as an

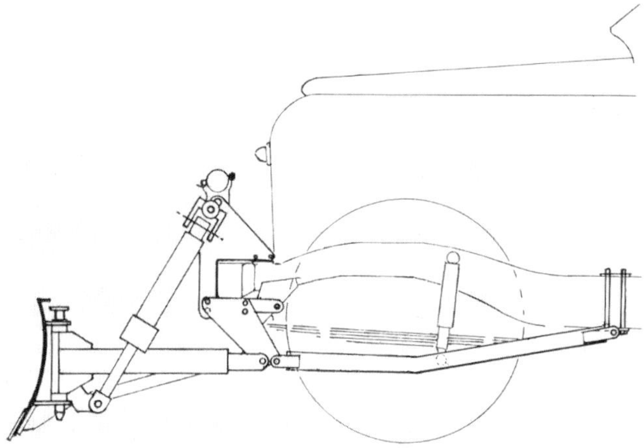

A schematic illustration of the Howie attachment.

alternative. The straight blade used the same attachments as Howie's bulldozer blade (*see* Bulldozers). The two were interchangeable and were sometimes supplied together as a set. The snowplough blade was considerably taller than the bulldozer type and was generally mounted at a 30-degree angle to the vehicle rather than the 25-degree angle of the bulldozer blade.

FAR LEFT: The Howie snowplough.
LEFT: A Howie straight blade snowplough.

Snowclear

Snowclear marketed American-made Meyer snowploughs. These had Land Rover Approval by July 1964 but had disappeared from the lists by June 1966; it is probable that their British distribution had been handed over to Rolba (*see* below). The Snowclear product had a spring trip and a reversible blade, and its cutting edge was a replaceable carbon steel blade. Three different blade widths of 72, 78 and 84in (1,830, 1,980 and 2,130mm) were available, and the blades were raised and lowered by Meyer's Electrolift system. The blades could also be used for light bulldozing duties.

LEFT: The Howie vee-blade snowplough.
BELOW: A Snowclear snowplough.

Rolba

Rolba offered a snow blower (*see* Chapter 7). By June 1966 they were also offering Meyer snowploughs in a variety of sizes, and it seems likely that they had taken over the British distribution from Snowclear (q.v.).

Meyer

By March 1966 the Rover Company of North America was listing a variety of Meyer snowploughs for use with the Land Rover. All had the Electrolift system as standard, although a hydraulic lift mechanism made by Western Hydraulic was optional at extra cost. A special mounting was also available to accommodate a winch. Listed were a vee-type heavy-duty blade, the standard model with spring trip and reversible blade (in two widths), the Royal Canadian model with full trip blade, and the Hydra-Turn with full trip blade.

SOIL SHREDDERS

Two types of soil shredder were made by Lawrence Edwards & Co. (Engineers)

TOP LEFT: The Lawrence Edwards Mk 2R soil shredder.
TOP RIGHT: The larger Mk 3R soil shredder.
ABOVE: A Brockhouse trailer.
LEFT: The Robertshaw trailer.

Ltd of Kidderminster in Worcestershire by January 1960. Of these, one had a shaft drive and the other a pulley drive; presumably both were operated by a Land Rover's rear PTO. Later sales literature still shows two types, this time the Mk 2R, which was a free-standing unit driven by belt from a pulley on the rear PTO, and the Mk 3R, which was attached to the Land Rover by a three-point linkage and was driven direct from the rear PTO. Both had disappeared from Land Rover lists by July 1964.

SPECIAL TRAILERS

Land Rover approved three types of special trailer. These were a 15cwt type made by J. Brockhouse & Co. Ltd of West Bromwich, a 1 ton type with a powered axle made by Scottorn Ltd of New Malden in Surrey, and a combined liquid and cargo trailer from M.F. Robertshaw Ltd of Bletchley in Buckinghamshire.

Brockhouse

The Brockhouse trailer had been introduced in 1949 and was designed specifically for use with the Land Rover. It remained in production until 1965, although only two examples were built that year, of which one was a 'special'. The design did change in details over a production run that has been calculated at 977 examples, and there is some indication that the later trailers were not actually built by Brockhouse but were sub-contracted to another company in the Midlands. Brockhouse trailers had an all-steel, open box body and a hinged tailboard. Some examples with special bodywork were supplied to the Auxiliary Fire Service and to other fire brigades. The trailers came with an eye type coupling or with a 2in ball coupling that was not compatible with the 'standard' 50mm ball coupling. The Brockhouse trailer was listed as Option E1098.

Robertshaw

By January 1960 M.F. Robertshaw Ltd were offering their 'Camel' Trail-Tank, a trailer that had separate compartments for carrying liquids and cargo. This approved accessory was no longer listed by Land Rover in July 1964. There were three models (known as the Mk I, II and III), and these appear to have had different combinations of load space. One trailer could carry 50gal and 2,000lb (228ltr, 900kg) another 100gal and 1,500lb (455ltr, 682kg) and the third 200gal and 500lb (910ltr, 227kg). There were also 250gal and 300gal (1,138 and 1,365ltr) units available.

Scottorn

Land Rover became involved in experiments with a powered-axle trailer during the early 1960s, mainly in anticipation of demand from the British Army. Development was carried out in conjunction with Scottorn Ltd, of New Malden in Surrey, and Scottorn brought the design to market as a Land Rover approved conversion. The trailer was known as the Bushmaster, had a 1-ton capacity, and was available by June 1966. It could be fitted with a variety of different bodies.

The trailer had a welded chassis with the drawbar bolted to it and rode on a Land Rover 109 rear axle with freewheeling hubs. The springs were standard Land Rover types with Aeon rubber assisters (*see* Spring Assisters). The basic Land Rover had to be fitted with a centre PTO, which drove a modified transfer gearbox just ahead of the rear cross-member. The splined output shaft emerged above the body floor and this was coupled to the trailer's drive shaft, which was separate from the tow hitch that attached to a towing jaw on the rear cross-member.

The Scottorn-powered trailer.

SPRAYERS

Two companies offered spraying equipment for use with the Land Rover. These were E. Allman & Co. Ltd of Chichester, and Evers & Wall Ltd of Lambourn Woodlands, near Newbury in Berkshire. The Allman field sprayer was available by November 1959 but was last listed in June 1967. It was initially called the Plantector Model 60, but was later simply known as the Model 60 Field Sprayer. It consisted of a 60gal (270ltr) tank mounted on a frame in the load bed of an 88 or 109, with a two-part boom fixed to the rear of the vehicle and extending outwards on both sides. The delivery pump was operated from the centre PTO.

ABOVE: An Allman crop sprayer.

LEFT: An Evers & Wall 'banker'-type sprayer.

An Evers & Wall crop sprayer in action.

ABOVE: An Evers & Wall contractors' sprayer.

RIGHT: The cab of an Evers & Wall fertilizer sprayer.

By June 1966 Land Rover price lists referred to a Model 50 Field Sprayer, which could be driven from either the centre or the rear PTO. There was by then also a 160gal (728ltr) version suitable for 109s only and driven from the rear PTO.

Evers & Wall had been supplying spraying equipment for use with Land Rovers since 1948. They offered a variety of different types for use with the Series II and IIA Land Rovers right through to 1968 and probably beyond. Early sprayers were driven by a centre PTO (with flange but with no pulley) while later examples were driven from a rear PTO.

The Evers & Wall exhaust nozzle sprayer on a Series II 109.

The Evers & Wall farmers' sprayer on an 88.

At the start of this period, boom-type sprayers that mounted on the front bumper were available with no tank, or with either a 65 or 100gal (296 or 455ltr) tank mounted in the back of the vehicle. These were all marketed under the Fortemist name. From at least January 1960 there was also an exhaust nozzle sprayer, activated by the vehicle's exhaust, which was intended primarily for killing locusts in desert regions. This did not use the Fortemist brand name.

By July 1964 the 100gal (455ltr) tank was standard (except where no tank was supplied), and the twin-boom crop sprayer had been supplemented by a verge sprayer with a single boom. This could be turned into a kerb sprayer by fitting a funnel-like device mounted on the nearside. A sheep spray race was also available.

By June 1966 the Fortemist brand name seems to have been confined to verge and kerb sprayers, which were available with either 100 or 160gal (455 or 728ltr) tanks. Other sprayers, including the sheep spray race, used the Evrall brand name. There were twin-boom sprayers with roller vane pumps and either 100 or 160gal tanks, some suitable for fertilizers and weedkillers and some for weedkillers only. Other types had diaphragm pumps. By this stage the exhaust nozzle sprayer was no longer listed.

By June 1967 the 160gal tank was no longer listed and the 100gal tank was standard. This range continued into 1968 and beyond.

ABOVE: An Evers & Wall rollervane pump.

LEFT: An Evers & Wall Fortemist kerb sprayer.

Aeon Products spring assister.

The Adams & Benson (Agricultural) tipping box.

LEFT: Adrolic Engineering's three-point linkage.
ABOVE: The vacuum trailer brake controls on a Feeny & Johnson conversion.

SPRING ASSISTERS

Spring assisters were sometimes needed on Land Rovers and conversions that carried extra weight, and by June 1966 Aeon Products Ltd of London had gained approval for their hollow rubber spring assisters. These remained available in July 1968 and probably later as well.

TAILBOARD TIPPING BOXES

By January 1960 Adams & Benson (Agricultural) Ltd were offering a tipping box that could be mounted in the back of the Land Rover. It pivoted on the lower half of the tailboard hinges and was held in place by brackets that fitted over the tailboard catches. The tipping had to be done by hand. This conversion was no longer listed by July 1964 and may have been taken over by F.W. McConnel Ltd (*see* Concrete Mixers).

THREE-POINT LINKAGE

A three-point linkage that enabled the Land Rover to use agricultural implements intended for tractors was manufactured by the Adrolic Engineering Co. Ltd of Milngavie in Scotland. This linkage was available by January 1960 but its last appearance in Land Rover price lists was June 1966. It was fitted to the rear of the vehicle in place of the tailboard and was raised and lowered hydraulically by a hand-operated pump.

VACUUM TRAILER BRAKES

Feeny & Johnson Ltd of Wembley in Middlesex gained approval for a vacuum brake control system, which could be fitted to Land Rovers that had to tow trailers fitted with vacuum brakes. On petrol models, there was a vacuum connection to the engine inlet manifold, but diesel-engined models had to be fitted additionally with an exhauster. A control lever was mounted on the steering column

ABOVE: The Feeny & Johnson vacuum trailer brake exhauster.

BELOW: A Hesford trailer winch.

BOTTOM: The Plumett winch.

to allow independent operation of the trailer brakes; a vacuum gauge was also fitted. This equipment was available by January 1960 and was still listed in June 1968.

WINCHES

In the Series II and IIA era winches were not the common accessory they have since become. Land Rover in Britain approved four different types. Of these, the Fairey capstan winch had been available since Series I days and was classified as an Optional Extra rather than a special attachment; it is therefore described in Chapter 6. The earliest of the other three was a trailer winch made by C.M. Hesford & Co. Ltd of Ormskirk in Lancashire. Next came one driven from the centre PTO and made by Plumettaz SA, of Bex in Switzerland; this was marketed in Britain as the Plumett by Fuller, Lucas & Co. Ltd of Crowborough in Sussex. The third was also driven from the centre PTO and was made by Mayflower Automotive Products Ltd of Tavistock in Devon, also known as MAP, which was later bought

out by Fairey. Also available, although apparently not an approved accessory, was a Turner winch. Different winches were listed by the Rover Company of North America, which mainly promoted locally manufactured types.

Hesford

The Hesford winch was mounted on a two-wheeled trailer winch that could be towed behind a Land Rover and was driven from its rear PTO. The winch could deliver a 7,000lb (3,200kg) pull when its own spade anchor was in use, and with the aid of an auxiliary ground anchor could deliver a 10,000lb (4,550kg) pull. This accessory seems to have been available only briefly. It was available by July 1964 but had disappeared from Land Rover lists by June 1966.

Plumett

The Plumett Auto-Capstan Winch was first listed in Land Rover literature in June 1966 and was still available in June 1968. A version to suit Forward Control models was listed from June 1967. The Plumett winch was operated from the Land Rover's centre PTO. Its cable drum was mounted between the front seats of the vehicle and faced sideways, but the cable was paid out underneath the chassis to a rotating pulley so that a pull could be achieved in any direction. The winch could deliv er a 4,000lb (1,820kg) pull; the drum held between 750 and 990ft (230 and 300m) of cable.

Mayflower

The Mayflower winch was mounted neatly between the Land Rover's front bumper and grille panel, and was driven by a shaft running forwards from the centre PTO. It was first listed in June 1967.

The winch offered a line-pull of up to 5,000lb (2,270kg), depending on the diameter of cable specified.

Turner

The Turner winch was a capstan type that was mounted ahead of the radiator grille. It was driven by a short propshaft from the crankshaft pulley, although the arrangement was different from that used for the Fairey capstan winch.

In North America the winches listed were the Fairey capstan winch, an electric winch from the Belleview Manufacturing Company of Portland, Oregon and a variety of winches from Koenig Iron Works of Houston, Texas, who used the brand name of King Power Winches.

Belleview

The Belleview was available by March 1966 and was one of the first electric winches. Belleview were later absorbed by Warn, who adapted the Belleview design and marketed it under their own name.

King

King made both front and rear drum winches, developed originally from winches used on drilling rigs in the 1950s. There were four main types of front-mounted winch: the LR-100 (also LR-100-D), LR-591 and LR-592 types all offered an 8,000lb (3,640kg) line-pull and were driven from the front of the engine's crankshaft. The L621 type was driven from the centre PTO. The rear-mounted winch also appears to have been driven from the centre PTO, but its other specifications are not known.

A schematic diagram of the Plumett winch.

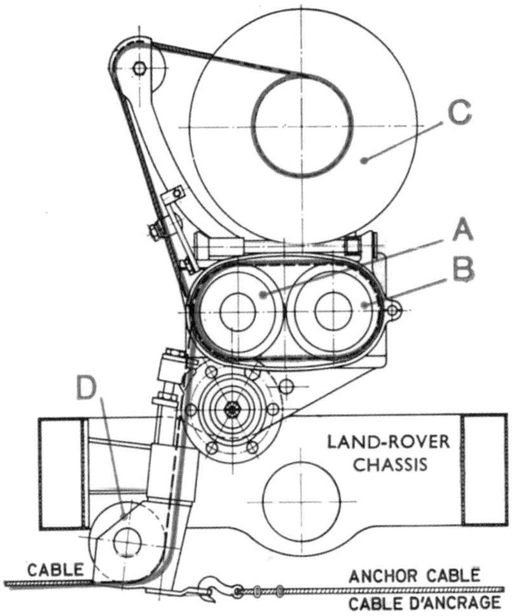

BELOW: The Mayflower winch.

9 British military models

Marshall's of Cambridge built the special four-stretcher ambulance body on 109 chassis. This is a Rover 9 version.

During the period of Series II and Series IIA production, the British armed forces took more Land Rovers than any other single user. The vehicles were used by all three services – the Army, the Royal Navy and the Royal Air Force – and it was with the Series II that they began to take increasing numbers of long-wheelbase models; during the Series I era, these models had been taken in only small numbers and for specialist roles.

The government department responsible for the armed services was known as the War Office during the early part of this period and became the Ministry of Defence in 1963. However, the Rover Company generally referred to British military vehicles as having 'WD spec', those letters standing for the title of War Department that was used for the military transport arm. In the period up to 1959 the vehicles were actually ordered by the Ministry of Supply (MoS), which handled procurement for the armed forces.

The military referred to four types of vehicle: CL types (commercial or almost to standard civilian specification), GS types (General Service, more militarized), FFW types (Fitted For Wireless, with screened electrical system) and FFR (Fitted For Radio, with a 24V electrical system). The vast majority of British military Land Rovers had three-quarter tilts and were configured as GS or FFR types.

However, there were also some 88 Station Wagons and civilian-specification hardtops (most delivered before 1968). Some 109s were configured as Wombat anti-tank gun carriers, Station Wagons, ambulances and fire tenders. There were also small quantities of 109 crash rescue tenders, drone recovery vehicles, van-bodied FFR types (some with DF equipment) and Vigilant anti-tank missile launchers.

Large numbers of battlefield ambulances were built on the 109 chassis, and a batch of 109s was specially equipped for long-range desert patrol and raiding duties for the Special Air Service Regiment. These and the Carmichael FT/6 forward-control fire tender conversions for civilian establishments attached to the War Department are described at the end of the chapter.

SERIES II

The standard British military Series II was a slightly modified civilian model. Petrol engines were standard, although there were some diesels for the RAF. All were delivered with 12V positive-earth electrical systems, although some vehicles were converted to 24V negative-earth for FFR duties in the early 1960s.

The 88in models were known as Rover Mk6 (or, more commonly, simply

Rover 6) types and were generally soft-tops used for cargo duties. They had a quarter-ton rating and were known as FV18021 or FV18021A types. The Army appears to have taken 860 in all, of which 580 were GS types, five were Station Wagons, and 275 were special 4×2 types (*see* below). All of them had 2.25-litre petrol engines.

RAF variants (not included in these figures) were used additionally for airfield lighting maintenance (FV18022) and for helicopter starting (FV18023) duties, in the latter case with a small platform built above the canvas tilt. Some early RAF deliveries had the 2-litre petrol engine.

The 109s were known as Rover 7s and were now classified as three-quarter-ton vehicles (earlier long-wheelbase types had been conservatively rated as quarter-tonners). The Army appears to have had 119 examples, made up of fifty-six GS soft-tops, fifty FFW Station Wagons (Rover 7, FV18042), and two more Station Wagons for other duties. The Station Wagons seem to have had twin underseat fuel tanks instead of the standard rear-mounted tank, with electric fuel pumps. Station Wagon chassis were also used for ten FV18044 field ambulances, which had aluminium-panelled, two-stretcher bodies by Mickleover, and there was a single fire appliance. The FV18043 mountain rescue ambulance for the RAF may have had similar bodywork, but could also have been a window hardtop equipped with stretchers.

The distinctive features of the GS Series IIs were as follows:

Body exterior

- bridge plate on right-hand front wing (except 4×2 models)
- rear reflectors on brackets bolted to rear cross-member (early models)
- rear reflectors mounted below lights (later models)
- wing-mounted bonnet catches, no central bonnet lock, grille without bonnet release cut-out
- rear-view mirrors on both front wings
- FV headlights (except on 4×2 models)
- civilian side and tail lights on most models; FV pattern on 1961 models only
- convoy lights (except on 4×2 models)
- Warner trailer socket

Body interior

- bracket fitted at front of rear body to enable use of the spare wheel recess as a jerrycan carrier

Cab

- Pyrene fire extinguisher in bracket on dashboard
- special FV ignition and lighting switch (late models; early models had the civilian type)
- turn indicator switch on dash (early models) or steering column (late models)
- horn button on steering column arm (early models) or steering wheel centre (late models)
- oil pressure and ignition lights swapped places on late models
- hand throttle on late models, possibly only on 24V conversions

Mechanical

- oil cooler fitted to very late models
- twin fuel tanks
- eight-bladed engine cooling fan
- chamois leather gaiters on steering ball swivels
- CV45 dynamo (but CL civilian-specification models with standard C40 type)

SERIES IIA

Rover 8 and 9 (1961–7)

The Series IIA models for the War Department were built to a distinctive specification agreed between Rover and the Fighting Vehicles Development Establishment (FVDE). Deliveries began in late 1961 with some 'quarter-ton' 88s, which were known as Rover 8 types. The 'three-quarter ton' 109s were Rover 9s. Both types had two main variants: the GS (General Service) cargo vehicle with 12V electrical system and the FFR (Fitted for Radio) with its 24V system. GS models had some features from the FFR types that enabled them to be adapted as radio vehicles in an emergency.

In 1967 Land Rovers switched over to a negative-earth electrical system and

Military Identification Plates

Series II and IIA Land Rovers in British military service normally carried a metal military identification plate attached to the passenger's side of the bulkhead. This was preprinted with the vehicle type, weight classification and other details. In addition, the contract number under which the vehicle was procured (such as WV10175) and the military registration number (such as 32 FK 33) were stamped into the plate.

Series II Military Registrations

The Rover 6 and Rover 7 models delivered between 1958 and 1961 had registration numbers in the series listed below. Dates are those of entry into service.

CL (1959)
DE (1959)
DL (1960)

The 4×2 Models

The War Department followed its purchase of 675 4×2 Series I 88s with an order for 275 Series IIs. These vehicles replaced its miscellaneous fleet of car-derived vans and utilities ('tillies'), and mostly served as camp runabouts, school vehicles and possibly on recruitment and driver training duties. All were soft-tops, with a largely civilian specification but with vertically-stacked front lights, twin wipers, a claw-type towing jaw, a Warner trailer socket and a fire extinguisher. Their chassis numbers ran from 1419-01445 in December 1958 to 1419-02210 in February 1959, and their military registrations were 17 CL 48 to 20 CL 22.

The engineering alterations were the same as on the Series I 4×2s: the front axle propshaft was omitted and the axle itself was replaced by a simple tubular type with no differential and with the hub carriers bolted to its ends. The transfer box front output housing was blanked off, low range was locked out by means of sleeves on the selector shaft and no transfer box levers were fitted; the holes for these were covered by blanking plates.

Military policy was to dispose of cars – and the 4×2s were classified as such – after five years, and so most of these Land Rovers were sold off in the first half of the 1960s. Some may have been bought by the Ministry of Public Buildings and Works (which bought a large number of the Series I types) and remained in service until around 1970 as general runabouts and tender vehicles at historic buildings and sites of the type now run by English Heritage and the National Trust. When they were eventually sold off to the public many of their new owners converted them to standard 4×4 configuration.

RIGHT: This 1966 standard Rover 8 GS model shows features typical of the breed. At the front are double-height outer bumpers, a military bridge plate, FV-type headlamps and vertically stacked lights, and a bonnet mount for the spare wheel. Note also the mirrors mounted on the door hinges (curiously turned round here) and, at the back, the emergency antenna mounts and the tilt with its extra flaps to accept co-axial cables for the antennae.

BELOW: The cab of a Rover 8 or 9 GS model. Note the rifle clips and the oil pressure gauge on the dash. The military vehicle identification plate is in the parcel shelf on the passenger's side, and under the dash are the brackets for the fire extinguisher. The thin piece of card below the chassis number plate is the build ticket.

military deliveries also had this. These later vehicles were classified as Rover 10s (on the 88in wheelbase) and Rover 11s (on the 109in wheelbase). There was no change in military classification associated with the switch to wing-mounted headlamps in 1969 for the Suffix G models.

The 88in models always outnumbered the 109s in British military service during the 1960s, but from 1968 deliveries of the civilian-derived 88 dried up as the new Half-Ton ('Lightweight') Rover 1 began to take over (*see* Chapter 12).

The characteristics of the Series IIA 'WD Specification' were as follows:

Body exterior

- bonnet-mounted spare wheel (blade-type bonnet on 88s, rolled leading-edge 'de luxe' bonnet on 109s)
- wing-mounted bonnet catches, no central bonnet lock, grille without bonnet release cut-out
- rear-view mirrors on both front wings (early models) or (late models) Winguard type mounted on top door hinge on each side
- double-height outer front bumpers incorporating lifting and towing rings
- lower front bumper drilled to accept a second NATO hitch (rarely fitted)
- strengthening plates on underside of front wings (to allow conversion to FFR)
- flaps in canvas tilt (for co-axial cables, to allow conversion to FFR)
- NATO-type rotating tow hook at rear
- reinforced rear cross-member (with squared ends instead of the standard tapered pattern)
- rear bumperettes bolted to the cross-member
- lighting switch with six positions
- front and rear vehicle lashing eyes
- split-rim wheels (early 88s only), with eight securing bolts around the rim; some units painted these nuts red; standard one-piece rims on later deliveries
- four-pin Warner trailer socket with a screw cap on a chain on the left-hand rear body panel (inboard); threaded 'keep' for this screw cap outboard of the NATO socket
- twelve-pin NATO trailer socket under a spring-loaded flap on the left-hand rear body panel (outboard)
- FV-pattern head, side and tail lights; flashing turn indicators always standard; front side and indicator lamps mounted in a vertical row (civilian standard was a horizontal row)
- NATO pattern tubular rear number-plate light
- convoy light and white-painted face for rear differential

LEFT: This 1961 Rover 8 FFR shows the military bumperettes, the tow hitch, towing socket and an aerial tuner on the front wing. Note the position of the red rear reflectors. The pioneer tools are missing from their tailgate mounting straps.

BELOW: The cab of an early Rover 8 or 9 FFR model is seen here without seat cushions, to show the mounting of the twin batteries between the seats and other details. Note also the warning plate on the seat box.

Body interior

- freight lashing cleats inside the back body
- rifle clips behind front seats

Cab

- Pyrene fire extinguisher in bracket on dashboard
- rifle clips on dashboard
- oil temperature gauge on passenger's side of dashboard
- military identification plate on passenger's side of dashboard
- twin 10gal (45ltr) fuel tanks under seat box; changeover tap on seat box front

Engine compartment

- toolbox on the passenger's side of the bulkhead
- eight-bladed engine cooling fan

Mechanical

- oil cooler
- chamois leather gaiters on steering ball swivels

FFR Models

There was a distinctive specification for FFR Series IIA models. These had a 24V electrical system with a negative earth rather than the 12V positive-earth system used on civilian and military GS models up to Suffix C.

These were the distinctive characteristics of the Rover 8 and 9 FFR types and were additional to those listed above for the GS models:

Body exterior

- special grille standing proud of front panel, to protect rectifier
- demountable HF aerial bracket bolted to the outer rear panel on each side
- flaps in canvas tilt (for co-axial cables)
- strengthening plates on underside of front wings
- aerial tuner unit bolted to each front wing (when equipped with VHF radio)

Body interior

- two radio batteries under metal cover against the bulkhead
- demountable wooden radio-operator's table across bulkhead
- Dexion slotted angle above bulkhead
- junction boxes for radio circuit
- single folding seat on passenger's side wheelbox (88s)
- folding seat on each wheelbox (109s)

Cab

- hand throttle
- warning plate for rectified AC electrical system on driver's side seat box

In this view of an FFR model's cab, the additional fuse box, twin ammeters, oil pressure gauge and hand throttle can all be clearly seen. In this case, the build ticket has been tucked behind the chassis number plate!

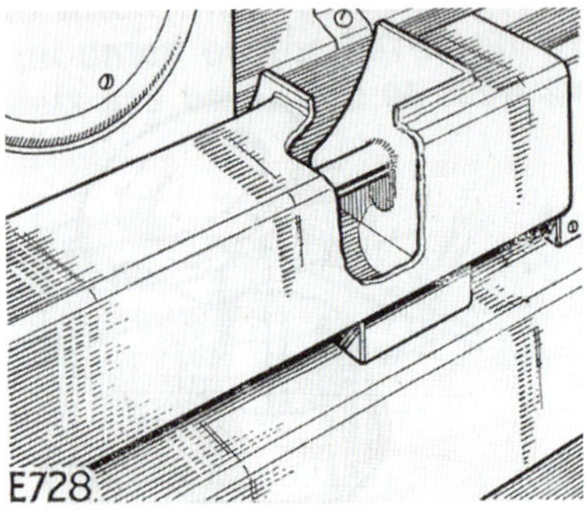

ABOVE: The upper front bumper sections originally included lifting and towing brackets. RIGHT: This 1961 109 GS has wing-mounted mirrors and the special bonnet spare wheel mount used on these models.

Special door hinges were made for military models with hinge-mounted mirrors. They were also an option on civilian models.

LEFT: *Rover 8 and 9 FFR models had a special grille which stood proud of the body to protect the rectifier box.*

BELOW: *The oil cooler (A) and rectifier (B) were mounted behind the grille on Rover 8 and Rover 9 FFR models.*

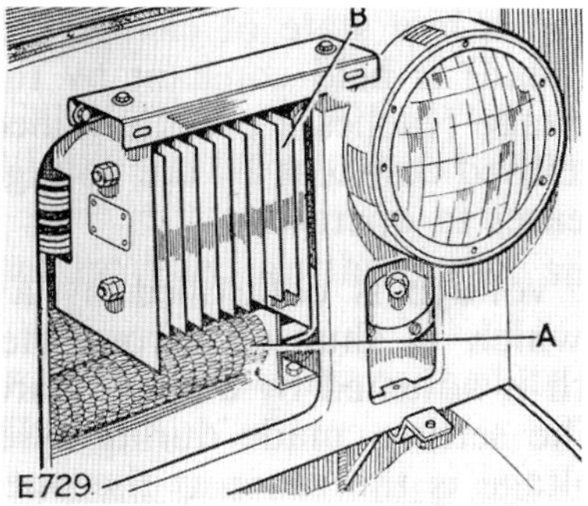

This is the layout of the batteries and associated electrical components in the rear of an early Rover 8 FFR.

The battery cover is in place in this picture of an early Rover 9 FFR. Note the twin seats for the radio operators.

There was a good deal of additional electrical equipment under the bonnet of an FFR model. This is an early Rover 8 or Rover 9.

ABOVE: Military light lenses were made of glass but had four lugs so that they could be twisted off easily.

LEFT: The wiper motors for pre-Suffix D FFR models were different from the civilian type.

- twin ammeters on passenger's side of instrument panel, upper labelled 'Vehicle' and lower labelled 'Radio'
- two vehicle batteries under metal cover between front seats; jerrycan holder on top of cover
- fuse box for the radio circuit on the passenger's side of the instrument panel

Engine compartment

- three fuse boxes on bulkhead, covering (i) NATO socket (and roof lights if fitted), (ii) flashers and stop lights, and (iii) wipers and engine auxiliaries
- 'keep' for VHF ATU cable (when fitted) on each inner wing
- relocated oil filler (to allow for 24V generator)

Mechanical
- engine-driven alternator with rectifier (located behind the grille)
- voltage regulator on left-hand inner front wing
- suppressed electrical system
- Lucas DZS 4A screened distributor
- Lucas type 5C 10 screened ignition coil
- screened spark plugs (originally Lodge SRL 14PC)
- upgraded differentials (35 per cent stronger than earlier types) and rear half-shafts (25 per cent stronger) from March 1964; these later models reclassified as Rover 8/1 and Rover 9/1 types, and earlier models without upgraded components became Rover 8/2 and 9/2 types

Rover 10 and 11 (1967–72)

The change to a negative-earth electrical system on the Solihull production lines occurred with the change to chassis Suffix D in 1967, and affected British military deliveries as well as civilian models. The MoD classified the revised negative-earth models as Rover 10 (88in) and Rover 11 (109in). There were in fact very few Rover 10s, because the model was superseded by the Lightweight or Rover 1 in 1968, and there were no Rover 10 FFR types. The final 109s were not delivered until 1972, but some were stockpiled and did not enter military service until 1975.

The production change to wing-mounted headlamps in April 1969 for Suffix G models did not lead to a further change of military classification. The military elements of the GS specification that had shaped the Rover 8s and 9s remained broadly unchanged, although 109 FFR models (Rover 11s) had the rectifier incorporated into the generator and there was therefore no need for the special protective grille. Like the Rover 8s and 9s, these vehicles were mostly delivered painted in dark green gloss, although the majority were probably overpainted with drab camouflage of one kind or another during their service lives.

This was the windscreen washer kit for later military models.

SPECIAL VARIANTS

Among the most interesting of the special military Land Rovers for Britain are the 109-based ambulances, crash rescue tenders, fire engines and special SAS vehicles. Each of these is fascinating in its own right, but there is space only for brief details here.

Carmichael Fire Engines

In July 1965 the War Department took delivery of twelve Carmichael FT/6 conversions (*see* Chapter 7) for civilian establishments attached to the War Department. These were initially given civilian registration numbers, but after a few months they were re-registered in the EP military series.

Foamite Crash Rescue Tenders

Foamite Ltd was an established builder of airport and airfield fire tenders based at Feltham in Middlesex. The company was a subsidiary of Tecalemit Ltd, who had Land Rover Approval for their mobile service units. A prototype Foamite crash tender on 109 chassis seems to have been approved in 1962, and the vehicles were delivered to the RAF over the next couple of years. They were truck cab models that were distinguished mainly by a series of additional equipment lockers let into the sides of the pick-up bed. The RAF examples had tropical roofs. It is not clear whether the same design was ever sold to other customers.

Marshall Ambulances

Marshalls of Cambridge was a specialist conversion company with a military vehicles division that built a number of conversions on Land Rover chassis. The company remains in business today as MCE (Marshalls Cambridge Engineering Ltd). The four-stretcher military ambulance that Marshalls developed for the British military had evolved from an earlier, two-stretcher Mickleover-bodied type on the Series II 109 chassis (see below). The angled cutaway at the rear allowed the vehicle to negotiate landing-craft ramps, and the low roof meant that it could be carried in RAF transport aircraft. There were

The SAS 'Pink Panthers' were all delivered in standard Bronze Green, and only those used in the desert were overpainted pink.

two windows on each side of the ambulance body.

The first Marshalls ambulances were delivered to the Army in 1964 as Rover 9s, and examples were also supplied to the RAF for mountain rescue duties. These had 'pusher' front bumpers, with a standard RAF-pattern brush guard, whereas the Army ambulances had the 'pusher' bumpers with an additional driving lamp mounted between the upper and the lower sections on each side. These vehicles were delivered in several large batches, and the final examples had the later headlamps-in-the-wings configuration. In the early 1970s, they were fitted with anti-roll bars on the front and rear axles.

Mickleover Ambulances

Just ten Series II 109 Station Wagon chassis were given aluminium two-stretcher ambulance bodies by Mickleover in 1960. These were classified as Rover Mk 7 types and were registered as 05 DE 35 to 05 DE 44.

Pink Panthers

Marshalls of Cambridge were again responsible for building the seventy-two 'Pink Panther' long-range desert patrol vehicles for 22 Special Air Service Regiment. All were based on Rover 11 109in vehicles with Suffix D chassis. Although the basic vehicles left Solihull in 1968, their entry into service was delayed until 1969 and they received registration numbers 10 FG 30 to 11 FG 01. Most were delivered in Bronze Green, but those used in the desert during the Oman Dhofar Campaign were repainted matt pink – a colour that blends into the desert haze. They were nicknamed 'Pink Panthers', after a popular film of the time. The Pink Panthers had heavy-duty suspension and a stripped-down, doorless body, which was modified to take twin 40gal (180ltr) fuel tanks behind the front seats. The navigator's seat was raised to allow him to double as the front gunner, and a second machine-gun was mounted on a pedestal in the rear. The rest of the body was kitted out with radios, sand ladders, smoke dischargers, navigation equipment and a vast quantity of other equipment, which put the operational weight of a Pink Panther up to more than 3 tons.

TACR-1 Crash Rescue Tenders

The TACR-1s were built by HCB-Angus Ltd to meet an RAF requirement (*see* Chapter 7). The acronym stands for Truck, Aircraft Crash Rescue, and after a Range Rover-based replacement was introduced as the TACR-2, they were renamed TACR-1 types. In the end, the TACR-1s were used by the Army and Royal Navy as well as the RAF. They were registered as 28 AG 00 to 28 AG 16, 03 FK 04 to 03 FK 05, and 05 FK 86 to 05 FK 88.

The twenty-two vehicles were built on 109 One Ton chassis, fitted specially with 4-cylinder petrol engines and fuel tanks under the seat box. Land Rover supplied them as truck cabs on a chassis fitted with military-pattern front bumper and rear cross-member, plus an RAF-pattern crash bar. HCB-Angus added a roof hatch to the cab and constructed a special back body. On a tray in the centre of the body was a 100gal (455ltr) water tank (sometimes used for foam). There was a 150lb/sq.in fire pump with side outlets, and the vehicle carried 100ft (30m) hoses with a 1.25in bore.

Around the tray for the first-aid tank was a structure containing open-side hoppers for the equipment and rear-facing lockers with roller shutters. Between these lockers was a rearward-facing crew seat. There was a ladder-rack on the driver's side, and most TACR-1s carried a blue beacon on a stalk, a 9in (23cm) Francis searchlight and a Plessey floodlight mounted on a telescopic mast that could raise it high above the scene of an incident.

Series IIA Military Registrations

The Rover 8 and Rover 9 models delivered between 1961 and 1967 had registration numbers in the series listed below. Dates are those of entry into service.

DM	(1961–2)
EK	(1962–3)
EL	(1963–4)
EM	(1964)
EN	(1965)
EP	(1965)
ER	(1966–7)

The Rover 10 and Rover 11 models delivered between 1967 and 1972 had registration numbers in the series listed below. Dates are those of entry into service.

ES	(1967)
ET	(1968)
FG	(1969)
FH	(1969–70)
FJ	(1970–1)
FK	(1971–3)
FL	(1972–5)

The airfield crash rescue tenders for the RAF were built by Foamite to a special military design. Note the heavy-duty front guard, typical of RAF vehicles.

Clear in this rear view of an RAF Foamite crash tender are the lockers let into the body sides.

10 overseas specials and CKD production

Most Series II and IIA Land Rovers were assembled at the Solihull plant in England. This shows Series IIAs on the lines in November 1964.

Most Land Rovers sold outside Britain were manufactured and assembled at Solihull, and there were dozens of minor specification variants to suit different regulations and user demands. There were also some special variants for the Benelux countries and for North America. In addition, many thousands of Series II and Series IIA Land Rovers were assembled overseas. In most cases, kits of parts were shipped out from Britain for local assembly. These assembly operations avoided taxes levied on fully built vehicles brought into a country and, at the same time, provided work for the local labour force. The Rover Company knew them all as CKD (Completely Knocked Down) operations, and there were three different varieties, which reflected the different levels of skill and equipment available in the destination assembly plant. CKD vehicles were usually, but not invariably, crated and shipped in batches of six. After 1964, CKD shipping was sub-contracted to Export Packing Ltd at Banbury in Oxfordshire, and no records have yet been found.

Some overseas plants used locally made items to supplement the parts shipped out from Britain. Typically these might be tyres, glass and batteries, and their inclusion would benefit the local economy; the arrangements in Zambia in the mid-1960s are shown below as an example.

At least three CKD plants – in Australia, South Africa and Spain – manufactured large elements of the vehicles themselves, and of these the one in Spain had an arrangement with the Rover Company under which it would eventually achieve full local manufacture and would be able to modify designs to suit local requirements as well.

SPECIAL OVERSEAS MODELS FROM SOLIHULL

Benelux Countries

Regulations governing headlight positions changed in the Benelux countries (Belgium, the Netherlands and Luxembourg) at the start of 1969. The traditional Land Rover headlamp position in the grille panel was no longer legal and so, for a few months in early 1969, Series IIAs for these countries had their headlamps mounted on the front of the wings. These headlamps had a bright-metal bezel and just a few hundred models were built with this specification, which shared some elements with the contemporary 'bugeye' specification for North America (*see* below). Also unique was a batch of around twenty-five 109s built for the Belgian Gendarmerie in 1967. These had Station Wagon bodysides with two doors on the driver's (left-hand) side and window hardtop bodysides with one door on the other. They seem to have been used as mobile incident control centres, and the 'long' window hardtop side had a fixed table used by the reporting officers.

A Canadian-built Kodiak heater was optional on North American models. This is the Mk III version on a Series IIA.

This badge was used only on North American models. It was located underneath the main Land Rover badge (like the Station Wagon badge) and seems to have been used for a period in the early 1960s only.

Canada

Land Rovers for Canada were always assembled at Solihull and were sold through Rover's combined North American sales company (*see* below under USA). Canadian Series IIs always had one-piece cab doors and the associated one-piece seals, which provided better weather-proofing than the standard type with removable tops. Vehicles with these doors had a C prefix added to their chassis numbers.

From around 1962 models for the Canadian market generally shared their specification with those for the USA and the same limited range of four paint colours was available. However, cylinder block immersion heaters were more commonly fitted in Canada, again as a precaution against the cold. Some vehicles in the early 1960s had an additional badge reading 'Four Wheel Drive' (*see* USA), but these appear to have been confined to the central region of the country only.

USA

As the Series II entered production Rover was in the process of winding up its North American distribution agreement with Rootes Motors, Inc. The last Land Rovers to be shipped to the Rootes distribution network left Solihull in October 1958. From then on – in effect, from early 1959 – sales in the USA and Canada were handled by the Rover Motor Company of North America. This initially had its headquarters in the Canadian city of Toronto, but a US branch was quickly set up at Long Island City, New York.

Both 88 and 109 models were available, with diesel as well as petrol engines, and there were soft top, hardtop, truck cab and Station Wagon variants on both wheelbases. An unpainted 88 window hardtop was displayed at shows in Canada and the USA during 1959. Early paint options were probably the same as for other markets, but by 1966 there were just four colours on offer. These were Blue (= Marine Blue), Light Green, Limestone and Red, the latter not an extra-cost option in this market. Wheels on North American vehicles finished in Red appear to have been painted Limestone.

From the start sales literature promised that any Land Rover could be equipped with 'pumping or spraying equipment, fire-fighting equipment, power take-off, winch or snowplow'. Some vehicles in this period had an additional badge, unique to North America, which fitted underneath the Land Rover oval like the Station Wagon badge and read 'Four Wheel Drive'. It appears that these were fitted to vehicles only in the northern Mid-West and in central Canada, possibly by a particular dealership chain.

Series IIA 88s and 109s followed the Series II types, and, from 1962, 109 Station Wagons for the USA were available with either the 'standard' ten-seater layout or the twelve-seater layout introduced for Britain. From engine number 251-63284, a 9.5in (240mm) diameter Borg and Beck clutch was standardized, although this remained an optional extra for other markets.

The USA began to take its own special models from mid 1966. From that point, the 109 range was reduced to a special ten-seat Station Wagon with the 6-cylinder engine, known to Solihull as the NADA (North American Dollar Area) 109. These were the first normal-control Land Rovers to have the 6-cylinder engine. However, this was in a higher state of tune than the engine later introduced for other territories (*see* Chapter 3), and had a big-bore (2⅛in/54mm outside diameter) single-silencer exhaust system.

Standard equipment on the NADA 109s included a Kodiak heater (made in Canada) and a Mot-a-Vac brake servo.

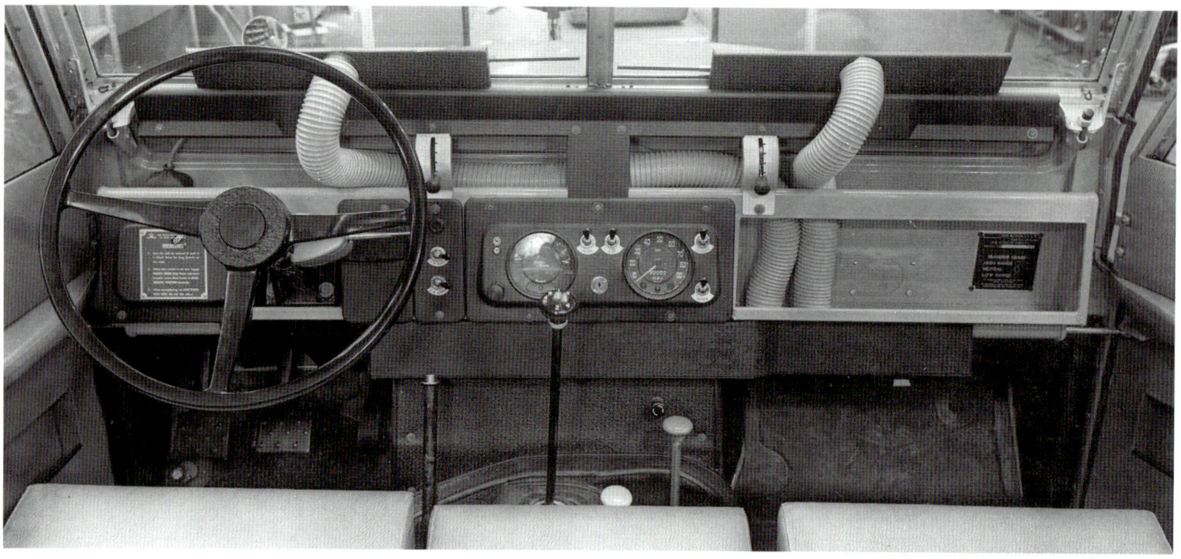

ABOVE: The NADA 109 Station Wagon pioneered several features later seen on other models, such as the black-painted instrument panel. Note here the labels for the switches, the large air distribution box for the Kodiak heater and the associated large demister nozzles. The chassis plate is also differently positioned and there is an additional instruction plate outboard of the steering wheel.

LEFT: The NADA 109 was the only Land Rover to have the Weslake-head version of the 2.6-litre engine. This view clearly shows the twin-intake air cleaner used on that engine.

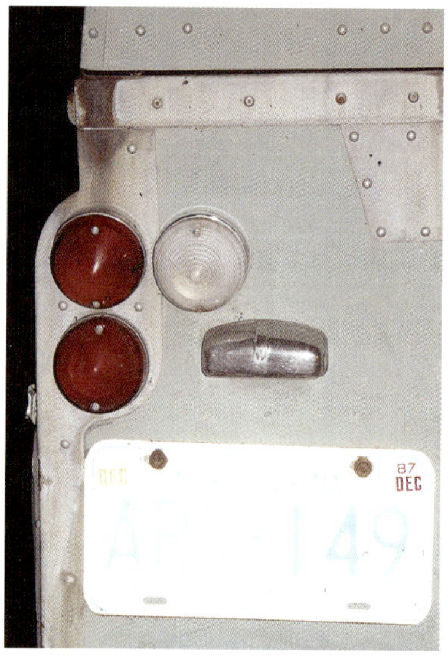

ABOVE: The NADA 109s also had a distinctive rear lighting configuration. The turn indicator lens was red, like the stop-and-tail lamp, there was a round reversing lamp, and the number plate lamp had a chromed housing.

LEFT: The first US Federal 88s were De Luxe hardtops (a hybrid of hardtop and Station Wagon), with 15-inch wheels and headlamps on the wing fronts. That wing-mounted air intake was unique to the Kodiak heater.

ABOVE: This close-up of the early Federal 'bug-eye' configuration shows the large-diameter turn indicator and the amber sidelight.
RIGHT: This is the rear lighting arrangement on a Federal 88. There is a large-diameter amber turn indicator, a 'square' reversing light, and a red reflective side marker. The number-plate lamp is again chromed.

These vehicles always had the 9.5in diaphragm spring clutch and a negative-earth electrical system with a C42 dynamo and an RB340 30A control box. The petrol pump was an SU electric dual-inlet type mounted under the seat box and a fresh air heater-demister and heated windscreens were both fitted as standard. The fuel tank held 16gal (73ltr), and a 10gal (45ltr) auxiliary tank under the right-hand seat box was available as an option. The chassis number plate was mounted on the right-hand side of the dashboard and there was an instruction plate on the left-hand side outboard of the driver. These were the first Land Rovers to have a black-painted dash panel; they also had reversing lamps as standard.

The 4-cylinder 109 models remained available during 1968, but were withdrawn at the end of that year because Land Rover was not prepared to meet the expense of changing them to comply with new Federal regulations that came into force on 1 January 1969. These regulations affected mainly exhaust emissions and lighting.

The new lighting regulations outlawed the traditional position of the Land Rover's headlights in the grille panel. Rover's short-term solution was a redesigned front end, which was shared with 88s and 109s for the Benelux countries (*see* above). The headlamps were relocated on the wing fronts, and a new grille and grille panel were drawn up. US customers have always called them 'bugeye' models. Production began in late 1968 to meet the New Year sales deadline and probably ended around April 1969 when the properly redesigned front end of the Suffix G models became available.

Unlike the Benelux models with this headlamp arrangement, the US 'bug-eyes' also had large-diameter amber indicator lamps (with a 4in/10cm

Lights and Reflectors on North American Models

Series II

Series II models were the same as for other markets.

Series IIA, Suffix A to F (1961–9)

Headlights	Lucas F700 with separate bulb	Chromed bezel and domed lens
Sidelights	Lucas 52602A	Separate chromed bezel
Front flashers	Lucas L594	Separate chromed bezel
Stop/tail lights	Lucas L692	Red lens
Rear flashers	Lucas L691	Red lens
Number-plate lamp	Lucas L467	On the driver's side tail panel; chromed body
Reversing lamp	Lucas L691	Clear lens; 6-cylinder 109 Station Wagon only

Series IIA, Suffix G to H (1969–71)

Headlights	Lucas F700 with separate bulb	Flat lens and no bezel
Sidelights	Lucas L594	Amber lens
Front and rear flashers	Lucas L833	Large-diameter lens
Side marker, front	Lucas L841	Amber lens
Side marker, rear	Lucas L841	Red lens
Stop/tail lights	Lucas L692	All-red lens
Rear side reflector	Lucas RER22	Rectangular
Number-plate lamp	Lucas L467	Always fitted to the tail panel on the driver's side
Reversing lamp	Lucas L798	Clear lens

diameter) front and rear, Lucas side reflectors and twin square reversing lamps, which were automatically operated when reverse was selected.

For 1969 the range was also reduced to a single model on the 88in chassis. Known as the De Luxe hardtop, this always had the 4-cylinder petrol engine and its body was a hybrid of hardtop and Station Wagon, with Station Wagon upper body sides and tail door, but a hardtop roof panel without Alpine lights or tropical roof panel. There were inward-facing bench seats in the rear instead of the four individual seats of the standard 88 Station Wagon. In their paint scheme, the De Luxe hardtops followed the style of ordinary hardtops rather than Station Wagons, with the upper side and upper panels painted in Limestone to match the roof.

The engine of the Federal 88s had an EGR system on its Zenith carburettor and a vacuum retard on the ignition to reduce exhaust emissions at idle. Wheels went down in size to 15in, as the 16in tyres were not easy to find in the USA. These models continued until Series IIA production ended in 1971.

THE CKD ASSEMBLY OPERATIONS

Very little is known about some of the overseas assembly operations, and much of the information here is based on research done by Land Rover's George Mitchell. Many CKD operations were related to military contracts and turned out only military vehicles for a limited period.

Australia

Rover Australia Pty Ltd was established in 1957 to set up an assembly operation. The impetus behind this was a major order for Land Rovers from the Australian Army, which was granted on condition that there was a higher than usual local content in the finished vehicles. The assembly contract was agreed with the Pressed Metal Corporation, a company that already had an assembly contract with BMC, and almost all Australian Series IIs and Series IIAs were assembled by PMC at Enfield, a suburb of Sydney, New South Wales. To meet shortages, small numbers of fully built Land Rovers were sometimes shipped in from Solihull.

From 1958, the Australians began to manufacture major elements of the vehicles' structure themselves, using jigs and tooling shipped out from Solihull. By the mid 1960s, the 'Rover' differentials were being made by Borg Warner Australia (these are recognizable by the words 'Rover Australia' cast into the differential casing).

Australian-built Series IIs and Series IIAs broadly followed the specifications of their British-built equivalents, but they always had vertically stacked front side and indicator lamps. Peculiar to

The CKD Assembly Operations

Country	Models	Start Date
Angola	109	1963
Australia		*see* text
Brazil		1955
Cameroons (later Republic of Cameroun)	88	1967
Ceylon	88	1959
Chile	88	1962
Congo	109	not known
Costa Rica	88	1963
Ecuador	88 and 109	1961
Egypt	109	1960
Ethiopia	88	not known
Ghana	109	1960
Greece	88	1969 or 1970
Indonesia	not known	1956
Iran	88	1960
Jamaica	109	1964
Kenya	109	1961
Lebanon	88	1959
Libya	109	1966
Madagascar	109	1964
Malawi	109	1969
Malaysia	88	1968
Morocco	88	1962
Mozambique	109	not known
New Guinea	109	not known
New Zealand	88 and 109	1960
Nigeria	109	1962
Pakistan	88	1959
Persia		*see* Iran
Peru	109	1964
Philippines	not known	1956
Portugal	109	not known
Rhodesia	109	1963
Saudi Arabia	88	1963
South Africa		*see* text
Spain		*see* text
Swaziland	109	not known
Tanzania	109	1964
Thailand	109	1964
Trinidad	109	1967
Tunisia	88	1959
Turkey	88	1962
Uruguay	88	1962
Venezuela	not known	1950
West Africa	109	1962
West Pakistan	88	1959
Yugoslavia	88 and 109	1960
Zambia		*see* text

Australia assembled its own Land Rovers from CKD kits at the Pressed Metal Corporation factory in Enfield. There was a substantial locally manufactured content, too.

LEFT: PMC-assembled Land Rovers had a special build plate attached to the bulkhead alongside the standard chassis plate.

BELOW: Australian-assembled Land Rovers had their own grille badge.

This 'Plus 35' badge was added in Australia to mark the arrival of reinforced half-shafts and differentials.

Australian 6-cylinders had this special grille badge in addition to the main Land Rover badge.

ABOVE: Later Australian Series IIAs had this special grille.

LEFT: Australia also had its own special grille for the Suffix G and later models with headlamps in the wings.

Characteristically Australian was the tray body. This is a 1959 example, as offered by Grenville Motors.

Australian military Series IIAs had cutaway front wings, drop-shackle suspension and no body sills. Note also the large roo-bar on this 88, to protect the radiator from errant animals in the bush.

The Australian military had its own design of tilt and its own rear bumperettes; note the protection for the rear lights.

ABOVE: The Australian military Series IIA 109 shared most of its special features with the 88s.
RIGHT: There were also FFR versions of the 109 for the military. The grille appears to be the same as on early British FFR models.

the territory was the 'tray top' body on 109s that was available by 1959. Initially advertised as the 'Table-Top' model, this was a flatbed body with removable sides and tailboard. These vehicles were delivered from the assembly plant as chassis-cabs, and the customer could choose a body manufactured by Pressed Metal or get one made locally. Australian dealers tended to have a favoured local bodybuilder and would recommend that company to clients who wanted a tray-top model. As a result, there are several varieties of tray top: steel-framed with timber deck, head, side and tailboards; all pressed steel; and all aluminium. The aluminium tray top introduced by Rover Australia in 1969 was promoted as a lightweight design that increased usable payload by 7cwt (784lb, 355kg).

The Australian armed forces also took a large number of Land Rovers during this period. The majority were on the 109 chassis but there were also large numbers of 88s. All had 4-cylinder petrol engines. From 1962 and the start of Series IIA deliveries, both 88s and 109s were delivered with 'drop-shackle' suspension (with extended spring shackles) to improve ground clearance. These also had an angular cutaway to the front wings. Among the special body variants were a locally manufactured ambulance on the 109 chassis and the 'gunbuggy' conversion of the Series II and IIA 88s, which turned them into portees of the American 106mm recoilless rifle. Later, some special 4-cylinder 109s were made for the Australian SAS Regiment.

The strengthened differentials and half-shafts introduced in March 1964 appeared slightly later in Australia, but their presence was advertised for the first twelve months or so by a special oval grille badge reading 'Plus 35'. Australian 6-cylinder models also had a distinctive grille and an oval badge reading 'Six', mainly to advertise the presence of the bigger engine at a time when Land Rover sales were suffering under the impact of the Toyota Land Cruiser with its 6-cylinder engine. From 1969, when the headlights moved to the wing fronts, Australian Land Rovers had yet another distinctive locally made grille.

Land Rovers assembled by the Pressed Metal Corporation had an additional build plate carrying the PMC logo and a build number. This was normally screwed to the bulkhead above the chassis number plate ahead of the gear levers.

Australian military 109s had a cut-out in a solid tail panel instead of a tailboard. The canvas was shaped to suit.

South Africa

Local assembly began there in 1950. Jigs and tools were shipped out to South Africa in early 1958 for the start of a military contract, which appears to have been mainly for 88s. The assembly plant was at Blackheath, in the Cape. Few details of these vehicles are available even now, mainly because the South Africans remain very tight-lipped about their military forces.

During the Series IIA period, local manufacture of both 88s and 109s began for the civilian market. Towards the end of the 1960s, a special extended-chassis 109 was developed to meet a South African Army requirement and this had a chassis extension of some 2ft (61cm) behind the rear axle to support its longer body. A version of this with the 6-cylinder engine, called the Sabre, was specially manufactured for the forward reconnaissance units of the South African Army. The chassis was further extended by some 2ft (61cm) with extensions on the front dumb irons, which carried a heavy-duty front bumper that contained storage

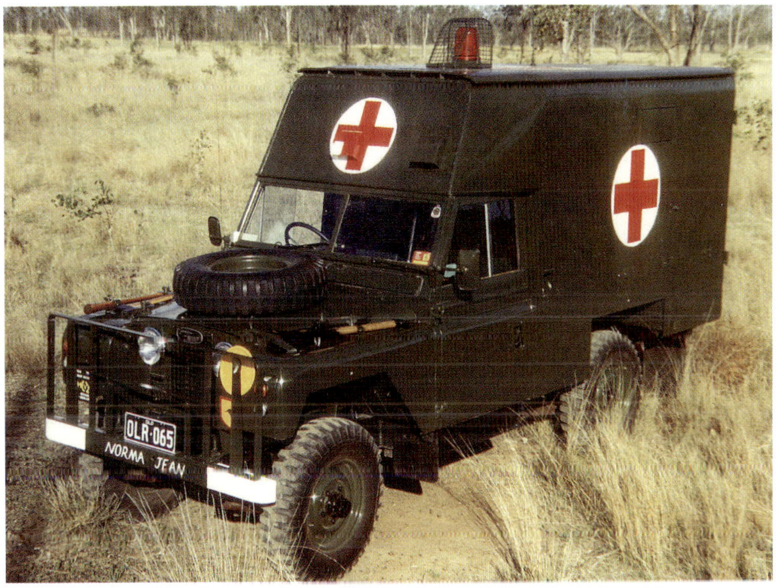

The Australian military ambulance was quite different from the British design. This is a 1965 example.

Overseas assembly facilities were often far more rudimentary than those in Britain. These are 88s on the assembly lines in Costa Rica in the early 1960s.

At overseas plants, Land Rover assembly was often carried out alongside the assembly of other marques. These 88s – and more in those packing cases visible on the left – are outside the New Zealand assembly plant.

boxes, rectangular headlamps and a massive mechanically operated winch. The engine's oil filter was remotely mounted on the left-hand inner wing for improved access, and a Donaldson canister-type air cleaner was mounted on the right-hand wing.

The transmission used the low-geared main and transfer gearboxes of the One Ton and Forward Control models, the axles were both Salisbury heavy-duty types and the heavy-duty road springs were carried on extended shackles. Tyres were 9.00×16s on robust split-rim wheels. The body carried water tanks, a large auxiliary fuel tank and stowage under a raised load floor.

The best estimates suggest that between fifty and sixty Sabres were built. No chassis numbers have been recovered from the few remaining survivors (although engines seem to have been in the usual 345-series), and it may be that these specially built vehicles were deliberately not numbered.

There was a special badge for South African-assembled Land Rovers.

The Sabre was a formidable military machine designed and assembled in South Africa for that country's special forces.

Spain

The Spanish CKD operation was run by Metalurgica de Santa Ana, whose headquarters were in Madrid although the assembly plant was at Linares in the south. The company traded under the name of Santana, and the Land Rovers they assembled wore Land Rover Santana badges. Jigs and tools were shipped out from Solihull in 1958 but assembly did not begin until 1959 and was initially of 88s only; 109s were later added to the repertoire and from 1967 Santana also assembled its own version of the 109in Forward Control, known as a Santana 1300.

In all important respects Santana-built Series IIs were identical to those built at Solihull. However, the Spanish-built vehicles had locally sourced instruments, trim, glass and probably tyres. In addition, they incorporated the Santana name below the oval Land Rover grille and tail badges. In due course, Santana introduced locally manufactured options, such as chromed hub-caps and body edge trim, and these appear to have been available before the end of Series II production.

The CKD packs sent out to MSA in Spain were to the Series IIA specification from some time in 1962. However, it looks as if Santana had already started to go its own way and did not refer to these vehicles as Series IIAs but continued to use the Series II designation.

Throughout the 1960s, the local content in Santana Land Rovers increased in line with Spanish government requirements. MSA was manufacturing more and more items to Solihull specifications but there were no significant differences between Santana Land Rovers and the Rover product. Some parts appear to have been dual-sourced, with a percentage being manufactured in Spain and the remainder being shipped out from Solihull.

Although both 88s and 109s were now available, there were no 109 Station Wagons before 1968.

It was at about this time that MSA attained their 100 per cent local content target, and from then on British-built and Spanish-built Land Rovers began to diverge much more. It is probable that they switched to new chassis numbering sequences at this stage, with three-figure prefix codes that were different from Solihull's and which were all preceded by the letter E. The E presumably stood for España (Spain).

A contract with the Spanish army led to the development of two special models whose production began in 1969. These were the 88 Militar and the 109 Militar, the former rated as a quarter-tonne model but the latter with a full one-tonne rating. Both drew on Solihull's own design work for the 88in Lightweight, but both had steel instead of aluminium bodywork. They appear to have been built only as GS soft-top models. The 88 Militar ran on 7.50×16 tyres and it is likely that both had (or were available with) twin fuel tanks and 24V electrical systems.

Changes for the civilian models began in 1970 but were initially confined to the 88 and 109 Station Wagons, which were badged as Especial types. MSA's aim was clearly to improve both the appearance and the comfort of these passenger-carrying models. Their headlamps were relocated in the wings (as on Solihull-built models from April 1969), the De Luxe bonnet with its rolled leading edge became standard and single-unit rear lamps were fitted. New parabolic leaf springs and upgraded seats and interior trim meanwhile improved comfort levels.

Other civilian models retained separate indicator and stop/tail lamps at the rear, as well as their grille-mounted headlamps. The Santana Series IIs also outlasted Solihull's own Series IIAs, remaining in production until they were replaced by Santana Series IIIs in 1974.

Zambia

Before the mid 1960s Land Rovers sold in Zambia were imported as fully built vehicles from either Britain or Rhodesia. Rover (Zambia) Ltd was formed in association with Central African Motors Ltd and began assembly operations at a plant in Ndola in June 1965. By 1966 it was geared to a capacity of 600 to 750 units a year and was building 88s with full tilts and truck cabs, and 109 hardtops, truck cabs and Station Wagons. All models were available with either 4-cylinder petrol or diesel engines, and during 1966 109 pick-ups with three-quarter tilts were being built for the Zambian Army. All models had heavy-duty dampers, uprated leaf springs and a steering damper as standard.

Locally sourced items by 1966 included canvas tilts (from the Canvas Company of Central Africa Ltd in Ndola), batteries (from Battery Makers of Zambia Ltd), glass (from Plate Glass & Bevelling Ltd) and paint (from Plascon Paints in Kitwe).

Santana models always had some differences from their Solihull cousins. This diesel 88 from the early 1960s is a window hardtop with fixed side glazing and a tropical roof.

The early Santana grille badge was a pressed metal plate.

Santana switched to a printed metal badge around 1963.

11 the Forward Control models

ABOVE: TTK 820 is a very early Series IIA Forward Control dating from December 1962. The headlamp peaks and twin grille badges are not original, but were added by its original owner, who still uses the vehicle, forty-seven years later.

LEFT: This rear view shows the wraparound rear mudguards, short cross-member and flush rear light mounting panel of the IIA models. The fairlead for the hydraulically operated rear winch ordered for this vehicle is also visible here.

The Forward Control models were developed to provide more load space within the same overall dimensions as the normal-control Land Rovers. By moving the cab forward so that the driver sat alongside the engine rather than behind it, Rover delivered a longer load platform. Chassis reinforcement in the shape of a box-section frame mounted above the main chassis allowed the payload to be set at 30cwt (1.52 tonne) on the road or 25cwt (1.27 tonne) off it. This extra space endeared the Forward Control models to aftermarket converters, and quite a high proportion of production was of chassis-cab and chassis-cowl versions, either with or without the extra frame above the rear chassis.

As introduced, the Forward Control Land Rover was a Series IIA, Suffix A type. Suffix changes followed their own course and did not match changes on the normal-control Land Rovers, even though similar changes were often introduced at the same time. The Forward Controls always shared a large number of components with normal-control models, but they also had many unique components. The VIN plate of a Forward Control is located on the parcel shelf ahead of the driver, outboard of the steering wheel.

The front chassis extension was bolted to the main frame. Also visible here is one of the 'hoops' supporting the upper chassis frame.

SERIES IIA 109in MODELS

The first Series IIA models all had the 2.25-litre petrol engine. A small number of diesel-engined models were built experimentally, but there was no volume production. From August 1963 the 2.6-litre 6-cylinder petrol engine became available as an option. In theory, this was available for export only.

Suffix A

The Suffix A Forward Controls were announced at the Commercial Vehicle Show in September 1962, but production did not begin until early 1963. All these first models had the 2.25-litre 4-cylinder petrol engine and were destined for export.

The gearbox cross-member was welded to the main chassis frame on the Series IIA Forward Controls.

Suffix B

The Suffix B models were introduced in March 1963 at the same time as the Forward Controls became available in Britain. They embodied a number of

ABOVE: Three of the wheel nuts on each front wheel had threaded extensions, to take the wheel step.

LEFT: On the Series IIA models, the axles were mounted above the road springs.

changes: lower gearing in the main and transfer gearboxes to improve pulling power, lighter steering from a lower ratio box, stronger shackle pins and bigger propshaft UJs. They also had a new diaphragm clutch in place of the earlier spring type, and they had the latest style of flat-lens headlamp and Wipac side and indicator lamp without a bezel.

Suffix D

There were no Suffix C models. The Suffix D models were introduced in August 1965 at the same time as the Suffix C normal-control Land Rovers. Their key features were a new steering column with the wheel fixed to the inner column with a tapered spline instead of the earlier straight spline, and a modified rubber gaiter for the transfer lever.

The Chassis Frame

Although the chassis frame of the Forward Controls follows the general configuration of the normal-control Land Rover 109 chassis, it is very different. At the front a forward extension is bolted to the main chassis frame, and bolted underneath this is an undershield. The forward chassis extension carries the pedals and steering column so that the driver can sit above and alongside the engine. The rear cross-member is similar to the military type used on the normal-control models and has no upward taper at the outer edge. The cross-member under the gearbox is welded to the main chassis frame.

There are also steel hoops welded to the side-members, and these provide supports for the massive girder-frame (Land Rover called it a 'body frame'), which runs above the main chassis for the full length of the vehicle to give extra rigidity. This raises both cab and load-bed higher, giving more clearance above the engine and so more room in the cab. Shims were used between the hoops and the 'body frame' to keep everything level.

The fuel tank is at the rear of the chassis, with its filler underneath the tailboard. Petrol and diesel tanks have minor differences, with different outlet and return elbows, and different sender units. The spare wheel is mounted in a clamp on the right-hand side between the main chassis frame and the upper girder frame. Angled brackets attached to the chassis frame at the rear carry the stop, tail and turn indicator lights.

The Transmission

Clutch

The Forward Controls were introduced with a nine-spring, 9in (23cm) clutch, and this was used on all Suffix A models. With the Suffix B chassis in March 1963 came a heavier-duty 9.5in (240mm) diaphragm spring clutch. In service, there were difficulties in obtaining the correct setting with the diaphragm spring clutch, and to alleviate this a packing piece was introduced in March 1964 for the clutch slave cylinder. This was introduced on 4-cylinder models at chassis number 286-01399B. The number given in service literature for the first 6-cylinder with this modification is 300-00379A, which appears to be incorrect; the chassis suffix should be a B rather than an A.

Main Gearbox

The first Forward Controls had the same four-speed gearbox as the contemporary normal-control models, but with the arrival of the Suffix B models in March 1963 came lower gearing to improve low-speed performance. These lower-geared units were also identified by a B suffix and were introduced at gearbox number 286-01133B. Anti-shunt bars were added at the same time, one on either side of the gearbox, to damp out unwanted fore-and-aft movement of the transmission. They could be retro-fitted to earlier vehicles. The gear linkage was improved in September 1963 by new set bolts with increased tensile strength to hold the selector levers to the linkage. These were introduced at chassis numbers 286-00295, 287-00364, 289-00242, 300-00002, 301-00036 and 303-00117. Then in February 1964 came a stronger tie rod bracket and some lugs on the bellhousing to provide a more positive attachment. This latter modification could also be retrofitted to existing vehicles.

As was noted, there was no gearbox Suffix C, and the numbering moved straight to Suffix D in August 1965. These final Series IIA gearboxes were characterized by a stronger layshaft, which had a shoulder instead of the earlier split ring and groove. This was another modification that could be retrofitted to earlier vehicles.

Transfer Gearbox

Suffix A models shared their transfer box gearing with normal-control types, but this was modified with lower gearing (1.53:1 High, 2.92:1 Low) at chassis Suffix B in March 1963. These transfer boxes are associated with Suffix B main gearboxes.

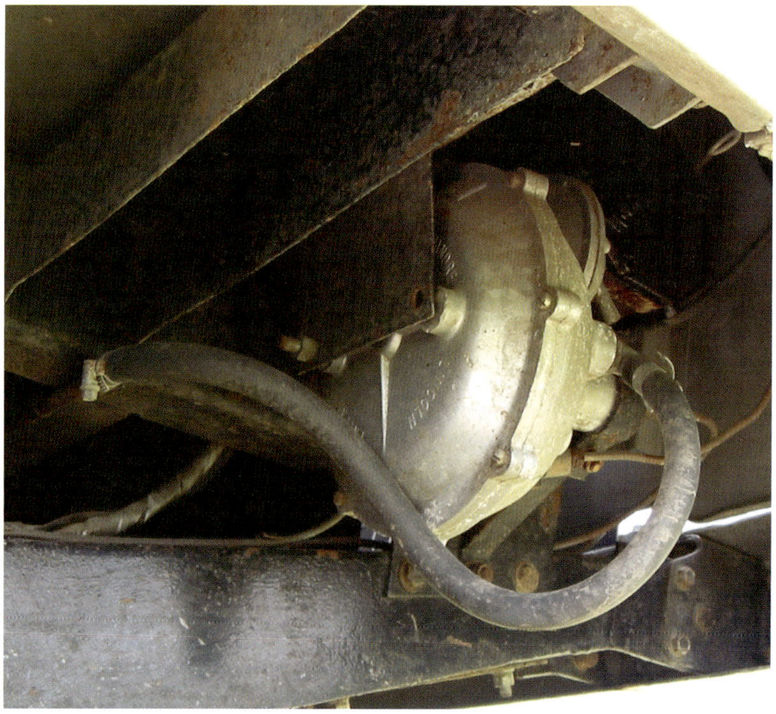

The Clayton Dewandre brake servo was fitted under the cab floor. One of the fixing nuts appears to be missing here!

ABOVE: This cover panel had to be removed to gain access to the rear of the engine. There was also a removable panel in the floor, and one in the cab between the seats.

Gearbox Identification Numbers

The gearbox number is located on the right-hand side of the casing, looking forwards.

286-00001A onwards	4-cylinder Forward Control gearbox
300-00001A onwards	6-cylinder Forward Control gearbox

The Axles and Propshafts

Neither the propshafts nor the original Rover-type axles were strong enough for the Forward Control models. Propshaft UJ and half-shaft failures were common. The first corrective action was taken when the Suffix B models arrived in March 1963, when propshafts with larger UJs were fitted. These could be retro-fitted to Suffix A models.

From the start of Suffix B production, differentials had different nose-pieces, and these were fitted to all 6-cylinder models from the start. However, the axle problem was not solved until February 1965, when heavy-duty axles made by ENV were standardized. It appears that the ENV front axle could foul under certain conditions on the 6-cylinder models. This was the reason why the axle was moved forwards an inch on the Series IIB models.

The brake and clutch shared a fluid reservoir, as on normal-control models, and the voltage regulator was also a common component.

The Steering and Brakes

Steering

The Series IIA Forward Control was introduced with a 15.6:1 steering ratio, but this gave heavy steering at low speeds, and from the start of Series B production in March 1963 a lower-ratio (19.6:1) steering box was fitted. At the same time, 3/8in (9.5mm) fixings replaced the original 5/16in (7.9mm) items on the steering unit; it was possible to fit these retrospectively to earlier vehicles.

The toolbox with its removable lid was concealed under the short bonnet.

Axle Identification Numbers

The axle number is stamped into the casing alongside the differential.

Front Axles

286-00001A onwards	Rover-type axles, all models, RHD
289-00001A onwards	Rover-type axles, all models, LHD
300-00001A onwards	ENV-type axles, 4-cylinder models only, RHD
303-00001A onwards	ENV-type axles, 4-cylinder models only, LHD

Rear Axles

286-00001A onwards	Rover-type axles, all models
300-00001A onwards	ENV-type axles, all models

BELOW LEFT: *The control layout of the IIA Forward Control was never very satisfactory, and became even less so when the arrival of static safety belts restricted the driver's ability to reach for essential items such as the handbrake.*

BELOW RIGHT: *Full door trims were standard in most markets, including the UK. Note the protective strip on the map pocket.*

BOTTOM: *A headlining and trim on the upper half of the cab was listed as part of the De Luxe specification, but was standard in the UK.*

ABOVE: *The side mirrors on early Forward Controls were mounted on brackets attached to the windscreen hinge plates on the bulkhead.*
TOP LEFT: *The modified front panel of the Series IIB models, with lower-mounted headlights, is clear in this picture. NXC 511D was the first production Home Market diesel Forward Control.*
LEFT: *From the rear, the wider cross-member, differently sited rear lights and straight rear mudguards of the IIB models are easy to see.*
BELOW: *The front mountings for the IIB's front springs are longer than those on the earlier IIA chassis.*

In March 1964 the steering relay shaft was modified, losing its oilway and filler plug hole. Then, with the arrival of Suffix D models in August 1965, a new steering column was introduced. The steering wheel was now fixed to the inner column on tapered splines instead of the straight splines used earlier.

Brakes

The Series IIA Forward Controls had 11in (28cm) drum brakes front and rear, with a Clayton Dewandre vacuum-operated servo as standard. Early models had a CB-type brake master cylinder, and a CV type was used on later examples. As on the normal-control models, the handbrake acted on a drum fitted to the rear output shaft of the transfer gearbox. The stop lamp switch was hydraulically operated.

This rear view of the IIB's chassis shows the fuel tank, the mounting bracket for the exhaust tailpipe, and the extended outriggers for the rear springs.

The gearbox cross-member on the Series IIB models was bolted to the main chassis frame and could be removed to facilitate work on the transmission.

As on the IIA Forward Controls, the spare wheel was carried in a cradle mounting between the main and upper chassis frames.

The Suspension, Wheels and Tyres

The Series IIA Forward Control models had semi-elliptic leaf springs on all four wheels, with the axles mounted above the springs. The Series A models showed up a weakness in the shackle pins, and so the Suffix B models introduced in March 1963 had stronger pins with a 9⁄16in (14.3mm) diameter thread and shackle plates modified to suit.

The Forward Controls had 16in steel disc road wheels with a 6.5in (165mm) rim width as standard and a five-stud fixing. These wheels were not the same as those used later on the One Ton normal-control models, which had a greater offset. Forward Controls shipped to Switzerland had 5.5in (140mm) rims to suit the smaller tyres standard for that country.

Each front wheel had a foot step ring bolted to it. Three of the securing nuts for each front wheel had a special threaded extension, which passed through the step ring. The wheel nut was tightened first and then the step ring was passed over the threaded extensions and was in turn secured by standard wheel nuts.

As on the normal-control Land Rovers, two different types of BSF-thread wheel nut were used. The first Forward Controls had a 59⁄64in (23.4mm) AF size and a length of 1in (25.4mm). Later Series IIAs had nuts of the same diameter but a length of 1 1⁄16in (27mm). The nuts on the special step-ring securing bolts changed in dimensions along with the main wheel nuts.

The standard tyres were 9.00×16s, originally manufactured by Avon or Dunlop (the RK2A type). However, Swiss Forward Controls had 7.50×16 Michelin XY tyres on narrower rims.

The Engines

Note that five pilot-production diesel-engined Series IIA models were built. No details of their engines are available, but they were probably similar to the diesel engines in contemporary normal-control models.

4-Cylinder Petrol Engines

The 2.25-litre 4-cylinder petrol engines were broadly similar to the versions used in contemporary normal-control Land Rovers. However, the Forward Control engines had their own sequence of suffix letters, and these differ from those on the normal-control engines. Forward Control 4-cylinder engines had a single Solex carburettor, either a type 40PA 10-5A or, when fitted with a heater element, a type 40PA PA 10-6. Alternative jets were available for high-altitude use.

The first engines were Suffix A types, and were broadly equivalent to the 251-prefix Suffix B engines fitted to normal-control models. They had a bellows-type thermostat and O-ring-type valve seals.

The Suffix B engines were introduced in March 1963 and were broadly equivalent to the Suffix D 251-prefix normal-control engines. They had lip-type valve seals (which could be retrofitted to earlier engines) and a wax-type thermostat with the simplified by-pass elbow. They also had non-adjustable ball joints on the carburettor control rod, plus linkage clips on the control rod between the relay shaft and carburettor relay. This modified carburettor control system could also be fitted retrospectively to earlier models. The oil filter was a short-bodied AC 72 type in place of the early long AC FF 50 type. At engine number 286-00957B in February 1964, they took on the strengthened left-hand engine foot that was also used on the normal-control models.

There were no Suffix C engines, and Suffix D replaced Suffix B in March 1964. The change signified a one-piece dipstick tube in place of the earlier two-piece type and the differently sized nut fixing this tube entailed a modification to the cylinder block.

The Suffix E engines that arrived in June 1965 equated to Suffix G types on the normal-control models, and had the simplified distributor drive shaft and a new front cover assembly. The final 4-cylinder engines in the Series IIA Forward Controls were Suffix F types; details are unclear but these probably corresponded to the Suffix H engines in normal-control models which dispensed with water pump locating studs on the front cover.

6-Cylinder Engines

The 2.6-litre 6-cylinder engine was introduced in August 1963, and in theory was available for export only. In practice, a few 6-cylinder Forward Controls did find owners in Britain. Modifications began in February 1964 at engine

RIGHT: The axles were mounted underneath the springs on the Series IIB models.

BELOW: Found only on diesel-engined models, the fuel sedimenter was located just ahead of the left-hand rear wheel.

BOTTOM: As on the IIAs, the front wheel steps were secured by three special fixings.

TOP LEFT: The special wheelbrace for the Forward Controls had a hollow within its socket to accept the threaded extension of the three special front wheel fixings. This is a late type from 1972; red wheels were used on fire engines.

BELOW LEFT: The Series IIB Forward Control gear linkage was modified to give a much better change. The cover panel has been removed on this fire engine, to show how the linkage runs above the six-cylinder engine.

BOTTOM LEFT: The rear lights on IIBs were mounted on a recessed panel for additional protection. Note also how the rear cross-member was wider than on IIAs.

number 300-00083A, when the core holes were deleted from the sides of the oil pump cover casting to prevent fractures between the fixing screw orifice and the core holes. The following month, Suffix B engines were introduced, characterized by enlarged crankshaft bearings and by new piston assemblies intended to reduce oil consumption.

However, oil consumption remained a problem, and at engine number 300-00674 in February 1965 the original Maxilite scraper rings were replaced by Duaflex rings in an attempt to cure it. These rings could be retrofitted to earlier engines. The parts catalogue lists a further change to these rings at engine number 300-00766, presumably again to help cure excessive oil consumption.

It is not clear whether the lock washers between the engine mounting feet and the cylinder block were replaced by spring washers in February 1966, as occurred on the 4-cylinder engines.

The Exhaust System

The Forward Control models had a different exhaust system from that used on the normal-control Land Rovers. On 4-cylinder petrol models, the system is in three parts with a single silencer incorporated in the tail section. The tailpipe emerges on the right of the vehicle. Early 4-cylinder models also had a butterfly valve in the exhaust manifold.

The 6-cylinder system is again in three pieces but with silencers in both the intermediate and tail sections; the tail section is also handed to exit on the driving side, away from a kerb; 6-cylinders also have a unique exhaust manifold with a rearward-facing outlet.

Engine Identification Numbers

The identification number of the 4-cylinder engines is located on the left-hand side, looking forwards, just ahead of the exhaust manifold:

286-00001A onwards	4-cylinder Forward Control petrol engines
300-00001A onwards	6-cylinder Forward Control engines

The Body

All varieties came with a truck cab, unless supplied to a specialist converter as a chassis-cowl model. The cab's roof, rear panel and windscreen frame (and their associated windows and fittings) were the same as on the normal-control models. However, the doors and all panels forward of them were different; there were also flared wheelarch panels, which acted as splash-guards.

Most obviously, the Forward Controls had a short 'nose' consisting of two side panels, a short hinged bonnet and a front panel. The doors were similar to those on normal control models but were shaped at the bottom to fit around the wheelarch. The bonnet was held shut by two spring clamps. There were two varieties of front panel on Series IIA models, one to suit the Suffix A headlamps with bezels and the other to suit the later configuration without bezels. Both set the headlamps between the side and indicator lamps. The stubby, T-shaped grille was unique to the Forward Controls.

As on the normal-control models, the cab seats were mounted on a transverse seat box. On the first 650 vehicles this had a strengthening plate running fore and aft under each seat. The plates were subsequently deleted.

Early models had a bracket on the windscreen frame to which a door mirror could be mounted. On later examples this bracket was deleted and a special upper door hinge was fitted with a drilled extension for the mirror mounting.

Standard body configurations were a fixed-side lorry, a dropside lorry and a flatbed lorry. A tilt was available for the rear of either dropside or fixed-side bodies, but was not supplied as standard. For export, the tilt could be fitted with perspex side windows. The rear 'mudguards' behind and in front of the wheels had curved outer edges.

The only paint colour available from the factory was Mid-Grey. Forward Control models supplied in chassis-cab or

RIGHT: Later side mirrors, as on this Series IIB, were mounted on special door hinges.

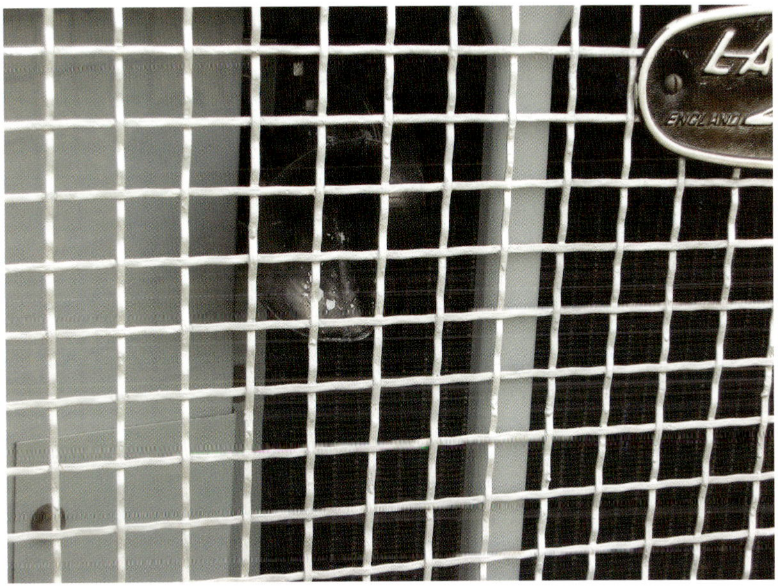

BELOW: The horn was mounted to the front panel, behind the radiator grille.

RIGHT: Many Forward Controls were specially converted, such as this Series IIA, which was fitted with a livestock carrier body by PD Stevens & Sons of Market Drayton.

chassis-cowl condition to the aftermarket converters had their body panels finished in grey primer.

The Interior

There were just two seats in the Forward Control's cab, the centre position being given over to a detachable engine inspection cover. Door trim panels, door armrest panels, floor mats, a tunnel cover and under-dash sound-deadening made up a De Luxe trim package that was standard on home market models and was probably also standard in most markets. The seats were upholstered in 'elephant hide' grey vinyl and the door trims were in grey to match. They had a rigid pull-handle in the centre.

The instrument panel was broadly similar to the one on contemporary normal-control Land Rovers (*see* Chapter 5). The main beam warning light was normally red, but on German export models it was blue. Swiss export models had a special version of the kilometres-per-hour speedometer.

The steering wheel was a spring-spoke type on Suffix A, B and C models, and from Suffix D in August 1965 changed to one with three black plastic spokes. Turn indicators were always standard, operated by a stalk switch on the steering column that was the same as the optional type available for normal controls. The pedals and dipswitch were the same as their normal-control equivalents.

The handbrake and transmission levers were similar to those on normal-control models (*see* Chapter 5) but were never very satisfactory in the Forward Controls because the driving position was different. At Suffix D in August 1965 the redesigned transfer box lever gaiter was fitted to reduce instances of tearing in service.

Tools

Like the normal-control models, the Forward Controls came with a set of hand tools in a hessian roll. This was kept in a toolbox with a removable lid under the 'bonnet' at the front. The box also contained the body of the jack and the wheelbrace. The jack handle and starting handle were secured by clips on the lower rear cab panel, behind the seats. There was a special wheelbrace for the Forward Controls. This had a cylindrical recess inside the primary socket, to allow tightening of the special front wheel nuts with their threaded extensions.

The Electrical System

The Series IIA Forward Controls had a 12V positive-earth electrical system. The single 12V battery was located on a tray mounted to the left-hand chassis side rail just behind the front wheel. As on the normal-control models, the wiring harness had a woven fabric sheath. The voltage regulator and Model 4J fuse box (with two fuses and two spares) were mounted on the front of the bulkhead, under the 'bonnet', while the starter solenoid was next to the battery. The starter motor was the same as on normal-control models; the dynamo was a Lucas C40-1 on 4-cylinder engines and a C42 on the 6-cylinders.

Coil

The distributor on 4-cylinder models was initially a Lucas DM2, but was changed to a Lucas 25 D4 in December 1963 at engine number 286-01124. The 6-cylinder engines always had a Lucas 25 D6 distributor. On early models, the plug leads entered at the side of the cap, but later ones had acorn-type screw connectors on the top; 6-cylinder models also had an SU double-entry electric fuel pump, although all 4-cylinders had a mechanical pump. The windscreen wiper arrangements were the same as on normal-control models, with only a driver's side wiper as standard.

Horn

The horn was mounted on a bracket attached to the grille panel. Both Lucas and Clearhooter types were used. French regulations demanded switchable two-tone horns, with a low note for town use and a higher note for the open road. So Forward Controls for France had an additional high-note horn made by Mixo and a changeover switch mounted on a bracket on the dash, labelled 'Route' (open road) and 'Ville' (town). French vehicles also had a rubber surround added to the interior mirror, additional padded crash rails on the dash and toughened glass in the windscreens.

Lighting

Lighting arrangements broadly followed those on the normal-control models, but all Forward Controls had both turn indicators and a separate rear number-plate lamp as standard. Front turn indicators (flashers) were mounted in the front panel above the headlamps, and sidelamps were mounted below them.

Series IIA Forward Control Lights

The Suffix A models had a unique set of lights, as follows:

Headlights	Lucas F700 with separate bulb
Sidelights	Lucas L638 or Sparto 5835, each with separate chromed bezel
Front flashers	Lucas L639 or Sparto
Rear flashers	Lucas L637 or Sparto 57103
Stop/tail	Lucas L581 or Sparto 57101
Number plate	Lucas L467/2 (L467 with different glass for France and Germany)

From Suffix B in March 1963, there were new lights:

Headlights	Lucas F700 sealed-beam type; F700s with separate bulbs were used on vehicles for Austria and France
Sidelights	Lucas L760, Sparto 62402 or Wipac WP 840, all without bezels
Front and rear flashers	Lucas L760, Sparto 62406 or Wipac WP843 (6-cylinder models for France always had the Wipac type)
Stop/tail	Sparto 62401/A or Wipac type with all-red lens; 6-cylinder models for France had Lucas L692
Number plate	Lucas L467/2 (L467 with different glass for France and Germany)

Vehicles for Switzerland had separate circular red reflectors at the rear. For further identifying details of all these lights, *see* the tables in Chapters 5 and 10.

Optional Equipment

By mid 1965 there was a long list of optional equipment for the Forward Controls. Many of these items were the same as those supplied for normal-control models. In theory, the cab was an optional extra, although this has been covered under the section relating to the body because it was part of the standard specification for Britain.

The list comprised:

- ashtray, telescopic
- altitude corrector for carburettor, 4-cylinder only
- centre PTO
- combined water temperature and oil pressure gauge; introduced in March 1964
- de luxe cab trim
- dust-proofed engine breather
- fire extinguisher
- flyscreens
- gaiters for steering swivels
- hand throttle
- heater-demister; introduced in June 1963
- immersion heater for cylinder block
- interior (rear-view) mirror
- inward-facing seats in the load bed
- lifting and towing rings
- locking door handles
- mirrors (mounted on special upper door hinges)
- oil cooler, 4-cylinder models only
- radio
- roof-mounted air cleaner (snorkel); not introduced for 6-cylinders until April 1965
- passenger's side windscreen wiper with separate motor
- pedal rubbers
- propshaft grommet
- safety belts
- speedometer with trip counter
- steering damper
- sun visor
- tilt (three-quarters type for standard dropside body)
- trailer socket, plug and leads
- tyres (various)
- UJ covers
- winch (hydraulic type, driven from centre or bottom PTO)

RIGHT: This blue-knobbed control protruding through the toeboard on the passenger's side was for the optional centre PTO on a Series IIA Forward Control. In this case, the PTO was hydraulic, and drove a Fairey winch, which emerged at the back of the vehicle.

BELOW: Fire tender conversions were popular, especially on the later models. This one was built in 1972 by Carmichael's, and became the Rover works fire engine.

Major Conversions

The Series IIA Forward Control was a versatile platform that formed the basis of several special one-off conversions. No full list of them is available, but the known ones include those listed below.

During the second half of 1963 Martin Walter of Folkestone brought to market a personnel-carrier body which seated eleven on wooden slatted seats. Relatively few seem to have been built. Shortly afterwards, Glover, Webb and Liversidge of Hamble in Hampshire offered a van body, which was intended mainly for cash in transit. The Rover Company used one as a wages van during the 1960s, and in 1964 one of these bodies was kitted out from new as a mobile caravan.

The British arm of the American company Boyles Brothers manufactured a drilling rig that could be fitted to the platform-body version of the Forward Control and P.D. Stevens of Market Drayton offered a stake-side livestock carrier.

The Series IIA Forward Control was also popular in the Alpine regions of Europe as a fire tender and was often used by volunteer brigades in the mountain villages of Austria and Switzerland. Most of these vehicles had the 6-cylinder engine. The primary builder of these fire appliances was the Austrian company of Rosenbauer, in Linz. Their conversion was known as the LLFA (Leichtes Löschfahrzeug-Allrad, or Light All-wheel-drive Fire appliance) and had a distinctive rounded body, which

overlapped the top of the rear wheelarches. There seem to have been several different internal configurations, but the body was generally laid out to include a crew compartment, equipment lockers and sometimes a portable fire-pump. Rosenbauer also offered a front-mounted fire pump, which was operated from the front of the crankshaft through a clutch arrangement of their own design. Fire tenders were also manufactured by L. Bücher in the German town of Rothenburg, just over the Swiss border. These had a squarer design than the Rosenbauer type.

Typical of the fire engines built by Rosenbauer in Austria for volunteer brigades in the Alpine regions is this Series IIA.

SERIES IIB 110in MODELS

Series IIB models were fundamentally similar to the Series IIA types they replaced, thus the notes that follow record only the differences.

Suffix A

As introduced in January 1967, the 110 Forward Controls had a 4in (100mm) increase in track and a 1in (25mm) increase in the wheelbase. Stronger road springs were mounted, this time above the axles rather than below them, and there were longer spring outrigger brackets to set the springs further outboard and reduce roll. A front anti-roll bar was standard.

There were 4-cylinder petrol and diesel and 6-cylinder petrol options, although the 2.25-litre petrol engine (now with Zenith 36 IV carburettor) was not available in Britain. A negative-earth electrical system was now standard. Diesels had a belt-driven exhauster to provide vacuum braking assistance, and their fuel sedimenter was now on the outside of the left-hand chassis member.

The rear body had a flared lower edge to cover the widened track and the tail lights were now recessed into corner panels; dropside models had stop buffers on the body sides and tailboard.

The dashboard had a new windscreen wiper and instrument layout and a warning light for the brake fluid level, which doubled as an indicator of low servo vacuum on diesel models. A longer handbrake lever and modified main gear lever made for ease of use; there was also a simplified gear change mechanism with its control tube running above the engine, and revised transfer gear change controls to suit.

The brake and clutch fluid reservoirs were now separate, and the clutch master cylinder had an integral reservoir. The 9.5in (241mm) diameter spring clutch was now standard, and the transfer box low ratio was changed from 2.92:1 to 3.27:1.

Suffix B (March 1968)

Suffix B Forward Controls had a larger (11in/280mm) handbrake drum to improve braking. Their 4-cylinder engines and all gearboxes took on Suffix B at the same time.

Suffix C (January 1969)

Suffix C brought the same larger capacity heater as on the normal-control models with its two-speed fan. The new permanent magnet wiper motor with improved rack tube was fitted and the mechanical stop-light switch replaced the old hydraulic type. Associated changes were the same as on the Suffix F normal-control models.

Suffix D (April 1969)

Suffix D introduced electrical changes: a new wiper motor, a new range of headlamps (now the same as those on the normal-control models) and the same new Lucas 8FL flasher unit that arrived on normal-control Suffix G models in April 1969.

Suffix E (February 1971)

These final Forward Controls had the 16mm (0.6in) wheel studs from the Range Rover and their brake drums were modified to suit. They also had modified front spring shackle plates.

The Chassis Frame

The chassis frame was broadly similar to that used on Series IIA models, and differed mainly in its removable gearbox cross-member, which was bolted in place, and in a wider rear cross-member, which reached the full width of the vehicle. The revised location of the front spring hangers is hard to detect. From June 1970 the frame was modified slightly to accommodate the strengthened handbrake relay shaft (*see* Brakes).

At the rear, the corner brackets to which the tail and indicator lights were mounted were set back from the cross-member to afford the lights more protection.

Diesel models had a fuel sedimenter mounted on a bracket on the body frame support just ahead of the forward rear spring hanger on the left-hand side of the chassis.

The Transmission

The Series IIB models had a 9.5in (241mm) diameter spring clutch as standard, and separate brake and clutch fluid reservoirs instead of the common fluid reservoir used on Series

IIA models. The reservoir for the clutch was integral with the master cylinder.

The gearbox was initially the same as in Series IIA models, but was identified by new serial number sequences with suffixes that started again at A. The Suffix B gearboxes had a modified speedometer take-off housing, and from October 1968 the mainshaft bearing housing was secured in position by Loctite; on earlier gearboxes it had been fixed mechanically with a peg, hole and groove, which were now all deleted. The later 4-cylinder and 6-cylinder Series IIB gearboxes also had a sealed clutch withdrawal unit. The final gearboxes had a Suffix C designation but appear to have been fitted only to very late models.

There was a modified transfer gearbox with a 3.27:1 low ratio in place of the 2.92:1 ratio of the Series IIAs. The right-hand rear mounting foot of this gearbox also differed from the earlier type.

The Axles and Propshafts

The wide-track axles fitted to the Series IIB models were all heavy-duty types made by ENV. There was an anti-roll bar on the front axle, with pick-up points on the chassis frame. The rear axle straps were originally 44in (1,117mm) long, but were later replaced by straps that were just 42.5in (1,080mm) long.

At chassis Suffix E in February 1971, there was a modification to the front propshaft.

The Steering and Brakes

The steering layout on the Series IIB models was the same as on the Series IIAs, but there was a different drag link with bracketry to take the steering damper, which was now a standard fit.

The brakes had the same 11in (280mm) drums and vacuum servo as the final Series IIAs. The transmission brake was initially the same as Series IIA types, but with the Suffix B models in March 1968 a larger 11in drum and associated shoes were fitted. The stop lamp switch was operated hydraulically on Suffix A and Suffix B models, but a mechanical switch was introduced with the Suffix C types in January 1969.

From chassis number 330-00077A in January 1968, the five-way front brake pipes were reshaped. Then in January 1970 came a new brake master cylinder and associated pipes to render them compatible with the normal-control models. These changes occurred at chassis numbers 326-00211D, 328-00038D, 330-00172, 333-00268D, 335-00136 and 338-00111D.

June 1970 brought a stronger handbrake relay mounting bracket in 8 SWG (4mm) steel rather than the earlier 12 SWG (2.6mm). The handbrake relay lever shaft was also thicker (now $^7/_{16}$in/11mm UNF, but earlier $^3/_8$in/9.5mm UNF) and a washer plate was added. These changes could not be made retrospectively to earlier models because of associated chassis frame modifications.

The Suspension, Wheels and Tyres

The suspension was once again by semi elliptic leaf springs all round, but the rear springs on Series IIB models differed from those on Series IIA types, and both front and rear dampers were different.

From December 1969, there were improved Silentbloc bushes for the rear springs. These could be fitted retrospectively to earlier Series IIB models (in complete sets), but not to Series IIAs.

The wheel and tyre combinations remained unchanged. Wheel nuts were initially 1$^1/_6$in (30mm) AF types with a BSF thread, a $^3/_4$in (19mm) length and a round face at one end only. With the Suffix H models in February 1971 came the 16mm M16 metric wheel nuts, also introduced on normal-control Land Rovers to make them compatible with Range Rovers.

Gearbox Identification Numbers

The gearbox number is located on the right-hand side of the casing, looking forwards:

325-00001A onwards	4-cylinder Forward Control gearbox
330-00001A onwards	6-cylinder Forward Control gearbox

Axle Identification Numbers

The axle number is stamped into the casing alongside the differential:

Front Axles

325-00001A onwards	ENV-type axles, all models, RHD
328-00001A onwards	ENV-type axles, all models, LHD

Rear Axles

325-00001A onwards	ENV-type axles, all models

The Engines

There were three engines available for the Series IIB models. The 4-cylinder petrol engine was reserved for export only, while the 4-cylinder diesel was sold only in Britain. 6-cylinder petrol engines were available both in Britain and for export.

4-Cylinder Petrol Engines

The engines for the Series IIB models had a new identifying prefix number and their suffix letters started again at A. Identifying characteristics were a Zenith 36IV carburettor, a water temperature transmitter at the front of the cylinder head and a different front side cover and oil filler pipe. The cylinder head bolts were also shorter, with a length of 5$^3/_{16}$in (132mm).

From April 1967, there were modified rocker shaft brackets with shorter set bolts; these became the standard service replacement issue but had to be fitted in complete sets. At engine Suffix B in March 1968, a timing pointer was added to the front cover. Then June 1970 brought the last modification, in the shape of a new exhaust manifold with plain instead of bowed fixing washers. There were also improved manifold clamps.

4-Cylinder Diesel Engines

The 4-cylinder diesel engine in the Series IIB models was broadly similar to the diesel engine used in contemporary normal-control models (*see* Chapter 4). A six-bladed cooling fan was standard, and the engines had an exhauster to operate the vacuum brake servo.

From engine number 335-00018A in May 1967 there was a new cylinder head gasket to improve the seal between the combustion chamber and water transfer

Engine Identification Numbers

The identification number of the 4-cylinder engines is located on the left-hand side, looking forwards, just ahead of the exhaust manifold. On the 6-cylinder engines it is also on the left-hand side at the front:

325-00001A onwards	4-cylinder petrol engines
335-00001A onwards	4-cylinder diesel engines
330-00001A onwards	6-cylinder engines

holes. A semi-sealed cooling system with overflow bottle was fitted from January 1968 at chassis number 336-00049A (an export model).

The Suffix B engines introduced in March 1968 incorporated a number of changes. They were recognizable externally by the new front side cover and oil filler pipe and by a modified breather filter. The fuel system had new injectors and a new spill rail, and there were new glow plugs designed to give quieter running. These could be retrofitted in sets of four to older engines. Much less visible were shorter bolts fixing the flywheel housing to the cylinder block and lip-type oil seals in the valve guides instead of the earlier O-rings.

A modified oil return pipe between the exhauster and the sump was fitted from engine number 335-00507B. The last running modification came in June 1970, when improved manifold clamps were introduced. These could also be fitted to older engines if required.

6-Cylinder Engines

The Series IIB 6-cylinder engines had a water temperature transmitter where the Series IIA engines had only a cover plate for this unit. A wax-type thermostat was fitted from engine number 330-00080A in September 1967 and could be fitted to older engines as well. Then in December 1967 the SU carburettor had a new jet needle securing screw.

March 1968 brought a new chainwheel, which shared its basic design with that used on 4-cylinder engines but had a thicker boss. This could be retrofitted to older engines. In May 1968 at engine number 330-00355A the sump was made deeper to make this component common with the 6-cylinder engine for the normal-control models. There was an accompanying extension piece on the oil pump assembly to bring the oil strainer closer to the pump. Once again, earlier engines could be modified to use the new arrangements.

Finally, in March 1969 the 6-cylinder engines took on an element-type fuel filter.

The Exhaust System

The exhaust system of the 4-cylinder Series IIB models is completely different from that on the Series IIA types. It is once again in three sections, but the silencer constitutes the centre section and the tailpipe is handed to emerge on the driver's side (away from the kerb). The 6-cylinder exhaust system is the same as the Series IIA type but has modified mountings.

The Body

The cab panels on Series IIB models are the same as those on Series IIA types with the exception of the front panel. This sets the headlamps lower down, with both sidelamps and indicators above them. (There are some indications that this panel may have been used on very late Series IIA models for some overseas territories, or possibly retro-fitted by dealers in those territories.) With Suffix D in April 1969 came a modified front panel to suit the new headlamps. This no longer had headlamp protection plates bolted to its inner surface.

From January 1968, at chassis number 333-00096A, a rubber fastener was added to the bonnet catch. This could also be fitted retrospectively to earlier vehicles.

Back body options were the same as those offered on Series IIA models. However, the engine cover panel at the front of the body behind the cab was much larger on Series IIB models than on Series IIA types. The rear 'mudguards' were also flat panels without the curved edges seen on Series IIA models.

The Interior

The earliest Series IIB models had grey upholstery and trim panels, but from October 1968 the colour changed to black. All Series IIB Forward Controls had a black-painted instrument panel and a black panel covering the new wiper motor at the left-hand end of the dashboard parcel shelf. The dials and switches on the instrument panel were rearranged in the same way as on later normal-control Land Rovers, and all models had a new amber handbrake warning lamp.

Diesel-engined Series IIBs had a T-handle engine stop control and an engine speed control quadrant as standard; on Suffix A and Suffix B models this was the horizontal type and from Suffix C a vertical quadrant was fitted. The diesels also had a new blue low-fuel warning lamp just above the key switch on the instrument panel. Swiss models once again had a special speedometer.

The control levers were very different from those on Series IIAs. Most obvious were the short, stubby main gearlever with its cranked stem that was now mounted between the seats, and the long handbrake like that on contemporary normal-control models. Both the front-wheel select and high-low range selector levers also differed from those on the Series IIA types. Pedals were unchanged but at Suffix C the brake pedal and its bracket were modified to suit the new mechanical stop lamp switch.

Safety belts were fitted as standard from chassis number 330-00023 and 335-00068 for the home market, but remained optional on export models. Both Britax and Irving types were used, in each case with grey webbing. Early buckles were released by lifting a plate and later types by a push-button.

The Electrical System

The Series IIBs had a negative-earth electrical system instead of the positive-earth type on Series IIAs. Diesel models had twin batteries, both carried on the tray behind the left-hand front wheel. All models had the rack-operated wiper motor with passenger's and driver's side wipers as standard. The motor was mounted behind a cover panel on the left-hand side of the dashboard. On

Suffix A and B models the motor was a Lucas DR3A, but the Suffix C and later models had a new permanent-magnet motor. Service literature records a change to the wiper arms in April 1969 at Suffix D, although the nature of that change is not clear. With the Suffix B models in March 1968 came a new fully-sealed starter motor.

Optional Equipment

The options listed for the Series IIA models were carried over for the Series IIBs, although there was obviously no call for a passenger's side windscreen wiper option. Additions were a twin fuel tank option, with a Lucas 45SA changeover switch, and a sealed-bearing dynamo that could be fitted to either of the 4-cylinder engines.

From October 1967 De Luxe front seats with black fluted PVC trim became available. When these were specified, the door trim panels remained in their original grey. These seats had a squab that was 75mm (3in) higher than on the standard seats. At the same time, an adjustable outer passenger's seat was made available.

Major Conversions

There were many one-off conversions on the Series IIB, including some with double cabs. Fire engines were numerous. In Britain there were conversions by Carmichael, HCB-Angus (who built a number for the Army Fire Service) and Merryweather, whose conversion was known as the Fire Warden. The Alpine market in Europe was served once again by Rosenbauer, and by 1968 Willi Müller of Romanshorn in Switzerland had developed a modern-looking, if rather boxy, special fire tender body, which was barely recogizable as a Land Rover.

Series IIB Forward Control Lights

The Series IIB Forward Controls inherited their head, side, tail and number-plate lights from the final Series IIA models. At Suffix D in April 1969 new head and sidelights were introduced, but the tail lamps remained unchanged. The Suffix D and later models had the same Lucas F700 sealed-beam headlamps as the contemporary normal-control models. These had a flat lens and no bezel. However, French and Italian regulations demanded F700 headlamps with separate bulbs.

The Suffix D and later models also shared their sidelights with the normal-control models of the time. There were three options: Lucas L760, Sparto 62402 or Wipac WP840. For identifying details *see* the table of lighting in Chapter 5.

Forward Control Production Breakdown

According to the records of Solihull's Despatch Department (now held by the Heritage Motor Centre at Gaydon), 3,194 Series IIA 109 Forward Controls were built in four years, which gives an average annual production total of just under 800. Of these, 2,091 had the 4-cylinder petrol engine, 1,098 the 6-cylinder petrol engine and just five the diesel engine. The diesels were probably all retained at Solihull and not sold to the public.

However, these records do not present the full picture, because the ones for CKD models do not go beyond the end of 1964. In the two years up to that date, 441 Forward Controls had been shipped overseas as CKD kits for local assembly, giving an average of 220 a year. Assuming the annual totals for 1965–6 to be similar, the grand total of 109 Forward Controls is therefore likely to be inflated by around another 440 to give a figure of around 3,630.

Our knowledge of 110 Forward Control production is also incomplete because the CKD records for 1966–8 and 1972 are missing. Surviving records show that Solihull assembled at least 2,603 examples (2,305 built at Solihull plus at least 298 CKD) in seven years, giving an annual average of just 371 vehicles. So annual production was clearly lower than that of the 109 models, even including the missing CKD examples.

Figures for 1969–71 suggest that around 100 CKD models were then being produced every year. If that figure was representative of all seven years of 110 Forward Control production, the grand total of 110 models would be inflated by around 400 to give a figure of about 3,600 – similar to the calculated overall total for the 109 Forward Controls.

In the surviving records for 110 Forward Controls the most common type is the 6-cylinder petrol, of which 1,254 were built. There were 527 4-cylinder petrol models and 524 with the diesel engine.

Forward Control Chassis Numbers

The Land Rover model year once again ran from September to August.

Series IIA

109in Forward Control	
286-00001A to 286-00353D	home market, 4-cylinder petrol
287-00001A to 287-00940D	RHD export, 4-cylinder petrol
288-00001A to 288-00303D	RHD, CKD, 4-cylinder petrol
289-00001A to 289-00459D	LHD, 4-cylinder petrol
290-00001A to 290-00036D	LHD, CKD, 4-cylinder petrol
300-00001A to 300-00002A	home market, 6-cylinder petrol
301-00001A to 301-00361D	RHD export, 6-cylinder petrol
302-00001A to 302-00096D	RHD, CKD, 6-cylinder petrol
303-00001A to 303-00633D	LHD, 6-cylinder petrol
304-00001A to 304-00006D	LHD, CKD, 6-cylinder petrol
305-00001A to 305-00005A	home market, diesel

Series IIB

110in Forward Control	
325-00001A (one only)	home market, 4-cylinder petrol
326-00001A to 326-00452A	RHD export, 4-cylinder petrol
327-series (records incomplete, 1)	RHD, CKD, 4-cylinder petrol
328-00001A to 328-00074A	LHD, 4-cylinder petrol
329-series (records incomplete, 2)	LHD, CKD, 4-cylinder petrol
330-00001A to 330-00360A	home market, 6-cylinder petrol
331-00001A to 331-00524A	RHD export, 6-cylinder petrol
332-series (no records)	RHD, CKD, 6-cylinder petrol
333-00001A to 333-00370A	LHD, 6-cylinder petrol
334-series (records incomplete, 3)	LHD, CKD, 6-cylinder petrol
335-00001A to 335-00168A	home market, diesel
336-00001A to 336-00176A	RHD export, diesel
337-series (no records)	RHD, CKD, diesel
338-00001A to 338-00180A	LHD, diesel
339-series (no records)	LHD, CKD, diesel

NOTES

1. At least 36 327-series vehicles were built in South Africa in 1969–71.
2. At least 54 329-series vehicles were built in 1969–70 in Morocco and Venezuela.
3. At least 158 334-series vehicles were built in 1970–1 in Morocco, South Africa and Venezuela.

12 the military Half-Ton or Lightweight

ABOVE: 72 FG 44 was one of the earliest Lightweights, built on the first day of production (11 November 1968). It is pictured here as it would have looked when serving with the Royal Marines of 41 Commando. Note that the glass section is missing from the door top.
BELOW: Later Series IIA lightweights had their headlamps relocated to a panel ahead of the wings.

The model that most people call the Lightweight was a variant of the 88in normal-control Land Rover developed specially for the British military. It is more correctly known as the Military Half-Ton or, in military language, as a Rover 1. Just under 3,000 Series IIA models were built between December 1967 and March 1972, and the Lightweight was further developed as a Series III type. Production overlapped with the start of Series III 'civilian' Land Rover assembly because outstanding orders had not been completed.

All the Series IIA Lightweights, with the exception of a small number retained by the factory, were delivered to the British armed forces. The first ones entered service towards the end of 1968. The majority were delivered to the Army, but there were also some for the RAF (132 between April and June 1969) and for the Royal Navy (for use by the Royal Marines).

LEFT: The chassis plate was attached to the bulkhead, ahead of the passenger and below the grab-handle.

ABOVE: There was an extra cross-member concealed behind the front bumper. Some units, as here, painted it with the vehicle's registration number.

BELOW: The front bump-stop bracket was separate from the vertical strips on the Series IIA Lightweight chassis.

Most had a 12V electrical system and three-abreast seating in the front, but there was also a sizeable number of 24V FFR models, which had a large battery box in place of the central seat in the driving compartment. The GS (General Service) models had the military type code of FV 18101 and the FFR models were known as FV 18102 types.

The main specification details given in this chapter are for Lightweights in 'as-delivered' condition. It is important to realize that vehicles were modified and adapted almost from the moment they entered service, and that different units had their own ways of doing this. Some units, for example, including the Royal Marine Commandos, would stencil the vehicle's registration number on to removable items such as the seats and tilt cover so that each vehicle could be refitted with all its original components. It is also important to remember that the job of military workshops was to keep vehicles serviceable, and they did this with whatever means they had at their disposal. If supplies of the 'correct' (that is, original) parts were unavailable, workshop staff would use anything that could be persuaded to fit, and typically this might have come from the Series III Lightweight parts inventory. As a result, many Series IIA Lightweights were released on to the civilian market in far from original condition.

The chassis number of a Lightweight will be found on a plate attached to the passenger's side of the bulkhead and is also stamped into the right-hand front spring shackle bracket.

THE CHASSIS FRAME

The basic chassis-frame was essentially the same as that of the contemporary military Series IIA 88. However, there was an angled metal strip welded across the front dumb-irons to retain chassis rigidity when the front bumper was removed for airlifting operations. The front lifting rings were bolted through this into the chassis dumb-irons. The gearbox cross-member (number 4 cross-member) could be unbolted to aid transmission removal and servicing.

An important feature that distinguishes a Series IIA Lightweight chassis from the later Series III type is the bracketry for the front bump-stops. On Series IIA models each bump-stop was mounted to a small bracket at the bottom of the chassis side-rail; on Series IIIs the vertical strips on the side rail were joined by a horizontal extension, which provided a stronger bump-stop mounting bracket.

The front bumper was narrower than the standard Series IIA type. It had four drilled holes to take a standard NATO lockable, rotating tow jaw if needed. As on other British military Land Rovers of the time, the bumper was fitted with double-height outer ends, but these were shorter than on other military Land Rovers to keep within the Lightweight's reduced width. The front number plate was normally bolted centrally to brackets on the top of the bumper.

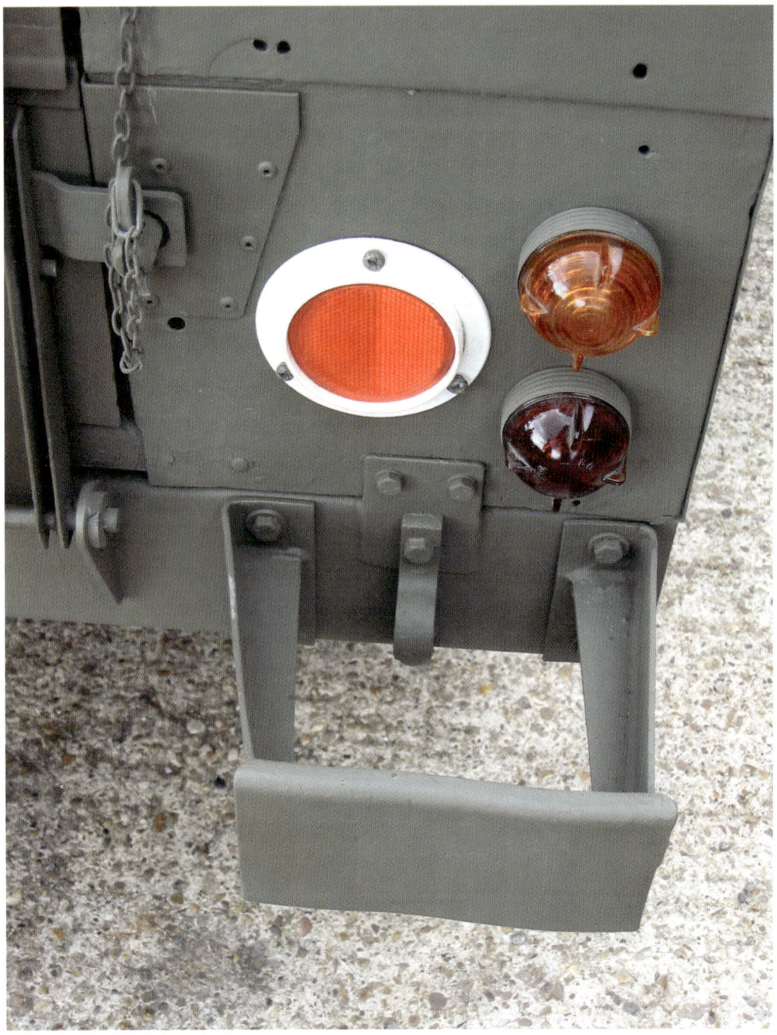

ABOVE: The front number-plate was bolted above the bumper, which has been painted over here but would have been delivered with a silver galvanized finish.

LEFT: The rear lifting and towing rings were mounted to the cross-member and protected by the bumperettes, which were delivered with a silver galvanized finish.

As delivered, the front bumper had an unpainted silver galvanized finish.

The rear cross-member had bumperettes bolted to its outer ends, and bolted to the cross-member inside these were lifting rings. These bumperettes were delivered with an unpainted, galvanized finish. The rear cross-member also carried a standard NATO lockable, rotating tow jaw. On its inner face was mounted a convoy light, which would shine on to the white-painted rear face of the differential casing.

Like other British military models, the Lightweight had twin 10gal (45ltr) underseat fuel tanks with a changeover switch.

THE TRANSMISSION

All Series IIA Lightweights had a 9.5in (241mm) Borg and Beck diaphragm spring clutch. They had the four-speed '76mm' gearbox without synchromesh on first or second gears, and the standard two-speed transfer gearbox.

Gearbox Identification Numbers

The gearbox identification number is located on the right-hand side of the casing, at the rear. All Series IIA Lightweight gearboxes had serial numbers with a 236 prefix. Specification changes generally followed those made to the civilian gearboxes, with the result that the first Lightweight gearboxes had an E suffix.

THE AXLES AND PROPSHAFTS

The Lightweights always had 'Rover'-type axles with the long-nosed differential casing. Front axles were handed to suit the driving position, and their steering ball swivels were normally protected by leather gaiters. Rear axles were fully-floating types with canvas restraining straps to prevent excessive axle movement. Both axles had shorter half-shafts and drive flanges than standard 88s to help to reduce the overall vehicle width, although both front and rear tracks had the same 51.5in (1,310mm) dimension as on the standard 88s. It appears that some vehicles were fitted with standard civilian-type half-shafts and drive-members in service, after the original width restrictions were relaxed. In other respects, both front and rear axles were the same as the contemporary civilian types, with the same 4.7:1 differential gearing. The rear face of the rear differential was commonly painted white, to pick up light from the convoy light fitted behind the cross-member.

Axle Identification Numbers

Axle identification numbers will be found on top of the axle casing on the left-hand side.

THE STEERING AND BRAKES

The steering box was always the same as that used in contemporary civilian models: a Burman recirculating type with variable ratio. The track rod carried the fitting for a steering damper, but no damper was fitted as standard.

The brakes had the same single-circuit hydraulic system as on civilian models. The wheel brakes both front and rear were Girling leading- and trailing-shoe types with a 10in (250mm) diameter. The handbrake drum on the transfer box rear output shaft had a 9in (229mm) diameter.

THE SUSPENSION, WHEELS AND TYRES

The suspension followed the civilian 88 pattern of semi-elliptic springs all round with hydraulic telescopic dampers. However, the Lightweights had lighter road springs. All variants had seven-leaf springs on the rear axle. The front axle on GS models had five-leaf springs and

The twin under-seat fuel tanks had filler caps painted red, to indicate that the required fuel was petrol.

Lightweights were built with special hub ends to reduce width. Also visible here is the date-stamp (4/68) in the wheel rim.

It was standard military practice to fit leather gaiters as protection for the front hub swivels, and the Lightweights were no exception.

ABOVE LEFT: *The carburettor was a Zenith 36IV. Note the liberal application of Duck Egg Green paint on this engine – although not on the exhaust manifold, where it would have burned off quickly. The engine number is just visible between the front of the manifold and the oil cooler take-off pipe.*

BELOW LEFT: *The oil cooler was mounted behind the radiator grille and ahead of the radiator itself.*

that on FFRs had seven-leaf springs. The original dampers were made by Woodhead-Monroe.

Some early vehicles delivered to the Royal Navy (but not to the Royal Marines) had split-rim combat-type wheels, but most Lightweights had single-piece disc wheels. The standard tyres on the first Series IIA Lightweights were Dunlop 6.50×16 Trakgrip types. These were later replaced by Goodyear Hi-Miler Xtra Grip tyres, again with a 6.50×16 size.

THE ENGINE, COOLING SYSTEM AND EXHAUST

All Series IIA Lightweights had the 2.25-litre petrol engine with a Zenith 36IV carburettor, an eight-bladed fan with twin drive pulleys and a semi-sealed cooling system with expansion bottle. The exterior of the engine was usually painted Duck Egg Green after overhaul in military service. An oil cooler was mounted behind the radiator grille and the original oil filter was an AC72 type. The oil and water temperature senders were both capillary types. The exhaust system was always handed, with the tailpipe emerging behind the rear wheel on the driver's side.

Engine Identification Numbers

The engine identification number is located on the left-hand front of the cylinder block, in front of the exhaust manifold. Suffix letters followed the system used on standard models, with the result that the first engines carried Suffix J. There were two engine prefix codes. The 236-series engines had a 7:1 compression ratio and the 237-series engines, introduced in April 1969, had a higher 8:1 compression ratio to give small increases in power and torque.

LEFT: *The bonnet slam panel escaped from the khaki drab applied elsewhere on this vehicle. Note the Negative Earth reminder plate.*

THE BODY

The body was designed to meet a maximum width need of 60in (1,520mm) – 4in (100mm) narrower than the standard 88. It was built up of flat panels around a unique narrow bulkhead with a demountable top section. These panels reduced width and weight, and also minimized tooling costs at a time when initial orders were expected to be small. The front wings were reduced to minimal flat-topped splash-guards and there were no separate body sills.

The design allowed for many elements to be removed to reduce the weight for airlifting operations. Thus the tilt, windscreen, bulkhead top panel, doors, top sections of the body sides and top half of the tailgate could all be unbolted relatively quickly. The spare wheel and the front bumper could also be removed if necessary. In practice, the vehicles were rarely stripped down to save weight for airlifting operations, but their top hamper and bulkhead top were sometimes removed to give a lower profile in operational use.

The first Lightweights had their headlamps in the grille panel, with sidelamps inboard of the turn indicators on the fronts of the wings. Some time in

Paint and Body Markings

All Series IIA Lightweights were delivered to their end-users with their body panels painted in Deep Bronze Green, chassis finished in gloss black and unpainted (galvanized) bumpers and body fittings. In service, they were commonly painted in all-over NATO drab, sometimes with black disruptive camouflage. Different military units also added their own markings, but it is beyond the scope of this book to list all the variants of these.

ABOVE: The expansion bottle alongside the radiator can be seen here, together with the twin-pulley drive for the cooling fan and water pump, and the braided take off hose for the oil cooler. The eight-blade fan would not have been yellow, as here; it would have been painted the same Duck Egg Green as the rest of the engine on overhaul.

BELOW: The exhaust emerged under the wheelarch on the driver's side. The rear face of the rear differential was usually painted white to reflect the convoy light, but appears not to have been so treated on this vehicle. The 'TP' (tyre pressure) markings were added in service at each unit's discretion.

1970, after around 1,500 vehicles had been built (the figure has not been confirmed but is an informed estimate), the design was changed to meet new lighting regulations in European countries where British forces were using Lightweights. The front wings gained extension panels and the headlamps were moved to these. At the same time, the side and indicator lamps were moved to positions outboard of the headlamps. The sidelamps were normally fitted above the indicators.

Series IIA Lightweights normally had round, black rear-view mirrors on the front wings, each one on a long cranked stem. However, replacements used in service depended on what the unit had available at the time, which would often have been a later type of mirror.

The special bonnet was always a distinguishing feature of the Lightweight. It was made from two sections riveted together and had deep sides to compensate for the absence of proper front wings. There was always a small semi-circular cut-out in the bottom of each side to accommodate the co-axial cable for an aerial tuner unit when one was fitted to the front wing. The spare wheel was mounted on the bonnet, where it was secured to cleats by three straps linked together above the wheel centre; the two rear straps had a fixed length and the front strap was adjustable and had a hook so that it could be detached from the cleat on the bonnet. There were variations in the mounting position on some special unit-converted vehicles, which are discussed below.

There was a tool locker inside the left-hand rear wheelarch, where it was accessible from outside the vehicle. Its lid was mounted on a hinged bracket and the turnbuckle latch could be secured by a padlock.

The tail-lights were carried on the tail panels on either side of the tailboard. The amber turn indicator was normally mounted above the red stop-and-tail light, and inboard of the lights was a large circular red reflector.

The tailgate was in two parts, the top section being demountable for weight reduction in airporting operations. The top section had brackets and straps for stowing a pick and shovel, and the right-hand hinge bracket had a metal loop which supported the blade of the shovel. The lower section carried the rectangular number plate on a hinged assembly, which allowed the plate to remain visible when the tailgate was open. There was a nylon clip under the plate, with a nylon receiver in the rear panel; this clip held the number plate in place against the rear panel when the tailgate was closed.

In normal use, the rear grab rail fitted into a bracket on the rear bulkhead and a socket in the lower tailgate. When not in use during stripped-down operations, it could be relocated in clips on the rear bulkhead.

The Series IIA Lightweights were supplied with a set of hood-sticks that slotted into sockets in the rear body, and with a tilt made of typical military khaki-coloured canvas. This was secured to the vehicle in the traditional Land Rover fashion with ropes that had to be looped over cleats attached to the body. The side and rear panels of the tilt could be rolled up and secured in position if required. These tilts always had flaps in the sides covering apertures through which the co-axial cables for radio aerials would be passed if the vehicle were carrying a radio station.

THE INTERIOR

The GS models had three separate seats in the cab, but FFR models had only two, the centre position being occupied by a black-painted metal cover over the batteries. GS models also normally had inward-facing bench seats in the rear over the wheelboxes; FFR types had a single radio operator's seat on the left-hand wheelbox; sometimes one seat was fitted on either side.

The Lightweight bulkhead lacked the parcels shelf found on standard 88

The original wing mirrors were black with metal bodies (this is a later plastic replacement) on cranked black arms. The cut-out for the co-axial aerial cable is clearly visible.

The spare wheel was held to cleats on the bonnet by three straps.

models and instead had a simple flat panel on the cab side. The main instrument panel was screwed to the middle of this, and there was a galvanized grab-handle bolted to it directly ahead of the passenger. Alongside the grab-handle was a plastic windscreen washer bottle in a bracket. The wiper motor was mounted direct to the bulkhead under a box-like aluminium protective cover, and was always at the left-hand end of the bulkhead, irrespective of the driving position. There were also aluminium cover plates for the wiper wheelboxes.

The two-dial central instrument panel fitted to Lightweights was broadly similar to the standard 'civilian' type, but there were several differences. The lower centre position was occupied by a starter button marked S, and the ignition keylock was on an auxiliary panel on the driver's side, in the centre of a six-way lighting switch, which had its own rubber cover that was attached to it by a chain. FFR models had a second auxiliary instrument panel on the passenger's side, containing one ammeter for the vehicle battery and one for the radio battery.

Alongside the six-way lighting switch, FFR models had a pull-out engine speed governor, which was used when the engine was being run with the vehicle stationary to charge the batteries. There was a changeover switch for the two fuel tanks in the driver's side footwell, and a fire extinguisher was normally mounted horizontally between the main instrument panel and the transmission tunnel.

The seat backs were attached to the transom panel by four press-studs, and on top of the panel itself were two clips to carry an SLR rifle.

TOOLS

The starting handle and jack handle were located in clips under the bonnet, and the jack was carried in the tool locker at the back of the left-hand rear wheelarch.

Series IIA Lightweight Dashboard Lights

	12V Models	24V Models
Instrument panel and speedometer	Lucas 937	Lucas 650
Flashers and trailer warning	Lucas 281	Lucas 283
Brake warning	Lucas 280	Lucas 283

ABOVE: The toolbox containing the jack was in the left-hand rear wheelarch. The door was sometimes difficult to open (as here), depending on how the body was mounted to the chassis. LEFT: Pioneer tools were carried on the tailgate. Also visible here are the NATO hitch and the towing socket. The hole to the left of the socket should have a 'keep' for the removable socket cover, and the large split-pin on the left-hand hinge-pin is not original. The wire running under the tailgate is for the convoy light.

Series IIA Lightweight Lights

All Series IIA Lightweights had military-pattern lights, those on the 24V models differing from their 12V equivalents. The table below lists the different types. Headlights were pre-focus types with a separate bulb and had military identification numbers in the centres of their lenses.

	12V Models	24V Models
Headlights	Lucas 367 (military i/d FV157942)	Lucas 368
Sidelights	Lucas 223	Lucas 149
Stop-and-tail lights	Lucas 380	Lucas 337
Turn indicators	Lucas 382	Lucas 339
Rear number plate	Lucas 233	Lucas 149
Convoy light	Lucas 223	Lucas 149

TOP: The rear number-plate bracket was hinged, and had a nylon clip to hold it in place.

ABOVE: This view of a left-hand-drive FFR dashboard shows the overall layout and the metal battery cover between the seats. The washer bottle was always on the right and the wiper motor under its cover always on the left, regardless of whether the vehicle had left-hand or right-hand drive. Note also the mushroom-shaped knob on the main gear lever.

LEFT: The indicator switch on the column and the washer bottle can be seen on this RHD model. The cover plate for the wiper wheelbox is missing.

LEFT: The changeover switch for the twin fuel tanks was mounted in the driver's footwell. Dangling on the chain is the rubber cover for the six-way lighting switch.

BELOW: The six-way lighting switch was a knurled knob around the key ignition switch and was mounted alongside the main instrument panel.

LEFT AND BELOW: The seat backs were attached to the transom panel by bolts through flaps attached to their back faces.

LEFT: Clips for an SLR rifle were mounted on the top of the transom panel. Visible on the dashboard is the centrally-mounted washer button; the washer tubing would originally have been black rather than transparent.

BELOW: The starting-handle was held in clips under the bonnet. The extra clip visible held the bonnet support rod when the bonnet was closed.

LEFT: The fuse box and electrical junction box were mounted on the bulkhead, while the coil was on a bracket on top of the engine rocker cover.

ABOVE: There was a 'keep' on each inner wing for the co-axial cable on radio-equipped Lightweights.

LEFT: The voltage regulator box was the familiar Lucas RB340. Alongside is the flasher relay.

THE ELECTRICAL SYSTEM

There were two types of electrical system, a 12V type for GS vehicles and a 24V type for FFR models. Both had a negative earth. All Lightweights were radio-prepared and therefore had a fully suppressed electrical system. All wiring and fittings were rendered safe for tropical conditions, and all lights had the standard military waterproofed pattern of the time. On all models the fuse box was mounted on the engine side of the bulkhead.

12V Models

The electrical system had a single battery charged by a Lucas 16ACR alternator. The distributor was a Lucas DM2, the coil a Lucas HA12 and the original spark plugs were Champion UN 12Y fitted with suppressors and waterproof covers. The starter motor was a Lucas 2M 100 type.

24V Models

The electrical system had twin 44A/h batteries charged by a 90A AC/DC generator (alternator) with a built-in rectifier. To the military, this was known as a 'Generator No.10 Mk2 90 amp'. The ignition system was fully screened and waterproofed; the distributor was a screened Lucas DZS 4A, the coil a Lucas 5C 10 and the original spark plugs were Champion RSN 101 or RSN 12Y. The starter motor was a CAV SCA/150 type. The 24V system was broadly similar to that used on earlier FFR Land Rovers. All cables were screened and armoured. The control units for the 90A generator were contained in a cast aluminium box under a cover panel, bolted to a bracket behind the bulkhead on the right. The military knew this control unit as a 'Generator Panel No.9 Mk3'. There was also a shunt box on the rear left-hand side of the seat bulkhead, with terminals to allow connection to the vehicle and radio batteries. Feeds from this shunt box operated the ammeters mounted on the dashboard.

FFR models had a special demountable modular radio station with its own mesh roof panel. This vehicle has been stripped of its top hamper and upper tailgate.

EQUIPMENT AND CONVERSIONS

FFR variants of the Lightweight were fitted with a demountable unitary radio kit in the load area. This was manufactured by DCM Products Ltd of Coventry and consisted of a Dexion framework incorporating a metal mesh canopy, which gave some protection to the radio equipment during airlifting operations. The radios, radio table, junction boxes and other items were bolted to this racking. A pair of sliding aerial brackets were attached to the top section and, when aerials were required, the brackets could be pushed through the apertures in the tilt sides. The batteries were housed within the radio table; there was provision for four, but normally only two were fitted, contained in a pair of fibreglass battery boxes that were clamped to sliding trays. The wiring had quick-release connectors.

As happens with all military vehicles, the Lightweight was adapted to perform a number of additional roles. Modifications would normally be carried out by unit workshops. Known modifications to the Series IIA Lightweight include those listed below, but there were probably many others carried out more or less on a one-off basis to meet specific requirements.

- Dual brake controls for driver training (from March 1978)
- Hardtop conversion, normally with Station Wagon-type tail door (from 1969)
- Linelayer conversion
- Mortar carrier conversion (for 81mm L16 mortar) (for the Parachute Regiment)
- Reconnaissance conversion, based on FFR with 7.62mm GPMG on a pintle mount in the rear; fold-down platform in place of tailgate; expanded-mesh metal basket on bonnet; jerrycan holder on each side of seat box; doors removed; spare wheel mount moved to side or on bracket ahead of front bumper (for the Parachute Regiment)
- Station Wagon-type hardtop conversion
- Stretcher-carrier conversion, with two stretchers and extended tilt (from March 1971)
- VPK (Vehicle Protection Kit) of GRP armour (for use in Northern Ireland, from 1971)
- Waterproofing kit (from May 1969)
- WOMBAT (anti-tank gun) carrier conversion (from March 1970) (initially for the Royal Marines)
- Some LHD vehicles bought under contract WV 8679 (these had registration numbers 53 FH 54 to 55 FH 40) were modified with a commercial heater-demister unit for use in north-west Europe.

Lightweight Chassis Numbers	
236-00001A to 236-01893H	RHD
239-00001A to 239-01096H	LHD

index